Capital Market Campaigning

Capital Market Campaigning

The Impact of NGOs on Companies, Shareholder Value and Reputational Risk

By Steve Waygood

Published by Risk Books, a Division of Incisive Financial Publishing Ltd

Haymarket House
28–29 Haymarket
London SW1Y 4RX
Tel: +44 (0)20 7484 9700
Fax: +44 (0)20 7484 9800
E-mail: books@incisivemedia.com
Sites: www.riskbooks.com
www.incisivemedia.com

ISBN 1 904 339 86 7

British Library Cataloguing in Publication Data
A catalogue record for this book is available from the British Library

Publisher: Laurie Donaldson
Assistant Editor: Lisa Reading
Designer: Rebecca Bramwell

Typeset by Mizpah Publishing Services Private Limited, Chennai, India

Printed and bound in Spain by Espacegrafic, Pamplona, Navarra

To Chloë and Max

Contents

Foreword

There was a time when captains of industry raised their capital in the smoke-filled rooms of gentlemen's clubs over long claret-imbibed lunches with financiers. Deals with profound repercussions for people in far-flung places would be struck by men of influence. And their influence was such that they would routinely ignore the impact their deals would have on society and the environment, for there was little comeback when things went wrong.

Capital Market Campaigning demonstrates that times have changed drastically. Today's instant information age has combined with the calls from NGOs for greater transparency, and has led to far greater scrutiny of companies and their investors. Globalisation has spawned a host of civil society organisations ready to intervene wherever socially and environmentally irresponsible behaviour manifests itself. We can now see which deals are struck by whom, and judge for ourselves where the responsibility lies for their impacts on society and the environment. Put simply, the smoke has lifted from the deals.

The significant increase in NGO capital market campaigning discussed in these pages highlights the fact that the capital market is critical to achieving sustainable development. Little wonder, then, that the CEOs of modern corporations must possess the skills of politicians as well as business people.

This need for successful companies to balance the financial interests of their shareholders with social and environmental concerns resonates with my own business experience. My work on the boards of a number of multinational companies taught me the importance of listening carefully to stakeholders when they express concerns – their views are important, sometimes influential, and their different perspective can be valuable.

Since I became Chief Executive of WWF-UK in 1999, I have been a strong advocate of capital market campaigning. My personal involvement in the Carbon Disclosure Project enabled me to see at first hand its considerable success in harnessing the influence of investors and increasing the disclosure of climate change emissions by listed companies.

WWF's recent report on sustainable finance shows that many financial institutions have a long way to go in developing a coherent response to sustainable development. But progress is being made – as this book demonstrates, some companies and investors have responded well to the challenge of sustainability.

Civil society now requires accountability and transparency from *all* powerful institutions – government and non-governmental organisations as well as financial and corporate bodies. But do NGOs have a legitimate role to play in the capital market? Of course they do – although, as Steve Waygood argues, we must stay within the boundaries of law and common courtesy when doing so.

The proposals in these pages are not only responsible but also commercially sensible, and I commend them to companies and investors alike. If the author's recommendations were to be broadly adopted, this would significantly reduce the extent to which civil society needs to confront capital market institutions – which in turn would reduce the risks to companies and investors from such challenges. Meanwhile, WWF-UK will continue to intervene in the capital market wherever we find irresponsible behaviour by captains of industry taking their mineral-watered lunches in today's smokeless rooms.

Robert Napier
www.wwf.org.uk

About the Author

Steve Waygood is a director in the Investor Responsibility Team at Insight Investment – the fund manager for HBOS plc. His work covers shareholder activism on corporate governance and corporate responsibility across Insight's £89 billion of assets, and leading the development of the ethically screened funds managed by Insight.

He is an elected vice chair of the UK Social Investment Forum, and is closely involved in the development of the United Nations Principles for responsible investment. Steve co-authored "A Capital Solution, Faith, Finance and Concern for a Living Planet", a book on faith-related responsible investment.

He joined Insight in 2001. Prior to this, he worked in the highly regarded governance and SRI team at Friends Ivory & Sime (now F&C), joining there from WWF-UK where he chaired its business and industry core group.

Steve holds a PhD in Socially Responsible Investment, a Post-Graduate Certificate in Environmental Management and Health, and a degree in Economics.

Acknowledgements

This book is based on my PhD thesis, entitled "NGOs and Equity Investment: a critical assessment of the practices of UK NGOs in using the capital markets as a campaign device". I conducted the research at the Centre for Environmental Strategy, University of Surrey, and I am greatly indebted to my supervisor, Walter Wehrmeyer, who was a constant source of inspiration. I also owe a significant debt of gratitude to both Craig Mackenzie and Les Jones for encouraging me to undertake a PhD whilst also working for them. My thanks also to my great friend Peter Denton for his help, and to my valued colleague, Rory Sullivan, both for convincing me to develop my thesis into this book, and for offering outstanding guidance on the best approach. Thanks to Laurie Donaldson and Lisa Reading at Risk Books for their sterling support on this project.

A great number of people also gave freely of their time when asked to be interviewed for this research. To that end, I would like to thank Meredith Alexander, Niaz Allam, Stuart Bell, Mark Campanale, Rob Cartridge, John Elkington, Peter Frankental, Duncan Green, John Gummer, Jo Johnston, Mark Mansley, Duncan McLaren, Brian Pearce, Rick Stathers, Raj Thamotheram, Stephanie Tunmore, and Helen Wildsmith. Their insights significantly contributed to the analysis within this book, which could not have been written without their help. However, I should emphasise that unless stated otherwise the opinions expressed are mine, and therefore the blame for any errors of judgment falls to me.

Without doubt the most important acknowledgement goes to my wife – Chloë – who gave me outstanding support during the original research, and readily gave again during its further development into *Capital Market Campaigning*. I am proud of everything we have achieved together – including this book – but I am particularly proud of our new son Max, to whom *Capital Market Campaigning* is dedicated.

List of Tables

List of Figures

List of Acronyms and Abbreviations

AGM	Annual general meeting
ANWR	Arctic National Wildlife Refuge
APO	Alternative Public Offering
ARC	Alliance of Religions and Conservation
CBI	Confederation of British Industry
CM	capital market
CSR	corporate social responsibility
DEFRA	Department for the Environment, Food and Rural Affairs
E-USS	Ethics for the Universities Superannuation Scheme
ECOSOC	Economic and Social Council (UN)
EIRIS	Ethical Investment Research Service
EPA	Environmental Protection Agency (US)
ERM	enterprise risk management
FI	financial institution
FoE	Friends of the Earth
FORGE	Financial Organisations Reporting Guidelines on the Environment
FSA	financial services authority
FTSE	financial times stock exchange
FUM	funds under management
GSK	GlaxoSmithKline plc
HLS	Huntingdon Life Sciences
IFA	independent financial adviser
IPPR	Institute for Public Policy Research
IUCN	The World Conservation Union
NGO	nongovernmental organisation
OECD	Organisation for Economic Cooperation and Development
OED	*Oxford English Dictionary*
OEIC	open-ended investment company
PIRC	Pensions Investment Research Consultants

PIRG	Public Interest Research Group
PSG	Pharmaceutical Shareowners Group
ROI	return on investment
SEE	social, ethical and environmental
SHAC	Stop Huntingdon Animal Cruelty
SIP	statement of investment principles
SSSI	Site of Special Scientific Interest
SRI	socially responsible investment
TRI	Toxic Release Inventory
Trips	Trade-Related Aspects of Intellectual Property Rights
UKLA	UK Listing Authority
UKSIF	UK Social Investment Forum
USS	Universities Superannuation Scheme

1

Setting the Scene

Over the past two decades, nongovernmental organisations (NGOs) have significantly increased their attempts to use the capital markets to change corporate practices. In some cases, these campaigners have influenced the target company's cost of capital, tarnished its reputation, and mobilised significant shareholder votes against management. In a few extreme cases, campaigners have also motivated company brokers to reject clients and stock markets to bar listings. This rapid growth in NGO capital market campaigning has created new risks for companies and their investors, and has not gone unnoticed. Indeed, the *Financial Times* listed "Growing pressures from international NGOs, armed with unprecedented resources, credibility, access to company data and global communications capabilities" as one of the five socioeconomic megatrends affecting the security and earning power of long-term retirement savings (2005a, p 6).

It is surprising, therefore, that there is a general lack of systematic research into the impact, effectiveness and legitimacy of NGO capital market campaigning. This is a very real issue for companies and investors, as the lack of analysis means that they are unclear as to what, if anything, they should do to avoid or respond to problematic confrontations.

There are also important welfare issues. While the short term consequences for companies and investors from these campaigns can be negative, they may generate longer term benefits for society. This is because the existing structure of rewards and incentives in the capital market can lead to short-term profit-maximisation behaviour by company directors that is potentially to the detriment of long-term financial performance. Such short-termism *can* motivate unethical behaviour, as while the rewards are frequently short term, the associated costs and sanctions – reputation damage, litigation and fines – tend to be longer-term in nature (Chapter 2 includes a more detailed discussion on short-termism). By acting as a "civil regulator" (see Zadek, 1998b), and policing unethical corporate behaviour, NGO campaigns can help to resolve this short-termism and generate outcomes that are both economically beneficial and welfare enhancing. However, this is not to say that all such NGO campaigns are to the benefit of society. There have been cases where the capital market has been harnessed by extreme pressure groups, such as the Animal Liberation Front, which use violence in an attempt to force their particular view on investors. There are therefore both positive and negative welfare issues arising from these campaigns that make them an important area for research.

OVERVIEW OF NGO CAPITAL MARKET CAMPAIGNS

The origins of NGO's use of the capital market in the UK can actually be traced back to the 19th century. For example, in 1888, the social reformer Dr Annie Besant (1847–1933) successfully drew attention to the low wages paid to the Bryant and May match girls by shaming shareholding clergymen.

Despite this early example, "professionalised" NGO attempts to use the capital market did not fully emerge until the 1970s, when the anti-apartheid movement used AGMs as a mechanism to publicly embarrass companies that had operations in South Africa.

In the period since then (1970–2005), there has been a dramatic growth in NGO use of the capital markets. Now more than 30 NGOs in the UK alone have used the capital market as part of their company campaigning. Examples of such campaigning include: Surfers Against Sewage questioning the board at South West Water's AGM about its policy in relation to marine dumping of sewage; Campaign Against the Arms Trade "naming and shaming" local authority pension funds with holdings in defence companies such as BAE; Friends of the Earth and the RSPB attempting to stop Fisons extracting peat from sites of special scientific interest; Greenpeace, Amnesty International and WWF-UK campaigning

for Shell to publish a corporate responsibility report to shareholders, as a result of the Nigerian government executing Ken Saro-
Wiwa, who had been campaigning against the devastation of the
Niger Delta by Shell and others; The Corner House campaigning
against Balfour Beatty's involvement in the Ilisu Dam in Turkey;
Christian Aid targeting BP and other institutional investors in
Petrochina, due to the latter's involvement in Sudan where an
oil-funded civil war was underway; and The Burma Campaign lobbying for the withdrawal of BAT and Standard Chartered from
Burma (myanmar), due to these companies' provision of finances
to a military dictatorship involved in human rights abuses.

The strategies that these and other NGOs have adopted broadly
fall into two categories:

❑ pressuring investors to invest capital in one company or sector
rather than another; or
❑ using the rights and influence associated with share ownership
to voice concerns directly with company directors and senior
management.

Figure 1 graphically depicts this flow of influence.

Figure 1 NGO capital market campaign mechanisms of influence

While the majority of early NGO capital market interventions
focused on AGM disruption – that is very hostile or antagonistic
approaches – NGO strategies have become much more sophisticated. Recent years have seen NGOs use a broad range of different
interventions, including: the production of investment analysis in
support of their campaign issues; direct attempts to move capital
into certain investment projects and out of others; ongoing programmes of communication with investors in relation to specific
issues of corporate social responsibility[1] (CSR); public policy advocacy on the rules that govern the capital market; and, in some cases,
formal programmes of collaboration between investors and NGOs.

NGO success with capital market campaigning has created something of a self-reinforcing circle as campaigners have promoted the benefits of capital market campaigns to each other. In the US, for example, Friends of the Earth produced *Confronting Companies Using Shareholder Power: A Hand-book for Socially Orientated Shareholder Activism* (see Chan-Fishel, 1999). In the UK, The Corner House produced *The Campaigners' Guide to the Financial Markets: Effective Lobbying of Companies and Financial Institutions* (see Hildyard and Mansley, 2001). Similarly, in the Netherlands, SOMO (the Centre for Research on Multinational Corporations) produced a wide-ranging review, *"Critical Issues in the Financial Sector"* (see Vander Stichele, 2004), focusing on the sector's impact on sustainable development and its contribution to environmental destruction, and is intended as a reference for NGOs working on these issues.

Perhaps most significantly, NGOs operating capital market campaigns have also produced the Collevecchio Declaration (named after the Italian town where it was written). This declaration is the most important collective contemporary statement of the changes that social and environmental campaigners would like to see (and is reproduced in Appendix 2), having been endorsed by more than 100 NGOs worldwide, including Greenpeace Italy; WWF national offices in Italy and the UK; Friends of the Earth national offices in Brazil, Germany, El Salvador, Australia, Canada, Czech Republic, Lithuania, Switzerland; and the Sierra Club in the USA.

Turning to the question of whether or not NGO campaigners have been effective, there are examples where a target company confirmed that it was influenced by the NGO campaign, which is a strong although not conclusive indicator of effectiveness. One such example was GSK, whose chief executive confirmed that he was responding to concerns raised by investors and campaigners when he decided to increase affordable access to its medication in developing countries following a campaign by Oxfam (see further the Oxfam "Cut the Cost" case study in Chapter 5).

NGOs have also had success when targeting financial institutions (FIs). In a significant development for all banks involved in project finance, in June 2003 a group of 10 banks published the Equator Principles (EP) (included as Appendix 3). These principles represent a set of guidelines for managing social and environmental issues related to the financing of development projects and were described by Chuck Prince, the chief executive of Citigroup, as "one of the most important things that the banking industry has done in the past couple of years" (see *Financial Times*, 2004, p 7). At the time of writing, 36 FIs have signed up, collectively arranging roughly three-quarters of the project finance loan market by volume of capital. BankTrack, a network of 14 NGOs monitoring the operations of the private financial sector and its effect on people and the environment, has stated that the Equator Principles has the potential to become the *de facto* standard on social, ethical and environmental (SEE) issues for projects finance. In an analysis of the consistency of the Equator Principles with the Collevecchio Declaration, BankTrack noted that "all the banks that drafted the EPs have been the subject of NGO advocacy" (see BankTrack, 2003), which again indicates NGO effectiveness in this area. Not only was capital market campaigning one reason why the original ten banks created the Equator Principles in the first place, but also the ongoing threat of being targeted by campaigners has been a major incentive for other banks to subsequently sign up.

Similarly, while the evidence of effectiveness is less clear it is increasingly recognised that NGO capital market campaigns can also impact governments "policymaking". For example, in 2001 the Congressional US–China Commission received a report into the national security issues arising from the capital markets – an issue that it termed "capital-market security". This report used NGO capital market campaigning in the US to demonstrate that capital market policy could be a useful government foreign-policy instrument and concluded that US NGOs have had significant influence on the capital market: "The government would be well-advised to understand more fully the impact of pressure campaigns by US NGO's ... which can significantly sway the markets and have shown escalating intensity and sophistication" (see Pener and Casey, 2001, p 75).

Nevertheless, while it is possible to point to a growth in UK NGO capital market intervention – and the evidence of influence presented above – due to the lack of a systematic analysis it is not at all clear that NGO capital market intervention has been generally effective or efficient. In addition, even where NGOs appear to have brought about change via capital market intervention, it is not clear that campaigners have always accurately understood the chain of influence that generated the success.

SCOPE, APPROACH AND OBJECTIVES

This book is an attempt to correct the lack of systematic research into NGO capital market campaigning. There are a number of questions that it seeks to address. For instance, has NGO capital market campaigning been effective? How does it work? What, if anything, makes it legitimate? What broader societal purpose does it serve? Is such campaigning on the increase? Can it influence votes at annual general meetings (AGMs), company share price and cost of capital? And finally, it really become a significant source of risk to companies and their investors?

The main overall objective is to identify lessons for companies and their investors that are targeted by – or wish to avoid being targeted by – capital market campaigns. To that end the book makes a number of recommendations aimed at decision makers within companies and investment institutions regarding the management of capital market campaign risk within the context of an overall enterprise risk management programme.[2]

As part of this work, the book charts – for the first time – the history of UK NGOs' capital market campaigning. Starting with the AGM disruption of the anti-apartheid era, it plots the evolution of capital market campaigning from the early media-friendly shareholder resolutions, through campaigns against large, high-profile, institutional shareholders, up to the collaboration with brokers on company reports and shareholder activism of today. By taking a close look at four specific cases, the book attempts to assess the nature and scale of the risks to companies and their investors from capital market campaigns.

In terms of scope, this book primarily studies UK-based local, national and international environmental and social NGOs' use of equities listed on the capital market to influence the practices of public limited companies (PLCs). It is important to emphasise that the campaign focus is a sub-set of NGOs' overall corporate campaigning, as the generality of NGO corporate campaigning often makes no attempt to target the capital market at all. Constraining the geographical focus to one country is important because different countries have different models of corporate law, different corporate-governance rules and different legislation underpinning their capital markets.

The analysis involves two main elements. First, a chronology of the main UK NGO capital market campaigns that occurred between 1990 and 2002 is developed and analysed.[3] This uses a model to classify each intervention, which enables us to see how NGO strategy changed over this time. However, this high-level analysis does not enable a detailed review of effectiveness. As a result, the second element is four detailed case studies of specific campaigns. Such detailed assessments are complex because NGOs focus on issues that are both difficult to measure, and often beyond their exclusive control. To simplify this complexity, each of the NGO interventions analysed in Chapter 5 is analysed against three criteria (building on Borkey and Leveque, 1998):

(1) *Viability and feasibility effectiveness*: How ambitious was the target? How realistic was it? What were the underlying aims? What dimensions were likely to work and why? Why might it fail?
(2) *Implementation effectiveness*: Were there any changes arising from the intervention? How did the change compare with stated aims? How significant a role did the capital market campaign play? What was the chain of influence and why did it work? Where did the chain of influence break down and why did it fail?
(3) *Efficiency*: What was the relationship between the effect of the intervention and the inputs or resources allocated to it?

STRUCTURE OF THE BOOK

There are six further chapters in this book. Chapter 2 provides the background to capital market campaign, and gives a general overview of the nature, role and legitimacy of NGOs in general. Chapter 3 develops a typology of capital market-specific campaign strategies and covers the various approaches to NGO capital market campaigning in depth. Chapter 4 uses the typology to analyse the history of UK capital market campaigning between 1990 and 2002. Chapter 5 presents the four detailed case studies. Chapter 6 is the main body of analysis and brings together the findings of the overall research in Chapter 4 with the more detailed research in Chapter 5. Chapter 7 distils the analysis into risk management lessons for companies and investors.

1   There are a number of alternative definitions offered for CSR. The use of the term here is consistent with the definition used by Business for Social Responsibility, USA: "Operating a business in a manner that meets or exceeds the ethical, legal, commercial and public expectations that society has of business. Social Responsibility is a guiding principle for every decision made and in every area of a business" (BSR, 2003, Internet).

2   Lam (2003) defines enterprise risk management as a comprehensive and integrated framework for managing credit risk, market risk, operational risk, economic capital and risk transfer in order to maximise firm value.

3   A mixed-methodology analysis using data gathered via a desk-based literature review and through a series of exploratory interviews conducted. For an explanation of a mixed-methodology approach see Bulmer (1984). In many cases, the NGO campaign was relatively high-profile. Where this was true, it was also possible to critically review the press coverage.

2

Background

WHAT ARE NGOs AND WHY DO THEY EXIST?

It is important to be clear about what is meant by "NGO", because it is an ambiguous term. "Nongovernmental organisation" is defined by the *Oxford English Dictionary* as "an organisation not belonging to or associated with a government". However, this covers more than 50,000 different organisations, aspiring to achieve a wide variety of aims.[1] Classifying an organisation by "what it is not" is unhelpful, since it does not specify what it is. Consequently, there have been a number of attempts at a more precise definition.

The term "NGO" derives from Article 71 of the Charter of the United Nations (1945), which states that "the Economic and Social Council may make suitable arrangements for consultations with non-governmental organisations". Willetts (1997, p 201) considers the United Nations process for assessing NGO eligibility for consultative status to the Economic and Social Council (ECOSOC), as having the status of customary international law. Among the provisions of the relevant ECOSOC resolution, Willetts states that for NGOs to be considered acceptable, they:

❑ must not be antithetical to the participatory democratic state;
❑ should be non-profit-making;
❑ should be nonviolent and noncriminal; and
❑ must not be directed against a particular government.

The use of the term "NGO" here is consistent with the UN ECOSOC protocol mentioned above, and it will be used later in the book during the case studies to assess the NGO's legitimacy. However, the protocol itself does not define the actual role of the

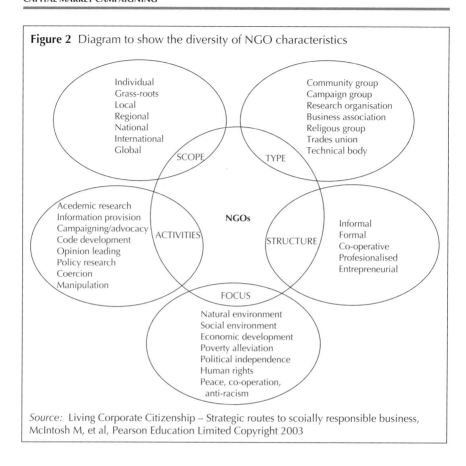

Figure 2 Diagram to show the diversity of NGO characteristics

Individual
Grass-roots
Local
Regional
National
International
Global

SCOPE

Community group
Campaign group
Research organisation
Business association
Religous group
Trades union
Technical body

TYPE

Acedemic research
Information provision
Campaigning/advocacy
Code development
Opinion leading
Policy research
Coercion
Manipulation

ACTIVITIES

NGOs

STRUCTURE

Informal
Formal
Co-operative
Profesionalised
Entrepreneurial

FOCUS

Natural environment
Social environment
Economic development
Poverty alleviation
Political independence
Human rights
Peace, co-operation,
anti-racism

Source: Living Corporate Citizenship – Strategic routes to scoially responsible business, McIntosh M, et al, Pearson Education Limited Copyright 2003

NGOs in question. In fact, the protocol is largely based on what NGOs should not be doing rather than what they are and what they do.

By way of providing structure to the question of NGO defin-ition, McIntosh *et al* (2003, p 64) broadly define the diversity of NGOs by geographical scope, type, structure, focus and activity and offer the diagram in Figure 2 of NGO characteristics.

Figure 2 demonstrates the diverse range of forms that NGOs can take and the broad range of focus. While the above is broadly con-sistent with the NGOs covered in this book, the specific purpose of the NGOs in scope here is captured in the following definition: "Groups whose stated purpose is the promotion of environmental and/or societal goals rather than the achievement or protection of economic power in the marketplace or political power through the electoral process" (see Bendell, 2000, p 16). Unlike either the UN or OED definitions, this definition illuminates what NGOs are, as well as what they are not.

However, two further refinements to Bendell's definition are required here. The first is that "the achievement or protection of economic power in the marketplace" is interpreted narrowly and taken to refer to the achievement or protection of economic power for commercial gain. This is because many non-profit-making NGOs – including, in particular, those in focus in this book – use the "economic power in the marketplace" to promote environmental and social goals. The second and arguably more important refinement is that the NGOs' "environmental and/or societal goals" are welfare-enhancing. In other words, those NGOs that are not generally regarded as working to improve overall social welfare are excluded. For example, some definitions of NGO (although, importantly, not the UN ECOSOC protocol that we use later as a proxy to test legitimacy) include organisations such as the Ku Klux Klan and the Animal Liberation Front. While it can perhaps be argued that such organisations are promoting environmental and/or societal goals of a sort, they are certainly not generally regarded as working to improve overall social welfare.

Therefore, NGOs that are in the scope of this book fall within the narrower definition of "groups whose stated purpose is the promotion of *welfare-enhancing* environmental and/or societal goals rather than the achievement or protection of economic power in the marketplace *for commercial purposes* or political power through the electoral process" (emphasis).

Exploring this welfare-oriented role of NGOs a little further, Edwards and Hulme claim that "NGOs are ... seen as vehicles for 'democratisation' and essential components of a thriving 'civil society'. Which in turn are seen as essential to the ... economy" (1995, p 4). NGOs are also said to act as an essential counterweight to state power with some claiming that their existence represents the failure of governments and companies to address some dissatisfaction with the contemporary condition of society. The UN also highlights a further welfare-related role of NGOs in global governance: "NGOs ... provide analysis and expertise, serve as early warning mechanisms and help monitor and implement international agreements" (see United Nations, 2003).

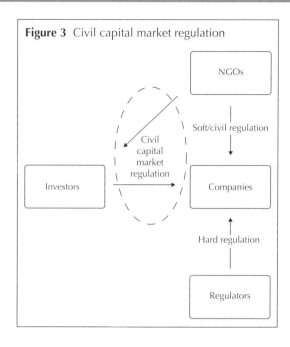

Figure 3 Civil capital market regulation

More specifically, Zadek (1998b) incorporates NGOs in the term "civil society" and argues that one emerging role of civil society is to regulate corporate behaviour, deeming such activity "civil regulation". This indicates that NGOs exist, in part, to ensure that the behaviour of other organisations, including companies, stays within generally accepted societal norms. The concept of civil regulator is important to this book because the capital market can be regarded as one mechanism through which NGOs regulate corporate behaviour – indeed, one might call it "civil capital market regulation" (see Figure 3).

WHY DO NGOs TARGET COMPANIES?

What is it that makes companies relevant to NGOs? From an environmental perspective, like any other organisation, companies use raw materials, consume energy and produce waste. They also produce products and services that contribute to resolving environmental problems. Therefore, as companies can both positively and negatively impact on the environment, this renders them relevant to NGOs with environment related missions.

Similarly, from a development perspective, companies can play a central role in enhancing living standards within developing countries. They provide foreign direct investment, enable the extraction of raw materials, create employment opportunities and facilitate the export and import of goods and services. While these actions can have significant development benefit and lead to higher living standards, they are not entirely without cost. For example, companies may treat their employees poorly: one study into labour conditions in Chinese factories producing goods for export to the US found up to 96 working hours per week, wages per hour as low as 13 cents, employees being fined if they did not work overtime and corporal punishment for talking at work. It also found clear evidence that these measures were having a significantly detrimental impact on employees' health (see Kemaghan, 1998).

Figure 4 depicts the various levels of corporate impact that render companies relevant to NGOs working on these broader issues.

The somewhat obvious implication of this analysis is that it is also the ability of companies to positively and negatively impact on

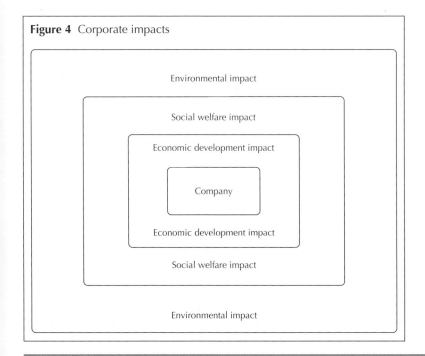

Figure 4 Corporate impacts

Environmental impact

Social welfare impact

Economic development impact

Company

Economic development impact

Social welfare impact

Environmental impact

economic development, social welfare and the environment that makes them relevant to NGOs with environmental, social or development-related missions. The scale of a company's obstruction or support can be a significant determinant as to whether it is possible for NGOs to achieve their mission. Wherever this is the case, it helps the NGOs in question to be able to change companies' business strategies in a way that either magnifies support or, more typically, mitigates obstruction.

NGOs have influenced corporate practices by deploying a range of strategies. The OECD, for example, identified (see OECD, 2001, p 22) that

> NGO activity in monitoring and shaping business conduct has been diverse. It has included monitoring of the activities of some multi-national enterprises and conducting public campaigns against those activities that are deemed to be inappropriate. They have also issued model codes of conduct (often in co-operation with the business community) and have provided expert advice in the field on managerial and strategic issues in the area of corporate responsibility.

In addition, and in particular focus here, NGOs mobilise "Shareholder Action" as part of their corporate campaigning. Mackenzie claims that this last approach – which is the focus for this book – can be highly effective: *"One of the best ways for people to ensure that their interests are represented in the corporate decision-making process is for them to buy shares and use them to take shareholder action"* (1993, p 9).

A TAXONOMY OF DIFFERENT CAMPAIGN BEHAVIOURS

When seeking to influence companies' business strategy, NGOs have adopted different stances in relation to their own approaches to business. Where they believe that the corporate form is immoral and beyond reform, they have worked to undermine the legitimacy of companies and bring the corporate form to an end. Alternatively, where NGOs have believed that the negative impacts of companies *can* be reformed, they have sought to work in partnership with those companies and help to promote their financial success. In the context of NGO capital market intervention, this choice of "stance" is important because it forms part of the capital market strategy deployed by an NGO.

This general stance is important because it significantly biases the kind of capital market campaign that the NGO is likely to adopt. As a result, it is useful to the subsequent analysis to have a framework of the range of stances that NGOs can adopt when intervening in the capital market, because the stance – or the extent to which it is "reformist" or "revolutionary" – may have an impact on success.

Such a framework has been developed by Elkington and Fennell (1998 – see Chapter 2). While this "taxonomy" was developed to model the NGO methods of engaging with businesses generally, it is used in this book to model the interaction between NGOs and the FIs that operate within the capital market.

In the Elkington and Fennell model, a distinction is first made between integrators and polarisers. Integrators place a high priority on developing productive relationships with business, and strive to identify non-confrontational win–win strategies. Polarisers, on the other hand, make a strategic decision not to develop close working relationships with business, preferring to concentrate their energies as a watchdog. These distinctions are similar to the "reformist" and "revolutionary" distinctions used above. Second, a distinction is made between discriminators and non-discriminators. Discriminators attempt to understand the issues facing a particular industry and track the SEE performance of individual companies compared with industry benchmarks. For non-discriminators, the focus is the environmental burden of the industry in general; a company's relative environmental performance is not of particular interest.

Hence, in this taxonomy, four distinct NGO business approaches emerge, as illustrated in Table 1.

Elkington and Fennell's idiosyncratically named taxonomy applies in this capital market context, as when an NGO engages with an FI to change the practices of the listed companies it holds, the FI intermediate investment institution also tends to be a company. In other words, where "companies" appears in the table above, the specific company here will be the FI.

This taxonomy does, however, have a number of limitations. First, by classifying an overall NGO with a fixed label, the model implies that individual NGOs always engage with companies in the same way. In reality, the mode of engagement with any one company changes over time. Similarly, NGOs often work simultaneously in

Table 1 A taxonomy of company–NGO relationship

ORCA (polariser, discriminator) Scrutinises relative performance of companies; attacks selected targets	*DOLPHIN (integrator, discriminator)* Scrutinises relative performance of companies, chooses to work closely with some of them
SHARK (polariser, non-discriminator) Ignores relative performance of companies; attacks most targets that present themselves	*SEA LION (integrator, non-discriminator)* Ignores relative performance of companies; willing to work closely with any of them

Source: Elkington and Fennell (1998, p 53).

different ways with different companies. Second, the designated taxa are shorthand for only two aspects of the NGO personality – whether it establishes partnerships, and whether it compares the relative performance of companies. Therefore, when used in this way, broader characteristics such as NGO policy in respect of trade liberalisation and the structure of the corporate form have to be inferred. Third, the label does not cater for NGOs that adopt a neutral stance – that is, those that neither develop productive relationships with business nor watchdog their activities. Fourth, it is difficult to use the label to classify one intervention by different NGOs working in a coalition. Finally, while there is perhaps some relevance, it is not immediately clear from the natural behaviour of these animals in the wild precisely to what NGO–business behaviour each label refers.

Nevertheless, notwithstanding the above limitations, the model does provide a useful framework for conceiving of the stance adopted by NGOs in their business relations.

THE CAPITAL MARKET AS A CAMPAIGN TARGET

But why might NGOs be attempting to use the capital market at all? The capital market is primarily of relevance to NGOs because it influences the practices of listed companies. This means that the capital market can be used by NGOs to increase corporate accountability and promote improved corporate social and environmental performance.

The influence of the capital market is relevant to NGOs in two distinct but related ways:

❏ as an instrumental mechanism for changing corporate practices that NGOs can seek to harness in different ways; and

❏ as a target for systemic change in itself because the influence of the capital market can undermine long-term sustainable development goals.

Why, though, might the capital market require systemic change? As Björn Stigson explained when president of the World Business Council for Sustainable Development, "Financial markets are key in the pursuit of sustainable development because they hold the scorecard, allocate and price capital, and provide risk coverage and price risks … if financial markets do not understand and reward sustainable behaviour, progress (in developing more sustainable business practices) will be slow" (2003, p 6).

The implication is that the capital market can be both a constraint and a facilitator in respect of improved sustainability practice within companies. Those that argue that the current structure of the capital market is a general constraint in respect of sustainable development goals use two main related arguments: short-termism and market failure.

The short-termism argument rests on the capital market being too near-sighted in the way it evaluates companies. The root cause is said to be that fund management organisations are evaluated by their clients – for example, pension funds – based on criteria that are themselves too short-term. This, in turn, motivates fund management institutions to incentivise and evaluate their individual fund managers and analysts based on performance over time frames that are excessively short, and lead to too much attention on short-term financial performance. The behavioural problem with this is that, when these individuals meet with company directors, the tenor of their questions and their consequent trading decisions leads company directors who wish to enhance shareholder value to focus too much attention on the quarterly earning figures at the expense of investing in the long-term health of the company.

One of the UK's largest pension schemes, the Universities Superannuation Scheme (see USS, 2003a), highlights the extent to which it believes that short-termism originates from the contract (or mandate) between institutional investors and their agents (ie, fund managers):

> There appear to be resistors to responsible investing which relate to deeply-rooted characteristics of the investment decision-making

system including: the mandates that pension funds and their investment consultants set; the systems for measuring and rewarding performance (which focus on peer comparison and beating benchmarks rather than on fulfilling the long-term liabilities of pension funds); and the competencies of service providers (eg, sell-side analysts). The effect of this resulting short-termism is that less attention is paid to responsible investment matters than is appropriate – these issues are too long-term in nature to affect the day-to-day behaviour of fund managers.

This apparent maximisation of short-term results is seen as a long-term problem for the economy as a whole: if the capital market does not sufficiently factor in long-term capital investment returns, then it undermines long-term investment decision-making by company directors as a whole and leads them to allocate insufficient capital to investing in the long-term health of companies overall.

Partly as a consequence, the UK government has proposed a Company Law Bill that, among other things, updates directors' duties and includes the "duty to promote the success of the company for the benefit of its members". In particular, directors must consider (where relevant and as far as is reasonably practicable) "the likely consequences of the decision in both the long and the short term". In addition, they "must take account of ... any need of the company to ... foster its business relationships with suppliers and others; consider the impact of its operations on the community and the environment, and maintain a reputation for high standards of business conduct".[2] In addition to the clear duty to balance the long- and the short-term performance contained within this draft bill, of particular relevance here is the explicit duty regarding impact on the community and the environment, and maintaining a reputation, which further underscores the relevance of SEE issues to business practices.

As many SEE issues are inherently long-term, such "short-termism" is also a particular problem for NGOs working on SEE issues as it results in the systematic erosion of incentives for company directors to invest in the resolution of SEE performance issues within their business.

While this problem of short-termism is conceptually compelling, it should be noted that the claim that the stock market *en masse* is overly short-term is not consistently borne out by the evidence. For example, Koller, Goedhart and Wessels (2005) published research that showed that deviations from a company's fundamental, or intrinsic, value based on financial performance and risk, tended to be short-lived. They concluded that while "some managers may believe that missing short-term earnings per share (EPS) targets always has devastating share price implications, the evidence shows that share price depends on long-term returns, not short-term EPS performance itself" (2005, p 69).

Therefore, a more nuanced and evidence-based view may be that any overall market short-termism is itself present only for short periods, but the perception by company directors of more pervasive market short-termism can lead them to behave as if the market did focus too much on quarterly EPS.

The second argument in favour of the current structure of the capital market being a general constraint in respect of sustainable development goals is that of market failure. Markets are said to fail where, if left unchecked, they would lead to suboptimal social welfare outcomes. Examples of such market failures include abuse of monopolistic influence, exploiting a lack of customer understanding in order to missell overpriced products they may not need, and the social costs of environmental externalities caused by companies that can pollute without incurring the clean-up costs. The specific market failure argument is that governments have failed to sufficiently internalise companies' environmental and social costs such that the consequent economic development is fully sustainable. As a result of government's failure to internalise these costs on company balance sheets, the capital market does not incorporate companies' full social and environmental costs. Indeed, until these market failures are corrected, it would be irrational for investors to incorporate companies' full social and environmental costs, as they do not appear on the balance sheet and, therefore, do not affect companies' profitability or EPS over the investment time horizon. The key sustainable development problem which this exacerbates is that in the very long term – perhaps more than 50 years – future generations will not be able to enjoy such high standards of living, because the stock of natural capital will have been irreparably depleted.

Therefore, returning to Björn Stigson's earlier comment, financial markets may be key in the pursuit of sustainable development, but they currently do not need to understand and reward sustainable behaviour either because the market participants are paid to be too short-term, or because market failure means that they do not need to worry about the very long-term costs as they accrue to future generations and these costs are not within current investment time horizons.

Having established why the capital market is relevant to NGOs, we now turn our attention to its chain of influence over companies. The following discussion describes the capital market institutions that facilitate the flow of capital from investors (which supply the capital) to companies (which demand the capital).

Figure 5 depicts the relationship between the FIs that operate the market between the demand for and supply of capital. The different roles of the FIs are important in the context of this book, as each role reflects the nature of the influence.

Figure 5 shows that, in the UK, the supply of equity capital originates from two main areas:

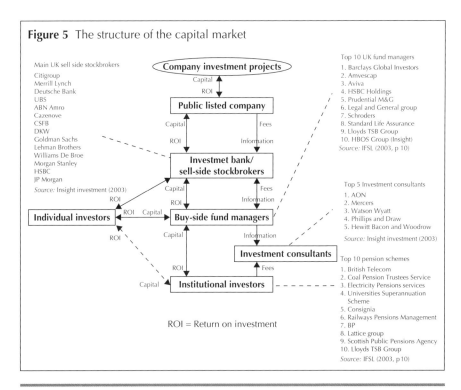

Figure 5 The structure of the capital market

Main UK sell side stockbrokers

Citigroup
Merrill Lynch
Deutsche Bank
UBS
ABN Amro
Cazenove
CSFB
DKW
Goldman Sachs
Lehman Brothers
Williams De Broe
Morgan Stanley
HSBC
JP Morgan

Source: Insight investment (2003)

Individual investors

Company investment projects

Capital
ROI

Public listed company

Capital   Fees
ROI   Information

**Investmet bank/
sell-side stockbrokers**

Capital   Fees
ROI   Information

Buy-side fund managers

Capital   Information

Investment consultants

ROI   Fees

Institutional investors

ROI = Return on investment

Top 10 UK fund managers

1. Barclays Global Investors
2. Amvescap
3. Aviva
4. HSBC Holdings
5. Prudential M&G
6. Legal and General group
7. Schroders
8. Standard Life Assurance
9. Lloyds TSB Group
10. HBOS Group (Insight)
Source: IFSL (2003, p 10)

Top 5 Investment consultants

1. AON
2. Mercers
3. Watson Wyatt
4. Phillips and Draw
5. Hewitt Bacon and Woodrow

Source: Insight investment (2003)

Top 10 pension schemes

1. British Telecom
2. Coal Pension Trustees Service
3. Electricity Pensions services
4. Universities Superannuation Scheme
5. Consignia
6. Railways Pensions Management
7. BP
8. Lattice group
9. Scottish Public Pensions Agency
10. Lloyds TSB Group

Source: IFSL (2003, p 10)

❑ *individual investors* – individuals, either as scheme beneficiaries or directly as "retail" investors, purchasing stocks and shares from an investment broker, or investing in pooled schemes such as open-ended investment companies (OEICs), unit trusts and investment trusts managed by fund managers; and

❑ *institutional investors* – such as company and local authority pension funds, insurance companies, trusts, charities and organisations operating unit trusts and investment trusts.

At the end of 2004, the UK fund management industry was responsible for around £3,000 billion of funds. Around 60% of these funds were managed on behalf of UK institutional clients.

The demand for UK equity capital comes from companies (PLCs) listed on the London Stock Exchange. These PLCs use the services of investment banks to underwrite the new issues of their shares. Investment banks also have a role in facilitating mergers, acquisitions and new placements on the exchange. Furthermore, many investment banks include sell-side broker operations that act as intermediary agents between companies and investors, maintain markets for previously issued securities and offer advisory services to fund managers.[3] In particular, this last advisory service role is what renders them important to NGOs working on SEE issues. Fund managers place considerable authority in the views of these analysts. Therefore, where the views of the most influential brokers change, markets also tend to move. Consequently, the broker's view on the NGO issue will be influential.

More generally, since the inception of the capital market, management and ownership of the capital have become increasingly concentrated among a few large institutions. At the time of writing, 50 FIs own approximately half the equities in the UK stock market. These FIs therefore represent influential targets for NGOs.

It is the job of the individual fund manager to make individual portfolio investment decisions in accordance with the stated goals of the investment fund. These depend to a large extent on the owners of the capital.

Similar to retail investors seeking the advice of independent financial advisers (IFAs), institutional investors place considerable authority[4] in the views of investment consultants who advise as to which fund manager has the most robust investment process and can meet the investment needs of the investment scheme. Therefore, being able to articulate a robust investment process that impresses investment consultants is of central importance to fund managers, because, in order to win institutional mandates, they need to be able to convince the investment consultants that, in addition to having the right people in place, there is also a process in place that should deliver consistent market outperformance. Consequently, fund managers spend a considerable amount of time and effort on the areas that investment consultants rate as important aspects of a good process.

Investment consultants are relevant to the NGOs in focus here because, if investment consultants believe that something is important, this will influence institutional investors' choice of fund manager and, as a consequence, signal its importance to fund managers.

Having now established why the capital market is relevant to NGOs, and what the precise chain of influence over companies is, we now examine the different forms of the capital market's influence over companies. The capital market's influence can be regarded as originating via two principal routes:

❏ *Economic influence*: The buying and selling of shares on the capital market influences the cost of capital for listed companies – this is the price the company has to pay to raise capital to finance its business. The more a company has to pay for capital, the less it can raise. This limits the extent of its activity. In addition, the financial value of the shares influences a director's remuneration and the degree to which the company is perceived as a candidate for takeover.

❏ *Investor advocacy influence*: Shareholders are the "principals" of the business and can exercise their rights of share ownership over their "agents", the company directors. They do this by sending explicit signals (referred to in the corporate-governance literature as "voice") regarding the management of the company. For example, at the end of a company director's term, the investor can vote for or against that director's re-election at the AGM.

As highlighted in the Introduction to this chapter, NGO capital market interventions to date have sought to utilise these two routes of influence in order to exert external pressure on companies via the investment decision makers (economic influence), or to exert internal pressure as members of companies via the rights associated with share ownership (investor advocacy influence).

The two routes above are alternatives because economic influence requires changes in the level of investment. When divestment occurs, the rights necessary for investor advocacy influence are no longer available. There are parallels between these two routes of influence and the alternatives of "exit" and "voice" through which management may find out about an externally perceived deterioration in performance of an organisation (see Hirschman, 1970, p 4).

However, while distinct, these strategies are linked via their long-term implications: where an NGO's strategy of investor-advocacy influence succeeds in persuading an investor to raise a concern with the directors of its company – and the company remains intransigent – then, if the investor believes the issue to be material it should ultimately re-evaluate its holding. If this re-evaluation leads to divestment on a sufficient scale, it could have cost-of-capital (that is to say economic influence) implications for the company.

Both the economic and investor advocacy routes of capital market influence are centrally important concepts in this book and are used in Chapter 3 to develop the NGO capital market intervention model. Due to their importance, Chapter 3 includes a more detailed analysis of the precise origin and nature of this influence.

In addition to the above main rationale of company influence for NGO capital market intervention, there are a number of subsidiary reasons why the capital market is of interest to NGOs. These include the following:

❑ *Generating fundraising income.* The need for financial services and investment products among an NGO's membership can provide it with an opportunity to raise funds via licensed financial products where the endorsing NGO receives a commission on sales from the FI. Examples of such an approach include the relationship of the Royal Society for the Protection of Birds

(RSPB) with Frizzel and the WWF/NPI Investment Fund. However, the commercial basis for such partnerships can be problematic. For example, there may be a conflict of values and the companies underlying the investment vehicles may come into conflict with the NGO's mission. Even so, depending on how the assets are managed, such partnerships can bring programmatic as well as financial benefits to the NGO.

❏ *Stewardship of financial reserves.* Some NGOs maintain financial reserves for continuity of project finance during downturns in fundraising income. The Charity Commission dictates that, in certain circumstances, good stewardship of these reserves involves the investment of a proportion in the stock market. For some charities this raises questions surrounding the appropriateness of the underlying investments, and there have been some instances where NGOs have been found to have arguably inappropriate investments. For example, the RSPB was found to hold investments in TotalFinaElf following an oil slick for which the company had been responsible, and which had killed a number of sea birds. In a study of more than 100 of the UK's largest charities and foundations, Green (2003, p 3) found that "60% of top charities surveyed have no written ethical or socially responsible investment policy".[5]

❏ *Raising capital.* A few NGOs have sought to use the capital market to raise investment capital for their activities. The *Financial Times* has christened such attempts "Alternative Public Offerings" (APOs). One such APO is Traidcraft plc, which is part of Traidcraft Exchange and Traidcraft Foundation (a registered charity). Traidcraft plc aims "to demonstrate that there is an alternative model of capitalism, [and] that a company can still provide a reasonable return without being exploitative, [by] working in the interests of all stakeholders" (see Traidcraft plc, 2002) and has raised in excess of £2 million (see Traidcraft, 2002, p 15).[6]

In summary, the capital market is primarily of relevance to NGOs because it can be used as a mechanism for changing corporate practice and because of its effect on long-term sustainable-development goals. In addition, it can be used by NGOs to raise capital and generate fundraising income, and to invest their financial reserves.

IS NGO CAPITAL MARKET CAMPAIGNING LEGITIMATE?

The above discussion demonstrates that the capital market is of relevance to NGOs because (i) it can be used as a mechanism for changing corporate strategy and (ii) it affects long-term sustainable-development goals. However, it says nothing about whether such NGO use of capital market influence is legitimate. This section considers this question of legitimacy from a broad societal perspective.

Many NGOs invest a proportion of their financial reserves in the capital market. Where the NGO is motivated by a concern about the future financial performance of its investment, that intervention is legitimised by the rights associated with the NGO's investment ownership. This is because these rights exist in order that the shareholders can protect their financial interests (see Chapter 3). If the NGO is a *genuine* shareholder, then it follows that the rights should apply.

However, as demonstrated in Chapter 4, the majority of NGO capital market intervention is conducted outside any genuine investment ownership. In other words, where the NGO has purchased the shares, or attempts to influence existing shareholders, in order to gain access to the shareholder rights, and is not interested in making a financial return on the investment primarily, this kind of NGO capital market intervention lacks the legitimacy derived from genuine investment ownership. In these circumstances, what, if anything, renders NGO capital market intervention legitimate?

There are three broad bases from which NGOs can derive legitimacy when intervening in capital markets:

(1) *Welfare-oriented legitimacy*: Perhaps the most important claim to legitimacy by the NGOs in focus here is their welfare-enhancing public-interest role, which society recognises as legitimate. When acting as civil regulators, NGO capital market intervention can be an effective and efficient method for NGOs to achieve welfare-enhancing social and/or environmental goals. Therefore, NGO capital market intervention is legitimate when it furthers the long-term welfare of society. Conversely, NGO capital market intervention that undermines welfare is, therefore, illegitimate. Davis, Lukomnik and Pitt-Watson (2006) use

this welfare-oriented role of NGOs to argue that NGOs have a specific role to play in participating in the creation of a more sustainable economy: "In a civil society, political parties, an independent judiciary, a free press, impartial law and civic bodies are the core sustainers of democracy. Parallel institutions of a civil economy can be understood as engaged shareowners, independent monitors, credible standards and civil-society organizations [NGOs] participating in the marketplace." The clear implication is that civil-society NGOs have an important, necessary and legitimate role to play in ensuring that FIs do not socially responsible management undermine the companies in which they invest.

(2) *Investment analysis legitimacy*: By enhancing information flows on corporate performance in SEE areas that may be material to share price, conceptually at least, NGOs could improve investment analysis. While there are no independent and verified analyses of this conceptual NGO benefit, when describing its "Sustainability of Securities" analysis process, HSBC (see Tyrrell, 2002a, p 10) states, "When assessing companies, we will build on [the knowledge of HSBC's mainstream investment analysts] by analysing any publicly available information from the company, public interest groups or the media ... In particular, we expect to establish and maintain links with a number of non-governmental organisations, think tanks and industry bodies." This indicates that at least one large capital market institution apparently believes there is value in maintaining links with NGOs. One practical reason why NGOs may be a useful source of relevant investment information is that they tend to spend time analysing and lobbying for changes to public policy on SEE issues. Consequently, NGOs may be a useful indicator of future public policy that could be material to company valuation. Where NGO capital market intervention contributes to enhanced investment analysis, that intervention is legitimate because it helps improve investment decisions and market efficiency.

(3) *Market trust legitimacy*: While NGO capital market intervention may serve to improve investment analysis, there are circumstances in which it has been detrimental to a company's share price (see Chapter 3). However, while NGO capital

market campaigning may represent a short-term financial burden for a company, this alone is not sufficient reason to render the activity illegitimate. This is because there is a case for NGO capital market intervention being in the long-term collective interests of listed companies and their shareholders: companies benefit from the existence of the capital market, and the existence of any market depends in part on society's trust in order to maintain its own legitimacy. As Korten (1995, pp 89–98) argues, "an economic system can remain viable only so long as society has mechanisms to counter the abuses of either state or market power". His preferred system is democratic pluralism, which combines "the forces of the market, government and civil society [including NGOs]". From the perspective of NGO capital market intervention, therefore, where such intervention serves to correct welfare-undermining aspects of the capital market, it also serves to maintain trust in the capital market. The implication of this analysis is that NGO capital market intervention is not only legitimate, but also *necessary* for the long-term viability of the capital market itself. So, in the long term, NGO capital market intervention as a civil regulator of unethical corporate practices maintains trust in the market and, therefore, helps to maintain the market itself. Consequently, it is in the long-term interest of companies and their shareholders for NGOs to undertake a civil regulatory role via the capital market.

Therefore, NGO capital market intervention is legitimate where it furthers the NGO's welfare-oriented role in society, where it contributes to investment analysis and where it maintains market trust.

However, are there any constraints on legitimate NGO capital market campaigns? Company law sets out the legal boundaries for shareholder advocacy (see Chapter 3). Most UK NGO capital market intervention so far has remained within the boundaries of what the law sets out as legitimate shareholder advocacy. However, there are occasions when NGO capital market intervention has been illegal and/or undermined welfare, and is therefore illegitimate.

One form of illegality is the relatively benign but nevertheless unlawful action typified by Greenpeace when it used a public address system in conjunction with a recording-device at the ICI AGM (it is illegal for anyone other than the relevant company to record an AGM) in 1991 (Intervention 4, Appendix 1). At the other end of the spectrum is the far more pernicious capital market intervention that involves death threats, arson, vandalism, intimidation and physical violence used by a minority of animal-rights activists.

One such campaign targets Huntingdon Life Sciences (HLS).[7] Publicly, the campaign against HLS has been led by Stop Huntingdon Animal Cruelty (SHAC). SHAC's motto is "Words mean nothing Action is everything" (SHAC's capitalisation), but it claims to adopt a moderate campaign approach. This approach involves targeting a broad range of secondary targets, including, essentially, any company that has dealings with HLS, and publicly embarrassing the company into severing contact with HLS. When violent tactics have been used, the Animal Liberation Front – not SHAC – has often claimed to be responsible.

As a result of these campaigns, and as SHAC (2005) reports on its Web site, HLS openly warns potential investors that

> The Company is targeted by animal rights activists ... These groups, which include Stop Huntingdon Animal Cruelty (SHAC) and the Animal Liberation Front (ALF), among others, have publicly stated that the goal of their campaign is to "shut Huntingdon". If they were to succeed in closing the Company or significantly adversely affecting the Company's business, you could lose all or substantially all of the value of your investment in the Company's Voting Common Stock ... The animal rights activists may target you individually for harassment if they learn of your ownership of Voting Common Stock.

While they have not yet closed the company, SHAC's campaign tactics have nevertheless been highly effective. Among hundreds of companies that SHAC lists as having "dumped HLS" are the following FIs: Allied Irish Bank, Citibank, Dresdner Kleinwort Wasserstein, HSBC, Legal & General, Marsh, Mercury Asset Management, Merrill Lynch and NatWest Bank. This created such a significant problem for HLS that in 2001 the UK government had to step in and allow it to use the Bank of England as its banker.

Similarly, in 2005, HLS postponed its stock market listing in the US "on the New York Stock Exchange at the NYSE's request because of potential protests from animal rights activists" (see Adetunji, 2005, p 1). SHAC had listed the names, email addresses and telephone

numbers of the NYSE board of directors on its Web site and encouraged its members to "make the good people of the NYSE aware ...
Please keep all communications polite."

Despite requests to keep the communications polite, there can of
course be no guarantee that such requests will be heeded. For
example, another of SHAC's campaign targets is a pharmaceutical
company called Phytopharm because it uses the animal-testing services of HLS. While SHAC may be moderate, in 2005, a Canadian
FI called Canaccord resigned as broker to Phytopharm after the car
of one of Canaccord's directors was firebombed.

In all likelihood, the main reason why so many companies have
severed contact with HLS following an approach by SHAC is probably the perceived threat of violence towards company employees
rather than public embarrassment at being connected with animal
testing. It is interesting to note that the US is using its anti-terrorism
laws to put SHAC on trial, and has suggested that the publishing of
contact details of companies that do business with HLS is an incite-
ment to others to commit crimes. For its part, SHAC USA argues
this is a violation of its right to free speech. At the time of writing,
the outcome of the trial is not known. Nevertheless, the US is taking an increasingly hard line on animal-rights activists in general,
with the Federal Bureau of Investigation including them among the
top domestic terrorism threats.

So, in conclusion, in a civil society, NGO capital market campaigns
can play a legitimate, economically valuable and welfare-enhancing
function. However, anti-corporate activists can also harness the
influence within the capital market, and, in so doing, undermine welfare. Consequently, the underlying aims, motivations and methods of
each NGO campaign needs to be assessed in order to establish
whether it is legitimate.

SUMMARY

This book focuses on NGO groups whose stated purpose is the promotion of welfare-enhancing environmental and/or societal goals
rather than the achievement or protection of economic power in the
marketplace for commercial purposes or political power through
the electoral process.

This chapter has established NGOs' societal role, including that
of civil regulator. It has argued that companies are relevant to

NGOs because their environmental, economic, political and social influence can impact upon an NGO's mission. It has also outlined the various strategies and stances that NGOs can adopt when conducting corporate campaigns, including attempts to harness the influence within the capital market.

This chapter has also established that the capital market has influence over companies via two principal mechanisms: (1) *economic influence* via the cost of capital and (2) *investor advocacy influence* via the rights associated with share ownership. It has also been demonstrated that the capital market is relevant to NGOs because of this influence and that this influence of the capital market is relevant in two related ways:

❑ as an instrumental mechanism for changing corporate practices; and
❑ as a target for systemic change in itself.

It has also been shown that there are a number of subsidiary reasons why the capital market is of interest to NGOs, including raising capital, generating fundraising income and the proper stewardship of financial reserves.

Finally, this section has argued that NGOs derive legitimacy for capital market intervention from their welfare-oriented role in society, their potential contribution to investment analysis and the maintenance of market trust derived from civil regulation. Consequently, it has been suggested that NGO capital market intervention that both operates within the boundaries of company law and aims to enhance welfare is legitimate and in the long-term collective interests of companies and their shareholders. Further, it has been shown that the United Nations NGO ECOSOC eligibility process has the status of customary international law. It is therefore used (in Chapter 5) as a proxy for the legitimacy of the NGOs under review.

1　The Union of International Associations has maintained a database of international organisations since its inception in 1910. The UIA produce a *Yearbook of International Organizations*, the 2005/2006 version of which states that there are 51,509 nongovernmental organisations (Union of International Associations, 2005, p 2966).

2　Company Law Reform Bill, Part B – Directors, Chapter 1, General Duties, B3 (3), DTI, 2005.

3　"Sell-side" refers to institutions that sell equities to investors for a percentage commission.

4   This is partly for legal reasons in that a trustee has the responsibility to represent pension fund beneficiaries, and partly for practical reasons in that some trustees do not have the professional skills to assess the investment processes of fund managers.

5   Unlike most other institutional investors, charities and charitable foundations in the UK are free to adopt SRI screening policies so long as the trustees take account of their responsibilities under trust law when making investment decisions. The legal position is outlined in the Charity Commission booklet CC14 – "Investment of Charitable Funds", which states, "Trustees of a charity may, of course, decline to consider investing in a particular company if it carries out activities that are directly contrary to the charity's purposes and, therefore against its interests and those of its beneficiaries" (p 3).

6   Organisational stakeholders are defined as "any group or individual who can affect or is affected by the achievement of an organisation's objective" (Freeman, 1984, p 46).

7   Because the CM campaigns against Huntingdon Life Sciences have involved physical violence and death threats, it is therefore illegitimate according to the criteria here. Therefore, they are excluded from the chronology.

3

NGO Capital Market Campaign Strategy

The main aim of this section is to develop the model for NGO capital market intervention and to explain in more detail the underpinnings of the capital market mechanisms of influence introduced in Chapter 1.

The principal role of the model is to provide a better understanding of the complex interface between NGOs and the capital market. As previously outlined, the model defines the capital market intervention strategies, and is used to classify the chronological list of NGO capital market intervention between 1990 and 2002.

This chapter commences with an outline of the model. Then the model's mechanism-of-influence components are reviewed in detail. This involves a review of the source of the capital market's economic influence, followed by an outline of how NGOs use this influence. The source of the capital market's investor advocacy influence is then reviewed, and is similarly followed by an outline of how NGOs use investor advocacy influence. The penultimate section includes an analysis of the theoretical limitations of NGO capital market intervention. The chapter closes with an analysis of which NGO capital market intervention strategies have the highest probability of success.

A TYPOLOGY OF CAPITAL MARKET CAMPAIGNING

As previously reviewed, the capital market influence listed companies via two principal mechanisms:

(1) *Economic influence*: The market establishes the cost of capital for listed companies. The more a company has to pay to for capital, the less it can raise. This limits the extent of its activity.

(2) *Advocacy influence*: Shareholders are the "principals" of the business and can exercise their rights of share ownership over their "agents", the company directors.

In the way that the influence of the capital market is realised via these two mechanisms, there are two associated strategies deployed by NGOs when they attempt to encourage the consideration of SEE issues by the capital market:

(1) an economic-influence strategy – where the NGO attempts to divert capital away from one area and into others so as to affect companies' share prices and, therefore, the cost of capital; and

(2) a strategy of investor advocacy influence – where the NGO uses the rights associated with share ownership to raise concerns with the company.

This NGO choice of mechanism of influence is one of the two main dimensions of the model and is described in detail in Chapter 3. The other main dimension arises from the route of influence: NGOs may buy and sell shares on their own account or they may attempt to magnify their influence by co-opting the influence of large institutional investors. Co-opting investors' influence is classified as "indirect". Conversely, "direct" involves an NGO (or coalition of NGOs) lobbying without having co-opted FIs.

When combined, these two main dimensions of "mechanism" and "route" result in four strategic options: direct and indirect economic influence, and direct and indirect investor advocacy. Indirect NGO attempts to co-opt the influence of FIs have included confrontational campaigns – particularly when the NGO has believed that the FI is impeding the progress of a corporate campaign – and the relatively recent emergence of formal collaborative partnerships between socially responsible investment (SRI) fund managers and NGOs.[1] To elucidate the NGO "stance" taken during indirect approaches, a classification element of this stance is added to the indirect route: a revised form of Elkington and Fennell's taxonomy (see Chapter 2) is used to classify the "stance" taken by the NGO in the indirect approach.

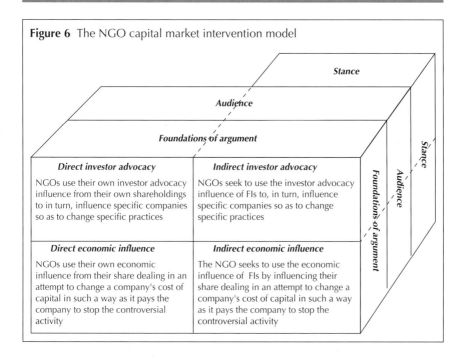

Figure 6 The NGO capital market intervention model

Direct investor advocacy	*Indirect investor advocacy*
NGOs use their own investor advocacy influence from their own shareholdings to in turn, influence specific companies so as to change specific practices	NGOs seek to use the investor advocacy influence of FIs to, in turn, influence specific companies so as to change specific practices
Direct economic influence	*Indirect economic influence*
NGOs use their own economic influence from their share dealing in an attempt to change a company's cost of capital in such a way as it pays the company to stop the controversial activity	The NGO seeks to use the economic influence of FIs by influencing their share dealing in an attempt to change a company's cost of capital in such a way as it pays the company to stop the controversial activity

In addition to "mechanism" and "route" and the subsidiary element of "stance" (which, as stated, applies only to the indirect strategic options), there are two final subsidiary elements to the model: "primary audience" and "nature of argument". Both apply to all four permutations of the two main dimensions (see Figure 6).

The audience element involves deciding whether to target companies and their investors and/or the public policy framework in which these capital market institutions operate. As demonstrated in the chronology (see Appendix 1), NGOs have attempted to use the strategic opportunities for sustaining long-term influence presented by the legislation governing the capital market. In theory, changes to legislation could influence the behaviour of all listed companies by changing economic influence or investor advocacy influence in some way. Changing the legislation therefore provides NGOs with a potential mechanism for influencing listed companies *en masse*. In addition to referring to the legislation underlying the capital market, this component of the model also refers to interventions where the ultimate target is changed legislation in general – strengthened construction-sector health and safety legislation, for example.

The argument component denotes whether the NGO primarily used business-case and/or moral-case foundations in the debate. A business-case argument uses conceptual, quantitative or qualitative financial analysis in support of a particular course of action – but a moral-case argument uses ethical principles such as "do no harm".

As both the latter primary-audience and nature-of-argument components are "and/or" options, each results in three possible classifications – primarily business case, primarily moral case, and both business and moral case.

The main two dimensions of "mechanism" and "route", when combined with the three subsidiary elements of argument, audience and stance, yield the model shown in Figure 6.

Figure 6's three-dimensional representation of the model highlights the central importance of the two main choices of "direct/indirect" and "economic/investor advocacy influence". The foundations of the argument, the primary audience and stance, underlie these two main dimensions. The lack of a third-tier direct-stance "box" in Figure 6 indicates that a direct intervention does not involve a stance because the NGO is not attempting to co-opt FIs and, therefore, does not adopt a stance in relation to them.

In summary, the two central dimensions of the NGO capital market engagement model are defined by the NGOs' choice of economic or investor advocacy influence, and the degree to which they seek to increase their own influence by approaching FIs. Underlying each strategy is the choice to confront investors and/or policy makers, and whether to use moral and/or business-case

---

PANEL 1

In order to help the reader understand how the model applies in practice, a pair of examples are provided below:

Example 1
Where an NGO attempts to influence a company via the capital market by attempting to encourage its institutional investors to divest from the stock – perhaps because the company's environmental practice is potentially detrimental to share price – and they do so confrontationally via targeted

correspondence with its main investors, the model would classify this as:

❏ *Economic influence*: "encourage a company's institutional investors to divest from the stock".
❏ *Indirect*: "via targeted correspondence with its main investors".
❏ *Business case*: "because the company's environmental practice is potentially detrimental to share price".
❏ *Capital market (CM) institutions*: "institutional investors".
❏ *Orca*: "confrontationally".

Example 2
Where an NGO attempts to influence a company via the capital market by purchasing shares in order to attend an AGM so that it can raise questions surrounding the moral integrity of a company's behaviour, then the model would classify this as:

❏ *Investor advocacy influence*: "purchasing shares in order to attend an AGM in order to raise questions".
❏ *Direct*: "an NGO... purchasing shares".
❏ *Moral case*: "questions surrounding the moral integrity of a company's behaviour".
❏ *CM institutions*: "in order to attend an AGM".
(As this approach is direct, the stance is not classified.)

arguments. For indirect strategies there is also a choice of four "stance" taxa. There are other ways to model this complex inter-action, but focusing on the relationship between NGOs and the capital market in this way is a useful means of categorising NGO behaviour that makes broad and intuitive sense.

There are clearly other components to the NGO capital market intervention that are not included in this NGO capital market inter-vention model. For example, the type of issue, type of NGO and scale and duration of the intervention are not incorporated. Nevertheless, this level of sophistication enables sufficient differen-tiation between different NGO strategies and provides a useful frame of reference for companies and their investors seeking to understand what strategy the NGO has adopted.

Having introduced the model, a more detailed review of the nature and origins of the two main mechanisms of influence – investor advocacy and economic – is now required.

THE SOURCE OF ECONOMIC INFLUENCE

Financial capital is of central importance to companies because they require it not only to meet operating costs, but also for investment in new projects. PLCs can raise new capital in the form of loans or equity – but capital costs money:

❏ *Cost of debt*: Providers of debt finance, such as banks or investors in Corporate Bonds, lend the money in return for a promise to pay a stated sum each year as interest and to repay the loan at some stated time in the future. The cost of debt to the company, therefore, is the interest on the loan.

❏ *Cost of equity*: Providers of equity finance – shareholders – may receive dividends and the possibility of capital appreciation, which is expected by shareholders. The cost of equity is the cost paid to attract and maintain investors. In addition to the costs arising from dividends and maintaining capital appreciation expectations, further costs in the form of underwriting fees arise at the point of new share issuance.

A company's cost of equity capital will be higher the more it has to pay in dividends or the less it receives as a price for its stock. The price is set by market expectations. All other things being equal, the more favourably the capital market views a company's prospects, the cheaper it will be for that company to raise equity capital to finance its growth through new investment projects. This is because the capital market will perceive the company security as a lower-risk and/or higher-return investment opportunity and therefore value the equity more highly.[2]

The cheaper the cost of capital to the company, the greater its ability to grow: it has to pay a lower proportion of the capital raised back to borrowers and investors, leaving more for investment projects and rendering it easier to generate a return on that capital. Conversely, if management fails to meet capital market expectations, the share price will fall, making it more difficult to raise new finance and exposing the company to unwanted predators. Herein lies the main part of the capital market's economic influence over corporate practice that is in focus in this book: the market for equities within the capital market sets a company's share price. This affects a company's cost of capital, which is an important business constraint.

While this cost of capital effect is the primary source of economic influence in focus here, there are others. For example, where a director has presided over a long-term depreciation in share price, and becomes generally regarded as part of the problem, investors may call for the director to resign. This potential for loss of income and damage to their professional reputation helps to motivate behaviours associated with good performance. Conversely, the intrinsic satisfaction arising from the prestige associated with having presided over a successful company is also a powerful motivational force. From a pecuniary-incentives perspective, some argue that it is in the long-term interests of shareholders to have their financial interests and those of the directors aligned by linking their incentive structure to measures of shareholder value. While there can be problems associated with taking such an approach too far, including share price, components in executive directors' remuneration packages is standard practice. As a consequence, economic influence also affects a director's personal remuneration and, therefore, acts as an additional motivating factor.

In summary, the principal source of the capital market economic influence is primarily the share-price influence on a company's cost of capital, but it also originates from takeover prospects and directors' remuneration packages.

HOW NGOs SHAPE ECONOMIC INFLUENCE

The previous section explained how investors influence companies through their economic influence. This section explains how NGOs attempt to harness this influence for their own ends when adopting an economic-influence strategy.

Individual NGOs do not have sufficient financial reserves to buy and sell shares on their own account to be material to the capital market. Therefore, an economic-influence strategy is typically attempted Indirectly.

Conceptually, as mentioned earlier, if NGO corporate campaigning on SEE issues negatively affects investors' views on the company, then, other things being equal, a rational investor would decide to divest (some of their shares) from the stock. If such action were repeated on sufficient scale, then this would drive down market demand for the share and, therefore, its price. This in turn would cause the cost of capital for the company targeted by the NGO to increase. In this hypothetical case of a highly effective NGO campaign, if a company decided not to change the cause of concern, it would become less competitive as its capital became more expensive – ultimately exposing itself to takeover. Consequently, the rational action on the part of the company would be to deal with the cause of concern in such a way as to bring the campaign to a close.

The above conceptual case demonstrates how an effective NGO campaign could influence corporate SEE performance via share price movements and cost of capital restrictions. However, in practice, two main questions arise:

(1) Investors buy and sell shares for a number of reasons – what evidence is there that SEE issues are integrated into their analysis at all?

(2) If investors do integrate SEE issues into their analysis, how in theory could NGOs working on those issues influence that analysis?

In relation to the first question, the Confederation of British Industry (CBI) recognises that "ethical considerations are influencing the decisions of a growing number of investors" (see CBI, 2000, p 2). Furthermore, many large fund managers have published policy statements that formally recognise that some SEE issues that NGOs work on can be material to equity valuation: "the investment world has recognised that many factors previously assumed to be extraneous to the generation of shareholder returns – business ethics, social responsibility and environmental sustainability – are increasingly material to financial performance"[3] (see Henderson Global Investors, 2003, p 2).

But does the empirical evidence in relation to share price movements arising from SEE issues confirm that investors integrate such issues to an extent sufficient to influence cost of capital?

There is a significant body of literature analysing the relationship between SEE issues and share price, and studies have taken a number of different approaches. The most relevant studies here are those that conducted an event analysis of some kind of SEE issues. The event analysed could range from disclosure of pollution inventory data through to catastrophes such as a major chemical spill and explosions.

From an environmental perspective, an influential study by Hamilton (1995) reviewed the impact on the share price of the US

Environmental Protection Agency's (EPA) release of companies' site-specific pollution data via the Toxic Release Inventory (TRI) in 1989. This is one of the few event analysis studies to look at how specific on-the-ground corporate environmental performance correlates with share price movements across an industry. The intention of the EPA was that by their subjecting the pollution data to public scrutiny, companies would be given an additional incentive to reduce emissions. The TRI placed data on some companies' toxic emissions to air, water and land in the public domain for the first time. This information was felt to be of potential relevance to investors, as it could be a forward indicator of civil actions and pollution convictions, and a general indicator of the quality of a company's management systems. Hamilton's analysis indicated that shareholders in firms reporting TRI pollution figures experienced negative, statistically significant abnormal returns upon the first release of the information: "the average abnormal return on the day [the TRI] information made public was negative and statistically significant... firms lost on average US$4.1 million" (1995, p 112). They also found that share price fell more when larger numbers of different chemical submissions were reported by the firms.

Separately, Blacconiere and Patten (1994) examined whether the catastrophe of Union Carbide's 1984 chemical leak in Bhopal, India, caused a market reaction in relation to other chemical firms. Their study found evidence of a significant intra-industry reaction. However, firms with more limited environmental disclosures in their financial reports prior to the chemical leak experienced a more significant negative reaction than firms with more extensive environmental disclosures. As with Hamilton's findings, Blacconiere and Patten concluded that their results suggested that investors include an analysis of the firm's environmental disclosures and regard them as a positive sign that the firm is managing its exposure to future regulatory cost.

From a social perspective, Knight and Pretty (2001) analysed the shareholder "ValueReaction"[4] to a number of corporate catastrophes. They identified "value reactions" arising from a number of corporate reputation crises that related to SEE issues. For example, the study found that 50% of value was eroded from Bridgestone shares following a product recall due to health and safety concerns.

From an ethical perspective, Gunthorpe (1997) examined whether the financial markets penalised public corporations for unethical business practices. It looked at 69 US corporations that were the subject of public announcements concerning a range of ethical misdemeanours such as fraud, price fixing, bribery and patent infringement. It found a statistically significant negative abnormal return upon the announcement that a firm was under investigation or had in some way engaged in unethical behaviour. Gunthorpe concluded that this suggested that firms were penalised by the capital market for their unethical actions.

Therefore, the above research indicates that there are circumstances where the capital market has included consideration of SEE issues to a sufficient scale to have implications for companies' cost of capital. This is not perhaps as surprising a conclusion as it may initially seem, as there are many circumstances in which a failure to manage strategically important SEE issues can result in significant brand damage, large-scale litigation or fines.

While the above analysis addresses the first question as to whether the market incorporates SEE issues at all, it does not clarify how NGOs shape the economic influence that the capital market has over corporate practice. The second question remains – how do NGOs actively attempt to harness the capital market's economic influence?

From the specific perspective of the NGO capital market intervention model developed above, when adopting an economic-influence strategy an NGO has a "nature of argument" option that it can use to motivate behaviour on the part of third parties. This nature of argument refers to whether the foundations of the overall intervention are rooted in business-case or moral-case (or welfare-case) arguments.

NGOs make moral arguments for divestment – and some individual investors may respond to this. However, in general, FIs can be constrained from responding to *purely* moral arguments (the legal origins of this constraint are covered later in this chapter). So, when considering how NGOs deploy an economic-influence strategy, the strength of the business-case argument and/or their ability to generate such a business case is a significant determinant of success and is therefore the focus of the discussion here. In general, there are two distinct scenarios arising:

❏ *capital market inefficiency*: the NGO issue is currently material to company earnings but the market is not considering the issue; and

❏ "immateriality": the NGO issue is not currently material to company earnings and therefore not factored into company analysis.

In respect of the "capital market inefficiency" scenario, if sustainability issues are to matter to companies, then one option for NGOs is to bring such issues to the fore – within companies – by accentuating to investors the positive financial implications of social agendas (where they exist) so that investment analysis of performance in this area becomes integral to company valuation and, therefore, the company's cost of capital. NGOs have made a number of attempts to tailor their campaign to the capital market by using business case and shareholder value arguments to support their moral standpoint.

The Corner House has implemented a number of different capital market campaigns (see Appendix 1), and has advocated (2002, p 3) to its NGO peers the use of the business case:

> The arguments that count in financial markets are not those based directly on ethics or environmental self-interest ("investing in this company means that your children are more likely to get cancer"), but on financial risk ("lawsuits arising from cancer cases will cost this company a lot of money and reputation, so your investment won't earn as much as you thought").

A practical example of an NGO's use of business-case arguments as part of a capital market intervention is Greenpeace, which commissioned an assessment of the share price impact of government responses to the threat of climate change on an oil and gas company's share price. Greenpeace commissioned Innovest, a specialist investment consultancy, to quantify the risks that BP faced from climate change. This analysis (see Whittaker and Brammer, 2001, p 14) was presented to institutional investors at the 2001 AGM and found that:

> under plausible scenarios, the discounted present value of potential future carbon liabilities within a single energy-intensive manufacturing firm could represent a substantial percentage of its entire market

capitalisation... As such, shareholders would be justified in seeking clarification of the company's risk mitigation strategy.

The key question here is whether this research encouraged shareholders to seek "clarification of the company's risk mitigation strategy". It appears that, by alerting the market to the potential materiality of climate change with this financial research, Greenpeace increased investor interest in BP's climate change. The evidence in support of this claim is as follows:

Investment analysis

The investment consultancy Global Risk Management Services (2001, p 6) referred to "BP going to unprecedented lengths [prior to the AGM]... The company held meetings with significant share-holders and SRI fund managers to stress its case, which indicates how seriously they took the challenges laid down."

Greenpeace claims

"It gave us a serious side – we had a reason to go and talk to investors and talk to them seriously about climate change and what BP were doing. It certainly put the wind up BP. They really didn't like us talking to their shareholders at all... if you put in a resolution you are entitled to circulate your argument, so we got in touch with one million people – at BP's expense – with our arguments about oil, pristine areas and climate change" (see Tunmore, 2001).

Investor activity

Following the AGM, a number of BP's largest institutional shareholders, including Barclays Global Investors, Schroders, Henderson, Jupiter, USS, Friends Ivory & Sime, and Morley Fund Management, met BP to review the detail of its strategy in relation to climate change. BP subsequently ran its first high-profile climate-change technology presentation to mainstream oil and gas ana-lysts, which reviewed the company's renewable-energy capacity and carbon sequestration technology. More than 18 months after the report, following a further BP presentation to investors, HSBC proffered the view that "BP leads the sector on its climate change strategy" (see Tyrrell, 2002b, p 3).

Clearly, this Greenpeace-commissioned business-case analysis was not the only source of climate-change-related influence on BP or its investors at the time. Such pressure would have also originated from the public policy debate, for example. However, there is *prima facie* evidence that investors were motivated to seek clarification of the company's risk-mitigation strategy as a result of Greenpeace's business-case arguments.

Therefore, in respect of the above immateriality scenario, where there is no *initial* business case for the NGOs' preferred course of action, they have attempted to influence corporate practice by targeting their campaign activity on the key business drivers underlying a company's cost of capital. These share price value drivers include earnings, access to raw materials, productivity and brand value. The result is that the NGO effectively "materialises" the business case for corporate change.

This concept that NGOs can materialise the importance of their issue deserves a little more explanation. The discussion below covers each of the aforementioned value drivers and sets out how NGOs have influence them:

Creating a business case via a focus on the earnings value driver

Where NGOs implement consumer boycott campaigns that change consumption patterns on a sufficient scale to be reflected in company earnings, the market picks up the earnings effect within the quantitative analysis and may then reflect this in the valuation. To the extent that this changed valuation affects investment decisions, it will also have an effect on the company's cost of capital for as long as the campaign is effective. One example is the impact on consumer purchasing behaviour from the NGO campaign against genetically modified foods, and the subsequent impact on the share price of Monsanto, the main company supplying the new agricultural technology: "Monsanto's share price has fallen from a high of US$51 earlier this year to just over US$42 yesterday as the consumer backlash against genetically modified foods in Europe has spread to the US" (see *Guardian*, 1999, p 16).

Creating a business case via a focus on the raw material value driver

Where NGOs have limited the availability of raw materials to a company by, for example, preventing access to a particular source, investors have included the financial impact of this activity in their analysis. NGOs are more likely to choose this route of action when the company in question does not have a "high street" brand that is susceptible to consumer boycott. One example is the integration of access to environmentally sensitive sites into an assessment of BP's exposure to political risks that was conducted by Société Générale Global Research brokers (see Ennis, 2002, p 11). SG constructed a quantified model of political risk. This defined overall risk to the oil and gas sector as comprising three main components:

❑ overall political risk;
❑ fiscal terms of the host country; and
❑ risks associated with exploration and production.

Overall political risk (component 1) comprises a number of subsidiary elements including the likelihood of imminent war, the stability of a country's regime and – of particular relevance here – "environmental sensitivity". This is defined as how much opposition there is within a country to the current development of petroleum operations. Ennis cites the opposition to drilling in the Arctic National Wildlife Refuge as an example (see case study in Chapter 5). The inclusion in mainstream financial analysis of the effect of the NGO campaign against drilling in the Arctic Refuge is noteworthy. It is also interesting to note its relative importance: the model assigns a weighting of 1% of the "total overall risk" from "environmental sensitivity", whereas the risks arising from "war" (defined as outright war and cross-border disputes) is 0.9% and the risks from "repatriation" and the "fiscal terms" risk (changes in a country's fiscal policy) is 1.2%.

Creating a business case via a focus on the employee productivity value driver

Where NGOs have affected employee morale in such a way as to be detrimental to productivity, investors have integrated this into their analysis via the productivity measures in the quantitative analysis. Greenpeace's campaign against the proposed disposal of the Brent Spar oil storage platform in the North Sea seems to have contributed to corporate change at Shell. A combination of value drivers appear to have been involved here: Svendsen *et al* (2001) say:

Shell estimated that the direct costs to change the disposal decision was US$200m. Boycotts and threats at the pump also cost the firm sales and market share. 50 Shell service stations were vandalised, 2 firebombed and one raked with gunfire. Employee morale plummeted . . . the Brent Spar North Sea oil platform incident cost Royal Dutch/Shell fully 30% of its market share in Germany within one month.

According to Mark Wade, a senior executive in Shell's Sustainable Development Group, employee morale was the single biggest factor responsible for the turnaround in Shell's decision (see Wade, 2000).

Similarly, Knight and Pretty (2001, pp 24–5) identify a Value Reaction in Shell's share price of almost –10% from this Greenpeace campaign against Shell. In this context, this research is particularly important because it clearly demonstrates that an NGO can have a significant impact on a company's share price (and, therefore, its cost of capital).

Creating a business case via the brand valuation driver

Finally, and most pervasively, NGOs have also targeted the share price value driver of a company's reputation. Management of reputation risk is an important business activity, since intangibles – which includes brand – now represent about 30% of FTSE100 company balance sheets. In some circumstances, a corporate brand can account for more than two-thirds of a company's market value (see Knight and Pretty, 2001, p 9). As a result, board directors are under increasing pressure from both the City and legislators to protect company reputations. Unsurprisingly, companies spend considerable time and money on protecting and enhancing the value of their brand.

In one example of an NGO campaign potentially impacting on the intangible value of a company's brand through reputation, Deutsche Bank's sell-side broker analysis on ExxonMobil (see Traynor, 2002, p 4) refers to the Greenpeace campaign and concludes, "While the company insists that it has suffered no fiscal impact from the boycott, being handed a reputation as environmental enemy number one for such a big customer-facing business has to be considered a brand risk."

This kind of effect is of sufficient scale for Morgan Stanley – the large sell-side investment brokers – to note, "We see links between corporate social responsibility and financial performance . . . stock markets respond positively to corporate disclosure on such issues, but negatively to disclosure by third parties (such as special-interest groups)" (see Dean and Garin, 2005, p 1).

In conclusion, this section has demonstrated that, where NGOs have either successfully advocated the inclusion of certain SEE issues into the investment analysis process or influenced key business value drivers, then NGOs have made their issue material to the company. The above analysis shows how NGOs have in some instances influenced the key value drivers of a business. It further demonstrates that, by influencing these key value drivers through their corporate campaigning, NGOs have "materialised" SEE issues for companies. This can subsequently encourage changes to corporate practice via the influence that cost of capital has over a company's ability to do business.

THE SOURCE OF INVESTOR ADVOCACY INFLUENCE

As set out above, the second of the two principal routes through which the capital market can influence the practices of listed companies is investor advocacy influence. The discussion below reviews the origins, nature and scope of this influence.

It has been demonstrated that economic influence arises from the trading activity on the capital market. Conversely, investor advocacy influence arises out of the law that has established the market itself. As previously mentioned, investor advocacy influence is distinct from an economic-influence strategy, because the latter is realised through buying and selling shares, whereas investor advocacy influence is realised via the ownership rights of shares which, when sold, are lost.

In the UK, the opportunity for shareholder influence is a legal attribute of the corporate form as established in UK company law. Consequently, when seeking to understand the theoretical foundations of investor advocacy influence, it is necessary to have a basic understanding of the legal context of investor advocacy. In particular, those sections dealing with the ownership, control and accountability of a company are important. The following discussion focuses on these aspects.

As identified above, the Companies Act regulates PLCs. The main legal principles of the modern form of a publicly listed company are as follows (adapted from Mackenzie, 1993, p 29):

The company
Once incorporated, the company becomes a "legal person" on its own account. The directors are appointed by the shareholders to manage the company.

The directors
The law variously considers the directors to be the agents of the shareholders, the controllers of the company and the company's servants. The articles of association confer on the board overall control of the company's activities. The board typically appoints executives to exert day-to-day management control. As a counter-point to this power, the Companies Act gives the board formal responsibilities to its shareholders, employees and the company as a whole.

The shareholders
Individual and organisational shareholders become "members" of the company when they buy the shares. At the annual general meeting, they are expected to oversee the activities of directors and may vote on their election or re-election. Shareholders may alter the articles of association – a founding legal document of the com-pany – and, in some companies and in certain circumstances, may direct the board to follow specific policies.

Despite the common impression to the contrary, in strict legal terms, shareholders do not own companies as a whole. In a 1948 landmark test case, Lord Justice Evershed concluded, "Share-holders are not, in the eye of the law, part owners of the undertak-ing [the company]. The undertaking is something different from the totality of the shareholdings" (see Gower, 1969, p 522). The intellectual basis of this judgment was, in part, the fact that in law a company is regarded as a "person", and is therefore beyond ownership.

Nevertheless, a large part of company law exists in order to pre-vent shareholders' interests being abused by company directors and confers on shareholders certain legal rights. As mentioned above, in company law, shareholders are expected to oversee the activities of directors. Directors are therefore supposed to be accountable for their performance to the shareholders who elect them to act on their behalf. It can be argued that the law conveys a collective responsibility on shareholders to ensure that "negligence and profusion" does not prevail in the management of the company.

The principle for these legal provisions can be traced back to Adam Smith, who argued that optimal market efficiency required the owners of capital to be directly involved in its management because they tended to be more vigilant with their own money (see Smith, 1776). Where a company lacked oversight by the owners of the money, Smith argued that company directors:

> being the managers rather of other people's money than of their own, it cannot well be expected that they should watch over it with the same anxious vigilance with which the partners in a private copartnery frequently watch over their own . . . Negligence and profusion, therefore, must always prevail, more or less in the management of the affairs of such a company.

So, while it is true that a company is more than a mere item of property, a legal relationship exists between company shareholders and company directors that provides shareholders with considerable investor advocacy influence over corporate practices.

The specific legal rights conferred on shareholders by company law include certain rights of access to the company directors: entrance to annual general meetings, the ability to vote on resolutions, the appointment of the directors, approval of the annual report, approval of the remuneration report and, in specific circumstances, the ability to table a shareholder resolution directing the company to take a particular course of action or call for an extraordinary general meeting.

As discussed in Chapter 1, company law also sets the parameters for legitimate shareholder advocacy. For example, in the UK, formally submitting a shareholder resolution requires compliance with the procedures intended to ensure that the issues discussed at an AGM are appropriate. Specifically, Section 376 of the Companies Act states that when a company receives a resolution from shareholders who collectively represent a minimum of either one-twentieth of the total voting rights, or 100 members holding shares collectively owning an average nominal[5] holding of £100 per member, then the company must circulate the resolution to its shareholders with the notice of its AGM.

In addition to the investor advocacy influence derived from the legal rights associated with the ownership of ordinary voting shares, a norm has been established whereby a company director's prime responsibility is to increase "shareholder value" (SHV). This provides a secondary source of investor advocacy influence.

The SHV doctrine is embedded in the principle that shareholders entrust the directors with running the company's business on their behalf. It has now become common practice among UK PLCs to refer to the importance that directors place on the generation of SHV. Consequently, it is possible for investors to raise concerns with the directors of investee companies on the grounds that their control over the company's activities is affecting SHV.

Investor advocacy influence is promoted by government-backed recommendations contained in the corporate-governance best-practice codes of conduct that encourage investors to play an active share-ownership role. The main reasons why corporate-governance guidelines are important to NGO capital market Investor Advocacy Influence are first, that they highlight the responsibilities of share ownership, and second, that they recognise that engagement on issues of corporate social responsibility is an appropriate activity for investors.

In respect of the responsibilities of share ownership, the Combined Code on Corporate Governance[6] (see Committee on Corporate Governance, 2003) recommends that FIs should take a more active role in corporate governance, and states that "institutional investors have a responsibility to make considered use of their votes" (p 20). It recommends that they "should be ready, where practicable, to enter into a dialogue with companies". It also levies a commensurate requirement on companies to speak with their investors: "Companies should be ready, where practicable, to enter into a dialogue with institutional shareholders based on the mutual understanding of objectives."

The Combined Code is particularly important to NGO capital market intervention because it is integrated into the UK Listing Authority stock exchange listing rules.[7] By way of sanction, a company risks losing its listing if it is found to be in breach of the listing rules and is not able to explain why this breach has occurred. A listing is important for any large company wishing to raise capital from investors, so such a potential sanction is a significant threat. (However, the question has understandably been raised as to whether the stock exchange would in practice withdraw a listing, since this would be deeply problematic for a company's share-holders who would find their share prices plummeting due to the significant decrease in the liquidity of their shares.)

In respect of the recognition within these corporate-governance guidelines that engagement on SEE issues is an appropriate activity for investors, the Combined includes the principle that "The board should maintain a sound system of internal control to safeguard shareholders' investment and the company's assets". The Turnbull Committee has produced guidance for directors on the internal control elements within the Combined Code. This guidance recommends that boards should identify and assess the significant internal and external operational, financial, compliance and other risks on an ongoing basis. It states, "Significant risks may, for example, include those related to market, credit, liquidity, technological, legal, health, safety and environmental, reputation, and business probity issues" (see Committee on Corporate Governance, 2003, p 39). This clearly suggests that corporate reputation on the SEE issues does matter to companies and, therefore, their investors.

Similarly, the International Corporate Governance Network (see ICGN, 2003, p 3) declares that:

> it is clear that institutions risk failing to meet their responsibilities as fiduciaries if they disregard serious Corporate Governance concerns that may affect the long-term value of their investment. They should follow up on these concerns and assume their responsibility to deal with them properly. Such concerns may, for instance, relate to ... the management of environmental, ethical and social risks.

The ICGN is a network of investors that works to promote better corporate governance worldwide. At the time of writing, ICGN members were estimated to hold assets exceeding US$10 trillion. These members include the founding pension funds such as the California Public Employees Retirement System (CalPERS), the College Retirement Equities Fund (TIAA-CREF), and institutional investors such as the Council of Institutional Investors in the USA, the Association Française de la Gestion Financière, Barclays Global Investors, Capital Group, CDC Investment Management, Deutsche Borse, European Association of Securities Dealers, European Federation of Investment Funds and Companies, Fidelity, Paris Bourse, Trust Company of the West and Unicredito Italiano.

Similarly, the Institutional Shareholders' Committee[8] has published "The Responsibilities of Institutional Shareholders and Agents – Statement of Principles" (2005). In addition to recommending the establishment of policies and systems for conducting, monitoring, measuring and reporting on activism,[9] this statement focuses on corporate governance but also recognises that engagement on issues of corporate social responsibility can be an appropriate activity for investors: "Many issues could give rise to concerns about shareholder value...Instances where institutional shareholders and/or agents may want to intervene include when they have concerns about... the company's approach to corporate social responsibility."

One further reason why corporate governance codes are relevant to NGO investor advocacy influence is that these codes recommend certain mechanisms for investor intervention through which influence can be brought to bear – see Panel 2.

One corporate governance code of particular relevance to the NGOs in focus here is the Association of British Insurers' (ABI) SRI Guidelines (October 2001). These take "the form of disclosures, which institutions would expect to see included in the annual report of listed companies. Specifically they refer to disclosures relating to Board responsibilities and to policies, procedures and

---

PANEL 2

ICGN (2003, pp 3–4) details the following list of intervention options:

The general objective is to stimulate the preservation and growth of the companies' long-term value... Appropriate actions to give effect to these ownership responsibilities may include:

❑ voting;
❑ supporting the company in respect of good governance;
❑ maintaining constructive communication with the board on governance policies and practices in general;

❑ incorporating Corporate Governance analysis in the investment process;
❑ stimulating independent buy-side research;
❑ expressing specific concerns to the board, either directly or in a share-holders meeting;
❑ making a public statement;
❑ submitting proposals for the agenda of a shareholders meeting;
❑ submitting one or more nominees for election to the board as appropriate;
❑ convening a shareholders meeting;
❑ teaming up with other investors and local investment associations either in general or in specific cases;
❑ taking legal actions, such as legal investigations and class actions;
❑ outsourcing any or all of these powers to specialised agents, for instance in the event the institutional shareholder concludes that it does not have the ability to muster necessary skills in-house;
❑ lobbying governmental bodies and other authoritative organisations;
❑ making appropriate statements concerning public policies affecting shareholder rights and Corporate Governance.

verification" (see ABI, 2001, p 2). They are a non-statutory document aimed at companies, and intend to encourage disclosure on corporate management of significant SEE risks within a framework of good corporate governance.

What makes these ABI SRI Guidelines particularly important in the context of investor advocacy influence by NGOs is their relationship with the interface between NGOs and FIs. At launch, the *Financial Times* (see Dickson, 2001, p 21) considered that the initiative "stands between companies and the wilder ideas of non-governmental organisations". Similarly, when explaining the rationale for the development of the ABI Guidelines, Peter Montagnon, head of investment affairs at the ABI, stated that "institutions have ... to be careful to avoid being obliged to take on the agendas of people with whom they have no contractual relationship ... In other words, they have to avoid being hijacked by particularly vociferous single-issue lobbies" (see Montagnon, 2002, p 3).

Therefore, in summary, investor advocacy influence originates from three principal sources: the mechanisms of the legal rights associated with share ownership; the duties of directors to serve the interests of shareholders; and the guidance contained in corporate governance codes of best practice.

HOW NGOs SHAPE INVESTOR ADVOCACY INFLUENCE

The previous section explained how investors influence companies through their investor advocacy influence. As before, this section now turns to how NGOs attempt to harness this influence for their own ends, when they adopt an investor advocacy strategy.

From a direct perspective, as previously mentioned, some NGOs routinely invest a portion of their financial reserves on the stock market. Some have used their own investor advocacy influence to persuade their fund managers to raise concerns with companies on their behalf. For example, WWF's fund manager has previously asked questions at company AGMs on its behalf. More typically, however, an investor advocacy strategy involves securing access to share ownership rights by investing in a particular company's shares specifically to gain the associated rights. As demonstrated in the chronology (see Appendix 1), NGOs have used the right to attend a company's AGM and raise questions to the board. From a direct perspective, the question of how an NGO shapes investor advocacy influence is a straightforward matter: with a direct strategy, it has no need to influence other investors, because, instead, it can simply use the influence it has acquired from its own investments in a manner of its own choosing.

But, from an indirect perspective, the situation is not so straightforward: the NGO must first persuade other investors of the importance of the issue before they will take it up. This section focuses on addressing the question of how NGOs shape investor advocacy influence from the perspective of indirect investor advocacy influence. When reviewing the practice of NGO capital market intervention from this perspective, four main questions arise:

(1) Do FIs use the investor advocacy influence open to them at all?
(2) If they do, is such influence effective?
(3) Does FI investor advocacy influence include the SEE issues that the NGOs in focus here work on?
(4) If so, how do NGOs working on SEE issues shape FI investor advocacy influence?

The first question can best be answered by considering the voting record. The annual Pensions Investment Research Consultants (PIRC) survey of proxy voting trends in the UK consistently finds that the median voting turnout for FTSE350 companies is over half of the available votes. But to what degree is that influence effective (question 2 above)? In an influential review of the activism conducted by the CalPERS – one of the largest US Pension Schemes – Smith (1996, p 251) concluded, "Overall, the evidence indicates that shareholder activism is largely successful in changing governance structure and, when successful, results in a statistically significant increase in shareholder wealth." Similarly, a review of twenty empirical studies attempting to measure the effects of shareholder activism on target firms' values, operations and governance structures concluded, "Activists have been successful at prompting some firms to adopt limited changes in their governance structures. The rate of activists' success in prompting some change in target companies has increased over time" (see Karpoff, 1998, p 27).

In respect of whether investors engage in dialogue with companies on SEE issues (question 3), as highlighted in Chapter 1, an increasing number of fund managers also use one-to-one company meetings to begin "engagement" with them on SEE performance issues. Some of these socially responsible investors explicitly recognise both the financial case for good corporate responsibility and the moral responsibility they share with the companies when they operate in the pursuit of shareholder value. Insight Investment,[10] for example, states:

> Shareholders have both substantial powers over companies and considerable responsibility for what companies do in their name. We believe that investors have both a moral responsibility and compelling long-term interest in providing support and encouragement to companies in their efforts to comply with global business principles.

Schroder Investment Management also identifies a moral dimension to investment:

> Equity investment is a moral activity if properly and responsibly undertaken ... Economic growth has been an important mechanism for increasing standards of living, and equity investment (and the ownership rights it confers) offers the best vehicle for sharing in, and influencing this growth.

Unlike investor advocacy influence on corporate governance, there is not yet a body of academic literature to reference that analyses whether Investor advocacy influence on the corporate-responsibility agenda can be effective. Nevertheless, while issues of corporate governance and corporate social responsibility are different in nature, they do use the same legal mechanisms for investor advocacy influence – so reference to the evidence supporting the ability of investors to change corporate governance practice suggests a potential for engagement in corporate social responsibility to be effective.

Some SRI teams publish public reports on their engagement, including, the Co-operative Insurance Society, F&C, Henderson Global Investors, Insight Investment, Jupiter and Morley Asset Management. In general, these reports attempt to demonstrate that their engagement has been influential. While such claims may be biased, the European Commission recognises their collective influence as follows: "Many factors are driving moves towards corporate social responsibility: new concerns and expectations from citizens, consumers, public authorities and investors... social criteria are increasingly influencing the investment decisions of individuals and institutions" (Commission of the European Communities, 2001, p 7). Similarly, the influence of SRI engagement is recognised more generally (see *Financial Times*, 2002d, p 18):

> The pressure on companies to improve their sustainability performance is mounting from... sources such as the growth of "socially responsible" investment funds, supply chain initiatives and the growing number of guidelines designed to foster corporate social responsibility.

There is also some evidence from research into the implementation of corporate governance codes that investor advocacy influence on SEE issues can work. In the UK, in a review of the aforementioned ABI SRI Guidelines, the ABI concluded that "there had been a strong response to guidelines it issued" (see Tassell, 2003, p 2) and that more than two-thirds of FTSE100 companies made "full" or "adequate" disclosure of the significant risks they faced from social, environmental and ethical issues.

As can be seen, therefore, some investors do use investor advocacy influence and there are circumstances in which this has been effective. Furthermore, it can also be demonstrated that some investors do raise SEE issues when conducting investor advocacy influence. Nevertheless, the fourth and final question from the above introductory list (and the main question for this section) remains unanswered: how do NGOs working on such issues shape their investor advocacy influence through an indirect approach?

NGOs have utilised an indirect strategy of investor-advocacy influence by exerting pressure on investors to "engage" with a company or sector on specific issues, as opposed to calling for outright divestment. Here are three examples.

Greenpeace

Greenpeace founded "BP Shareholders Against New Exploration", which argues, "Shareholders are the primary regulators of the companies in which they invest. They have a right and a responsibility to challenge decisions made by the directors" (see www. sanpebp.com, accessed 2000).

Friends of the Earth

According to Friends of the Earth (2000a, p 4):

> Institutional investors have a moral responsibility not to fund the destruction of the environment and the exploitation of people. Now it is time for [institutional investors] to face up – systematically and proactively, not just when occasionally goaded by protest groups – to the morality of investing in companies that collaborate with authoritarian regimes' mass-murder of native peoples; or who poison people's water; or who contribute to climate change that contributes to the deaths of thousands in hurricanes and floods.

WWF

Robert Napier of WWF-UK said in a speech (2000):

> WWF's call to action to you is "engage with companies in your portfolio on issues of social responsibility. We do believe it is better to engage rather than to screen. It is no good simply walking away from companies. It is much more important to seek to engage with them. If in the end, engagement fails, then walk away rather publicly".

The main point here is that NGOs have argued that the existence of investor advocacy influence places a moral responsibility on investors to change what they regard as immoral corporate behaviour (which is consistent with the analysis in the preceding section).

The key group of investors to share this view are the previously defined "socially responsible investors". Such investors are of particular relevance to NGOs working on SEE issues because these investors explicitly claim to integrate SEE issues into their investment process in some way, and market their products to clients on this basis. Recognising the opportunity to their campaigns, NGOs have targeted SRI investors in two principal ways:

❏ as interested audiences for the NGOs' corporate SEE performance information and lobbying activity; and
❏ as a lobbying target to test the authenticity of their claims to "social responsibility".

NGOs have also targeted non-SRI investors in order to persuade them to adopt SRI strategies (see, eg, the USS and Norwich Union case studies in Chapter 5). When effective, this increases NGO capital market influence.

As to what NGOs seek to gain from this approach, McLaren (2002, p 5) claims that most NGOs need to work with SRI investors:

> Where asymmetries of power [between companies and NGOs] persist, this precludes a dialogue of equals...For most stakeholders to obtain an equal position requires effective collaboration with SRI, who can exercise power, and mobilise a credible threat within the current system.

Dresner (2001, p 21) found that all the SRI fund managers surveyed claimed to be "responsive to issues brought by third parties such as NGOs" but that "all fund managers caveat[ed] their responses with the need for discretion and balance". There are a number of possible reasons for this caveat. For example, Sparkes (2002, p 36) expresses the view that:

> it seems quite legitimate for [NGOs] to want to cause financial harm to a company, perhaps by encouraging consumer boycotts, if that is seen as the most effective way to achieve their aims. On the other hand, it is hard to conceive of any circumstances in which SRI fund managers would actually want to see a decline in the value of the shares that they hold.

The reason why this is likely to impede collaboration between SRI investors and NGOs is that the interests of the NGOs' "clients" (ie, membership) in changing the company may well not be aligned with the clients of the socially responsible investors who are also interested in making a return on their investments. The investors' and NGOs' client interests are aligned only when there is a clear business case in favour of the company adopting the course of action proposed by the NGO (we will return to this point later in this chapter).

Turning now to consider conventional rather than socially responsible investors, NGO campaigns to influence such conventional investors are based on formal and informal shareholder-rights-based initiatives. The discussion below analyses how these NGO campaigns differ.

In respect of NGO capital market interventions attempting to use the formal system of "legal rights" mechanism, interventions here have typically involved NGOs submitting shareholder resolutions. This encourages institutional investors to take the issue into account as they consider whether and how to vote.

As demonstrated in Appendix 1, despite having to comply with the requirements of company law, UK NGOs have successfully filed resolutions at AGMs. However, no NGO SEE resolution in the UK has yet succeeded in generating the support of more than a fifth of voters.[11] Therefore, what evidence is there that they can be influential?

Despite the fact that no SEE shareholder resolution has been carried, or approved, at an AGM, there is considerable evidence from voting levels that resolutions have been successful in changing the investor advocacy influence of large FIs. Among those resolutions that have been filed in the UK, it is not uncommon for in excess of 10% of votes to either support the shareholder resolution or abstain, and votes of this level typically require at least a few large institutional investors to vote in favour.

As an example of a SEE resolution that did influence FIs, in 2001 Balfour Beatty received a resolution submitted by the Ilisu Dam campaign (the dam was controversial due to human rights infringements by the host government of Turkey and the displacement of significant numbers of people whose homes were to be flooded by the dam). While the majority of shareholders who voted expressed support for the company management, with only 1.9% voting in favour of the campaigners, an unprecedented 40.9% abstained. As to the ultimate impact on the company from this resolution, Balfour Beatty subsequently announced, "After thorough evaluation of the commercial, environmental and social issues it is not in the best interests of our stakeholders to pursue the project further" (see Balfour Beatty, 2001).

While this resolution was one part of a broader campaign, it can be seen that a sufficient number of investors appear to have had some sympathy with the NGO aims.[12] Furthermore, it also suggests that it is misleading to judge the ultimate success or failure of resolutions by reference to the AGM vote alone.

In respect of NGO capital market campaigns that take more informal approaches to the shareholder-rights-based initiatives system, an increasing number of NGO capital market interventions using a strategy of indirect investor advocacy influence are conducted outside of a company's AGM. One example of an NGO that successfully adopted this approach is Oxfam's Cut the Cost campaign against GSK. As can be seen from the case study in Chapter 5, it was ultimately successful, which indicates that such investor advocacy influence can be influential.

In conclusion, NGOs may attempt to influence corporate practice via a direct or indirect strategy of investor advocacy influence. Direct involves securing access to share ownership rights by investing in a particular company's shares. With an indirect strategy, in order to access the influence of other investors, the NGO must first persuade them of the importance of their issue. As to the extent of investor advocacy influence, some FIs exert their investor advocacy influence and, when they have, such intervention has been shown to be influential. In the specific context of this book, there have been occasions where FI investor advocacy influence has included the SEE issues that NGOs work on. NGOs have attempted to shape this FI investor advocacy influence by exerting pressure on investors to "engage" with a company or sector on specific issues. In particular, NGOs have argued that the existence of investor advocacy influence places a moral responsibility on investors to challenge what they regard as immoral corporate behaviour.

WHICH CAPITAL MARKET CAMPAIGN STRATEGIES RAISE THE MOST SIGNIFICANT RISKS?

The following discussion uses the model to deduce which capital market campaign approach is likely to be more problematic for companies and their investors.

Conceptually, the risks to companies and investors may be higher when NGOs adopt an investor advocacy influence rather than an economic-influence mechanism. This is because investor advocacy influence is arguably more precise in that a company can better heed explicit concerns raised by investors than attempt to interpret implicit signals from small variations in cost of capital. Similarly, NGOs can more readily use arguments based on morality, which is an observable NGO strength (particularly when compared with business-case arguments). Finally, the associated limitations to NGOs can be more readily overcome – particularly those of fiduciary obligation and pension case law.

In respect of the source of influence, theoretically, co-opting FIs influence should magnify the influence of the NGO – regardless of which primary audience is being addressed. Individually, NGOs' direct influence is limited by their relatively minuscule investment reserves.

This suggests that the probability of an NGO campaign being successful may be increased by its adopting an indirect approach. However, as indicated above, where an indirect approach is adopted, the NGO also needs to decide upon what "stance" should be adopted. The two main dimensions of the Elkington and Fennell taxonomy (Chapter 2), used to measure NGO stance are integrators *versus* polarisers and discriminators *versus* non-discriminators. Conceptually, whether the chances of success with an indirect approach are increased by a confrontational (polariser) or cooperative (integrator) approach should depend on an analysis of the issue and the likely response of the capital market institution. For example, if it is likely that the FI will not respond to a cooperative approach, a confrontational campaign may be required. However, it is reasonable to suggest that a targeted and more analytical approach is more likely to succeed than a non-discriminatory approach. This is because the relatively limited resources of the NGO will be more focused and better informed. Therefore, if this is true, then the dolphin and orca stances should, in general, be more successful than shark and sea lion.

Regarding the nature of argument, conceptually, the probability of successfully changing corporate practice is increased by striking a balance between moral and financial arguments. This is for two main reasons: first, purely moral arguments run into conflict with the fiduciary legislative obligations that form part of the structure of the capital market; second, purely economic arguments can lack the force of popular compulsion that is inherent within clearly articulated moral arguments. The two arguments can therefore be regarded as complementary rather than contradictory.

CHECKS AND BALANCES ON CAPITAL MARKET CAMPAIGNING

Having detailed how NGOs may use the mechanisms of influence underlying the model, and deduced the strategies most likely to succeed, this section explores what the practical checks and balances on alternative NGO capital market strategies might be. The model provides the structure, as this discussion considers the limitations of the four main components in the following order: (1) direct, (2) indirect, (3) economic influence, (4) indirect investor advocacy.

Direct

Perhaps the most significant limitation of a direct approach is the relatively minuscule investment reserves of most individual NGOs. For example, the total reserves of a relatively large NGO such as WWF-UK equate to less than one-hundredth of one per cent of BP's market value. As previously discussed, both investor advocacy influence and economic influence will be most influential when the holders of large numbers of a company's shares either divest or use their investment to raise their concerns. As individual entities, NGOs do not have the financial reserves necessary to wield significant direct influence.

Nevertheless, from the NGO perspective, there are reasons why an NGO may wish to deploy a direct strategy. These include:

❑ *Internal consistency – "to practise what they preach"*: Where the NGO has investment reserves and advocates responsible ownership to large institutional investors, it is sensible to ensure that its own house is also in order if it is to avoid embarrassment and a reduction in its own credibility.

❑ *As a tactical measure to draw the attention of a company's board and/ or the media to an ongoing NGO campaign*: This could involve purchasing a token share in order to attend the AGM (see Chapter 3).

❑ *To acquire campaign information*: Some companies have a policy of openness with their shareholders that does not extend to other stakeholders.

NGOs have attempted to overcome this lack of significant direct ownership influence by strategic use of the media and through attempts to co-opt the influence that other investors have. This latter approach entails an Indirect strategy.

Indirect

The discussion earlier in this chapter identified that institutional investors are influential targets for NGOs. However, factors limiting the extent to which NGOs can induce such FIs to use this authority include:

❑ *lack of professional motivation*: the investment professionals' remuneration structure motivates a focus on financial performance rather than SEE issues *per se*, which themselves may be viewed as tangential to the core business of investment valuation;

❑ *lack of client interest*: quarterly performance meetings with institutional clients focus on financial performance; institutional investment clients tend not to check on performance in relation to SEE issues; and

❑ *lack of personal motivation*: due to a lack of personal interest, some investment professionals can be uninterested in NGO SEE concerns.

These factors can result in significant NGO resources being required to persuade FIs to use their authority. From the NGO perspective, this may not be an efficient allocation of its resources.

Economic influence

As previously established, it is potentially advantageous for an NGO to adopt an economic-influence strategy: if it can divert capital away from a company that it has deemed to be detrimental to its goal, this can increase the target company's cost of capital, which, in turn, will result in a marginal reduction of its ability to do business. Conceptually, at least, if an NGO can exert significant long-term influence over the distribution of capital, it will be able to incrementally redistribute some resources away from some business activities and into others.

The NGO capital market intervention model highlights the fact that NGOs can make moral arguments for divestment – but FIs, generally speaking, are constrained in their ability to respond. More specifically, this limitation occurs where an NGO call to sell the totality of a holding is made on purely moral grounds, and the company represents a profitable investment and/or a significant part of a financial index. This is a major limitation for NGO capital market intervention and requires further analysis.

When an NGO calls for FIs to sell the totality of a company holding on purely moral grounds, this runs against three distinct but interdependent practical constraints:

(1) *Fiduciary obligation*: The Financial Services and Markets Act (2000) sets out that a fund manager has an obligation to attempt to maximise the financial returns for its clients. Similarly, ICGN (2003, p 2) states that "institutional shareholders have a general responsibility to ensure that investments are managed exclusively in the financial interests of their beneficiaries, as amplified – where relevant – by contract or law". In particular, where these beneficiaries are represented by pension fund trustees, the trustees must consider the financial return above any purely ethical concerns (see the Megarry Judgment below).[13] Consequently, where a particular stock has good investment prospects, the fund manager is compelled to maintain its holding.

(2) *Index-tracking funds (similar to point 3 below), where fund managers' clients have invested in passively managed index-tracking funds*: In such circumstances, it is the job of a fund manager to mirror the index constituents within the portfolio so as to maintain the tracking error within specific boundaries.[14] This does not mean that the fund manager must hold all the companies in an index, but it does mean that very large companies will need to be included in order not to breach the tracking-error constraints. In other words, an institutional fund manager of passive index-tracking funds does not have the discretion to divest holdings, and simply tracks an index.

(3) *Load difference*: Large active fund managers tend not to take absolute buy or sell "bets" on most of the biggest FTSE100

listed companies.[15] This is partly because institutional clients tend to stipulate an outperformance target based on an index as the benchmark (eg, exceeding the FTSE UK All Share by 1% on a three-year rolling average). In practice, for reasons similar to the above case, this limits the extent to which the fund manager can divest from the largest companies that reflect a significant proportion of the benchmark. Therefore, actively managed funds with such performance and risk objectives tend to make a relative bet, going over- or underweight when compared with a company's presence in the benchmark index (this is sometimes referred to euphemistically as "closet index tracking" – see point 2 above).

The last two points allude to the difficulties of total divestment from large companies in an index when the index is set as the benchmark. To demonstrate how heavily biased indices are towards companies near the top of the index, the combined market capitalisation of the 699 companies in the FTSE UK All Share is collectively worth £1,102,692 million[16] but the top 100 of these represent 85.58% of this figure. This shows the relative importance of companies inside the FTSE100 relative to the rest. Furthermore, within the top 100 is a significant emphasis on those in the top 10. Figure 7 depicts the market capitalisation of the companies in the largest 100 companies in the UK FTSE All Share (the FTSE100).

As can be seen from Figure 7, companies inside the top 25 positions represent a considerable part of the FTSE UK All Share, so totally divesting from such companies has significant risk-and-return implications for portfolio performance.

The above three limiting factors of fiduciary obligation, load difference and index tracking combine to prevent institutional investors from responding to calls from NGOs to sell the totality of a holding on purely moral grounds. Furthermore, the load difference and index-tracking constraints identified above also limit the extent to which divestment can take place on financial grounds.

While these load-difference and index-tracking constraints are relevant, the most important of the above limitations to NGO calls on investors to divest on purely moral grounds is the legal fiduciary obligation. The discussion below analyses this legal check and balance in more depth.

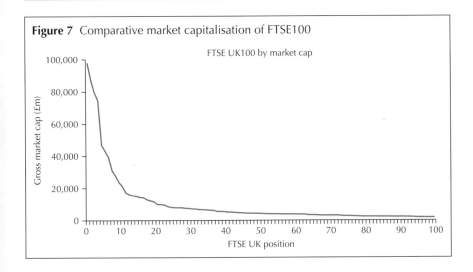

Figure 7 Comparative market capitalisation of FTSE100

Fund managers cater for a range of different clients. While individual (or "retail") investors are free to choose which ethical concerns they wish to be considered and how they would like this to be done (eg, divestment *versus* engagement), this same freedom does not apply to all the fund manager's clients. Occupational pension funds, for example, elect trustees who are charged with acting in the best interests of the beneficiaries as a whole. These trustees do not have the same scope as retail investors to incorporate ethical concerns (see below). Pension funds are among the fund management industry's most significant client groups: UK clients' pension fund assets totalled £625 billion at the end of 2002, representing 25% of the £2,600 billion of funds for which the UK fund management industry was responsible.[17]

The most relevant case law regarding the scope of pension fund trustees to incorporate ethical concerns is *Cowan versus Scargill*, 1984. The question under consideration by the judge, Sir Robert Megarry, was whether it was legitimate for trustees to restrict funds to investments in the UK and prohibit investments in industries competing with the coal industry. In what has come to be referred to as "the Megarry Judgment", Sir Robert made the following observations (*Cowan versus Scargill*, 1984 (2 All ER 750)):

❑ A trustee must take "such care as an ordinary prudent man would take if he were minded to make an investment for the benefit of other people for whom he felt morally bound to provide".

- ❑ It was the main duty of trustees "to exercise their powers in the best interests of the present and future beneficiaries".
- ❑ If the trust provided financial benefits, then "the best interests of the beneficiaries are normally their best financial interests".
- ❑ "Although a trustee who takes advice on investments is not bound to accept and act upon that advice, he is not entitled to reject it merely because he sincerely disagrees with it, unless in addition to being sincere he is acting as an ordinary prudent man would act."
- ❑ "In considering what investment to make, the trustees must put on one side their own personal interests and views."

This putting to one side of personal interests and views has been interpreted as constraining the extent to which trustees can prohibit certain companies from investment on the basis of ethical concerns. However, since the Megarry Judgment, other rulings have taken a slightly more lenient view on the application of negative screening – or divestment criteria – on purely moral or ethical grounds. They indicate that it is not prohibited, provided it does not affect returns. In practice, this means that ethical criteria can be used by the fund managers selected by pension fund trustees to distinguish between two investments that are equivalent on purely financial grounds – unless it would be better to hold both to ensure sufficient diversification.

When considering what reforms to the 1995 Pensions Act were required following the Robert Maxwell pension fund debacle, the Goode Committee stated that pension fund trustees must "treat the financial interests of Scheme members as paramount" and manage the fund "consistent with proper diversification and prudence", but, provided they do so, "trustees ... are perfectly entitled to have a policy on ethical investment and pursue that policy" (see E-USS, 1999).

While these cases were decided on their own merits, the implications for NGO capital market strategy are that pension fund trustees are not legally able to respond to NGO calls to divest on purely ethical grounds and must instead operate in the best financial interests of the pension fund beneficiaries.

Partially as a consequence of these limitations of moral arguments, NGOs have developed divestment arguments based on a business-case analysis of their issue. When deploying a business-case route of argument, the NGO attempts to demonstrate that integrating an analysis of its issue into the stock selection process is in the best financial interests of the beneficiaries of the investment fund. Furthermore, where business-case arguments are successfully deployed, they may become integrated into the core functioning of the capital market and, therefore, are more capable of providing the long-term influence referred to at the outset of this section. Therefore, as noted earlier in this chapter, when considering how NGOs deploy an economic-influence strategy, the strength of the business-case argument and/or their ability to generate such a business case is an important determinant of success.

However, there are situations where, in the absence of an NGO campaign, a business case for an ethical issue does not exist. For example, as Pearce and Mills (2002, p 28) identify, "an arms exporting company is unlikely to create value for its shareholders by stopping sales of weapons to the third world [oppressive regimes]". Where the business case arises from the brand being put at risk through the NGO campaign, if NGOs allocate campaign resources to represent the business case – at the cost of representing the ethical case – they may paradoxically reduce the business case in support of the issue.

Conversely, even where a positive "business case" for the NGO issue exists, in practice convincing investment professionals of its compelling nature is not without its own limitations. NGOs have been confronted by three main limitations (see Waygood and Wehrmeyer, 2003, p 376) associated with an economic advocacy strategy:

❑ *information overload*: supplying new information into an already information-saturated market;
❑ *perceived bias*: investors habitually discounting information provided by intermediaries with biases or potential conflicts of interest; and
❑ *materiality*: not only does the business case need to be compelling, but the issue also has to be sufficiently relevant to the financial valuation of the company ("material") to warrant the attention of busy fund managers.

Nevertheless, when successfully presented, business-case arguments can be influential.

Investor advocacy influence

As previously established, it is potentially advantageous for an NGO to use investor advocacy influence: if it can encourage holders of sufficiently large numbers of shares to engage with a company on their issue, then the NGO can change corporate practice.

In practice, however, when an NGO attempts to use either business- or moral-case arguments within an indirect strategy of investor advocacy influence, it is confronted by one main limitation: many institutional investors in the UK have not carried out an effective long-term ownership function. In a recent government-commissioned review of the industry practices, Paul Myners concluded that "fund managers are reluctant to intervene in companies where they own substantial shareholdings, even where this would be in their clients' financial interests" (see Myners, 2001, p 3). As previously noted, there is some evidence that an increasing number of UK institutional investors take their effective long-term ownership role seriously, but with average voting levels still at less than two-thirds of the issued shares, there remains some way to go.[18]

Part of the problem is that, while there is a collective interest in holding company directors to account, individually it is possible to "free-ride" on the activity of other shareholders, saving time and money involved in policing company directors' stewardship of investee companies. As Aristotle observed, "For that which is common to the greatest number has the least care bestowed upon it ... For besides other considerations, everybody is more inclined to neglect the duty which he expects another to fulfil." In the context of this book, the institutional expectation that others will conduct sufficient corporate governance activism has arguably resulted in the public good dimensions of such activism being undersupplied.

However, there are some signs that this may be changing. In addition to the proclamation of responsibility set out by the Institutional Shareholders' Committee (see Institutional Shareholders' Committee, 2005), the annual PIRC survey of proxy-voting trends in the UK, included earlier in this chapter, found some evidence of change in ownership accountability by institutional investors and their agents – suggesting that this limitation may be diminishing in scale. In addition, there is currently a threat of further regulation in this area from the UK government. The Secretary of State for Trade and Industry, Patricia Hewitt (2003, p 10), has stated that:

> it's time to assert the principle that fund managers – as trustees, for us, the savers – have a responsibility, as well as a right, to be active owners ... Beneficial investors need clear, concise and regular inform-ation on how fund managers are acting and voting on their behalf. Whether through voluntary codes or regulation, we need to create a chain of transparency and accountability that stretches from the boardroom to the individual shareholder and saver, via the pension fund manager, trustee and institutional investor.

SUMMARY

The NGO capital market model uses the two main components of *mechanism* and *route*, and combines them with three subsidiary elements of *argument*, *audience* and *stance*.

NGOs have attempted to influence corporate practice via two routes: direct or an indirect strategy of investor-advocacy-influence. In the context of investor advocacy influence, direct involves securing access to share-ownership rights by investing in a particular company's shares. With indirect, to access the influence of other investors, the NGO must first persuade them of the impor-tance of their issue. In the context of economic influence, direct involves the NGO trading on its own account, whereas indirect involves attempts to persuade FIs to trade.

The principal source of the capital market economic-influence mechanism is primarily the share-price influence on a company's cost of capital, but it also originates from takeover prospects and directors' remuneration packages. NGOs have in some instances influenced the key value drivers of a business, and "materialised" SEE issues for companies. This has had cost of capital implications for the company in question and in some cases changed company practice.

The source of the capital market mechanism of investor advocacy influence is primarily the legal rights associated with share owner-ship, but the duties of directors to serve the interests of shareholders and the guidance contained in corporate governance codes of best practice further support this mechanism. There are instances where

NGOs have shaped this FI investor advocacy influence by arguing that its existence places a moral responsibility on investors to challenge what they regard as immoral corporate behaviour.

Regarding the limitations of NGO capital market intervention, the main limitation of a direct strategy is the relatively small financial reserves of most NGOs. Conversely, one limitation of an indirect approach is the scale of NGO resources required to co-opt FI influence. The economic-influence mechanism's main limitation is that some FI's will be unable to respond to an NGO's purely moral arguments because of the FI's fiduciary obligation. Whereas the most significant limitation with an investor-advocacy-influence approach is the lack of ownership responsibility on the part of many UK FIs.

1   Mansley (2000, p 3) defines SRI using the text of the UK reform of the 1995 Pensions Act as follows: "investment where social, environmental or ethical considerations are taken into account in the selection, retention and realisation of investment, and the responsible use of rights (such as voting rights) attaching to investments".

2   A complete treatment of the process of professional investment analysis, asset allocation and portfolio construction can be found in the seminal work by Graham and Dodd (1940).

3   There have been a number of attempts to define materiality in the context of the capital markets. In the US, the Securities and Exchange Commission (SEC) – the capital market oversight body – has set out that information is material if "there is a substantial likelihood that a reasonable shareholder would consider it important" in making an investment decision. To fulfil the materiality requirement, there must be a substantial likelihood that a fact "would have been viewed by the reasonable investor as having significantly altered the 'total mix' of information made available" (SEC, 2000).

4   This is not a measure of absolute share price movements but "the extent to which the firm's share price outperformed or underperformed market expectations" (Knight and Pretty, 2001, p 14).

5   "Nominal" refers to the value that is assigned to the share certificate itself for legal purposes, rather than the price at which the share is trading which is generally significantly higher.

6   "Corporate Governance is the system by which companies are directed and controlled" (Hampel Report, 1998, p 1). A more comprehensive definition is the OECD (1999): "Corporate governance involves a set of relationships between a company's management, its board, its shareholders and other stakeholders. Corporate governance also provides the structure through which the objectives of the company are set, and the means of attaining those objectives and monitoring performance are determined."

7   The Financial Services Authority is the "competent authority" for the UK Listing Authority and therefore sets out the rules for companies wishing to be listed (UKLA, 2002).

8   In 2005, the members were the Association of British Insurers, the Association of Investment Trust Companies, the Investment Management Association and the National Association of Pension Funds.

9   An alternative term for institutional investors' engagement with companies on issues of corporate governance and corporate responsibility.

10 The fund manager for HBOS plc with £79 billion under management at 31 July 2005 – and the author's employer at the time of writing.

11 At Rio Tinto's AGM in 2000, the ICFTU won 17.3% of votes with a resolution encouraging the company to adopt a code of conduct guaranteeing internationally recognised labour rights.

12 Sparkes (2002, p 39) describes abstentions thus: "Abstentions should usually be read as shareholders who sympathise with the resolution but don't want to go the whole hog."

13 The law as it relates to institutional investment by Charities or Trust Funds is different in that an investment may be excluded on ethical grounds if it conflicts with the objects of the charity and/or accepts a lower return on specific investments if, in so doing, the objects of the charity are furthered.

14 The tracking error is a statistical measure of the difference between the configuration of the investment portfolio and the configuration of the index.

15 The load difference indicates the extent of the active "bet" in the fund against the index used as a performance benchmark.

16 Excluding unit trusts, OIECs and investment trusts. Stock market figures at 31 December 2002 (HSBC, 2003).

17 Data sourced from IFSL (2003).

18 In 2004, the annual PIRC survey of proxy voting trends in the UK found that there had been a significant improvement in UK voting turnout with the median turnout for FTSE350 companies up to 57% (from 55% the previous year) and an increase from 7% to 9% in the number of votes opposing resolutions. In addition, the level of abstentions increased from 9% to 16.4%.

4

The History of
Capital Market Campaigns

This chapter analyses the chronology of UK NGO capital market interventions arising during the 12-year period 1990–2002 (Appendix 1 – readers are encouraged to skim the Appendix before reviewing this analysis). The main reason for developing the chronology was to establish whether there are any underlying trends in the way that campaigners have used the capital market to campaign against companies and their investors. It also enables the NGO case studies (Chapter 5) to be viewed in the broader context of overall NGO capital market intervention.

Regarding the analysis, the key questions considered here are: whether capital market campaigning has changed in scale; whether NGOs explored a range of strategies; whether it has changed in nature over time and whether it has become more successful. The following analysis is therefore structured around these key questions.

HAS THE NUMBER OF CAPITAL MARKET CAMPAIGNS INCREASED?

Figure 8 plots the overall number of UK NGO capital market interventions that took place between 1990 and 2002.

As can be seen, NGO capital market intervention increased from average levels of 2.8 interventions per annum during the first six years to 10.1 interventions per annum in the last six years. Bearing in mind that many of the campaigns had multiple company and investor targets, UK NGO capital market intervention

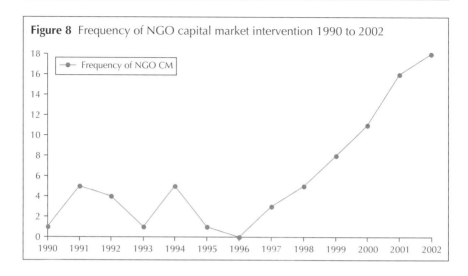

Figure 8 Frequency of NGO capital market intervention 1990 to 2002

significantly increased over the time period. This suggests that the risk of being targeted by such a campaign has similarly significantly increased.

However, it is noticeable that the trend is not positive throughout the time period. In particular, while the first half of the period contained a relatively low level of NGO capital market intervention, there is a significant increase in NGO capital market intervention after 1996. Does the chronology provide any clues as to what happened to catalyse the increase in NGO capital market intervention at around this time?

Intervention 30 (February 1999) on the chronology involved the establishment of a requirement on trustees of occupational pension funds to publish a statement regarding the extent to which SEE issues were taken into account in the investment process. This capital market intervention was led by the UK Social Investment Forum (UKSIF) and included informal collaboration with other NGOs including Friends of the Earth, Traidcraft Exchange, War on Want and WWF-UK.

Despite opposition – for example, from the influential National Association of Pension Funds – UKSIF's campaign was successful: the Pensions Act was amended to place a requirement on trustees to declare via a SIP "the extent (if at all) to which SEE considerations are taken into account in the selection, retention and realisation of investments; and the policy (if any) directing the exercise of the rights (including voting rights) attaching to investments" (HMSO, 1999, Section 35(3)(f)).

One specific benefit to NGOs has been the increased scope for capital market intervention provided by the positive statements on SEE issues. Following the reform, the *Financial Times* (21 June 2000, p 16) reported, "Britain's top companies risk becoming targets of environmental activists unless they act urgently to give their pension fund trustees advice on socially responsible investment." However, while lacking a statement would raise such risks, publication of statements of this sort would also have increased the scope for NGO capital market intervention on SEE issues. This is because such statements provided a SEE policy against which NGOs could hold the occupational pension funds to account. While it is probable that this reform did contribute towards an increase in NGO capital market intervention, the reform did not come into effect until halfway through 2000. However, the trend of increased NGO capital market intervention began some years before. Does the chronology include previous interventions that may have catalysed the original growth in NGO capital market intervention?

The chronology lists two earlier successful NGO capital market interventions with significant aims that may provide the answer: the international environment and development NGO coalition to stop Asea Brown Boveri (ABB plc) constructing the Bakun hydro-electric dam in Sarawak, Malaysia; and the intervention by PIRC in conjunction with Greenpeace, Amnesty International and WWF-UK[1] surrounding Shell's disposal of the Brent Spar storage buoy (see also Chapter 3) and its human rights record in Nigeria (Interventions 17 and 18). As a result of this success, it is probable that these NGOs would have been more likely to repeat a capital market intervention strategy and, more significantly, other NGOs looking for effective campaign strategies would have been more likely to deploy a capital market intervention themselves. However, to substantiate the claim that these interventions catalysed the increase in NGO capital market intervention, the precise nature of these interventions, and the extent of apparent success, requires some analysis.

Hildyard and Mansley (2001) reviewed the NGO intervention against ABB and the Bakun dam.[2] They highlighted that the dam would have entailed the involuntary relocation of approximately 10,000 indigenous people and the flooding of 70,000 hectares of land. They argued that the key to the campaign's success was "the lobbying of potential investors in the dam – and of the financial analysts who advise these investors" (p 7). FoE had used business-case arguments to warn potential investors that "Investment in Bakun is unlikely to offer the return you require" due to antici-pated project delays, questionable predicted power output and risks that an inequitable power-purchasing agreement would be renegotiated. The project failed to raise the necessary finance and was eventually indefinitely postponed.

Whether or not the NGO capital market campaign played a major role in the downfall of the Bakun dam (and, on the face of it, it certainly seems to have been highly effective), the perception among NGOs was that the campaign had been a major success and that the capital market intervention had been a significant contributory factor. This perception alone would have been suffi-cient to contribute towards other NGOs exploring whether a capi-tal market intervention could benefit their own campaigns in some way.

The second of the two successful contemporary interventions cited here is also singled out as catalytic by Sparkes (2002, p 34):

> The real beginnings of UK shareholder activism on SRI issues can be precisely dated to 14 May 1997. This was the date of the 1997 annual general meeting of the Shell Transport and Trading Company. Shell had already received negative publicity in 1995–96 over its planned disposal of the Brent Spar oil platform, and concern over human rights abuses in Nigeria culminating in the execution of Ken Saro-Wiwa. In 1997 an NGO-led coalition was able to assemble enough support from local authority pension funds (coordinated by PIRC) and church investors led by ECCR to file a shareholder resolution.

As can be seen from Figure 8 and from the ABB case above, it would be wrong to suggest that no shareholder activism on SRI issues had taken place before May 1997. However, Sparkes is right to single out this intervention as a turning point: not only were the

Brent Spar and Ken Saro-Wiwa cases very high-profile, but this capital market intervention was also highly successful in achieving its objectives.

PANEL 3 TEXT OF 1997 SHELL AGM SHAREHOLDER RESOLUTION

[I]n recognition of the importance of environmental and corporate responsibility policies (including those policies relating to human rights), to the company's operations, corporate profile and performance, the directors are requested to:

❑ Designate responsibility for the implementation of environmental and corporate responsibility policies to a named member of the Committee of Managing Directors.
❑ Establish effective internal procedures for the implementation and monitoring of such policies.
❑ Establish an independent external review and audit procedure for such policies.
❑ Report to shareholders regularly on the implementation of such policies.
❑ Publish a report to shareholders on the implementation of such policies in relation to the company's operations in Nigeria by the end of 1997.

Panel 3 contains the resolve clause of the resolution and the following discussion briefly assesses the extent of the campaigner's success.

Shell recommended voting against the resolution. However, ultimately, 17% of the investors that voted withheld their support from the board.[3] While this represented a formal failure of the resolution, *The Times*'s city editor (1997, p 23) summed up the significance of the lack of support thus:

> The fact that 11% of Shell's shareholders were persuaded to vote against the company's board was a huge blow to the company and carries a strong blow to industry generally ... for the opposition to have reached that level means that some substantial funds voted for change. The grey men who run the institutional funds joined with small shareholders to deliver a drastic condemnation of the company.

Perhaps as a consequence of this scale of apparent support for the resolution, over the course of the next 18 months Shell was to take actions that substantively met the five requests contained in the resolution. PIRC was later to state that "we consider that Shell has, in a relatively short period of time, moved as requested by the resolution 'to the head of the movement for corporate responsibility' " (see PIRC, 1998, p 32). While arguing from an understandably biased position, PIRC also states (*ibid*) that it believed the resolution, and the work around it, were catalytic in Shell's making these changes:

> PIRC considers that the programme of research, meetings and discussion with the company, followed by the resolution, have had a constructive and significant impact upon the company. We welcome Shell's progress since the resolution and consider it a tribute to the ability of the directors, executives and other staff to respond positively to pressure for change both within the company and from shareholders and other groups in recent years.

As can be seen, relative to previous interventions, both of the above were significant in scale and had substantive targets that have been achieved. The success of these capital market interventions would have indicated to other NGOs looking for strategies to increase their influence that the capital market could be a useful campaign device. Therefore, the apparent success of these two contemporary interventions probably goes a long way to explaining the increase in NGO capital market intervention since 1996. It also demonstrates that the risks to companies and investors that NGOs were able to create were sufficient in two cases to both change the practices of the target company and, at least in the Shell case, to influence the views of a sufficient number of investors.

HAVE NGOs EXPLORED A RANGE OF STRATEGIES?

Tables 2–4 highlight the relative frequencies with which NGOs sought to deploy each of the components of the model mechanisms of company influence, route of influence, primary audience, nature of argument and the relative success of the intervention.

Table 2 demonstrates that an investor advocacy approach was the most commonly used mechanism of influence, and was more

Table 2 Frequencies of mechanism

Valid	Frequency	Percent	Valid percent	Cumulative percent
Investor	47	60.3	60.3	60.3
Economic	18	23.1	23.1	83.3
Both	13	16.7	16.7	100.0
Total	78	100.0	100.0	–

Table 3 Frequencies of route of influence

Valid	Frequency	Percent	Valid percent	Cumulative percent
Direct	13	16.7	16.7	16.7
Indirect (dolphin)	34	43.6	43.6	60.3
Indirect (orca)	29	37.2	37.2	97.4
Indirect (shark)	2	2.6	2.6	100.0
Total	78	100.0	100.0	–

Table 4 Frequencies of nature of argument

Valid	Frequency	Percent	Valid percent	Cumulative percent
Business	29	37.2	37.2	37.2
Moral	17	21.8	21.8	59.0
Both	32	41.0	41.0	100.0
Total	78	100.0	100.0	–

than twice as popular as the economic mechanism of influence. NGO capital market interventions that attempted to use both were the least commonly deployed with only 16.7% of the overall number. Insofar as the analysis in Chapter 3 suggested that this would be a more successful strategy, this may indicate that NGOs are learning from mistakes in previous interventions.

Table 3 demonstrates that an indirect route of influence was more than four times more commonly used (43.6% + 37.2% + 2.6% = 83.3%) than a direct strategy (16.7%). It also highlights that, within indirect, only the dolphin and shark stances have been used. A shark stance has been used in only 2.6% of interventions and a sea lion stance has not been used at all. The potential reasons for this are discussed below.

Table 4 demonstrates that the frequency distributions within nature of argument are more evenly distributed than the apparent choices made within any of the other components of the model. However, given the "moralising" nature of the NGOs in question, there has been a surprising lack of purely moral nature of arguments – most interventions have incorporated business-case arguments in some way. As before, the analysis in Chapter 3 suggested that this would be a more successful strategy. In particular, it suggested that interventions that used both business- and moral-case arguments would be more successful. Consequently, this result may indicate that, once again, NGOs are learning from mistakes in previous interventions. A move towards a "both" classification over time would indicate the consideration of lessons learned from previous interventions, which will be considered later in this chapter.

Overall, these tables demonstrate that, with one exception, UK NGOs conducted interventions utilising the full range of alternative strategies within each component of the model during the time period in question. This suggests that NGOs have used a broad range of alternative strategies in their capital market intervention. The exception is that of a sea lion stance within an indirect strategy, as there were no instances of an NGO adopting such an approach during the period in question. Why might this be so?

As highlighted in Chapter 2, the sea lion's stance "ignores relative performance of FI; willing to work closely with any FI". The popularity of the dolphin (which is also willing to work closely with some companies and scored 34% within route) indicates that it was not reluctance on the part of NGOs to work with FIs that led to the unpopularity of this strategy. Furthermore, the lack of popularity in the shark (which also ignores the relative performance of companies and scored 2.6% within route) indicates that NGOs were discerning in their selection of FI partner/target. This result indicates that NGOs have carefully selected which FI to target/work with. This makes some sense as it could reflect a concern among NGOs of the dangers of being compromised – or being seen to have been compromised – by the FI in question.

The frequency tables above also demonstrate that, while NGOs have deployed a range of capital market intervention strategies, there has been a predominance of certain strategies over others. In particular, there has been a high proportion of:

❏ investor advocacy over economic influence (60% within mechanism);
❏ indirect over direct as a route of influence (83.3% of the interventions were indirect) – and a preference for a dolphin stance within indirect; and
❏ a marginal preference for "both business- and moral-case arguments" (rather than focusing on one or the other) within nature of argument (41%).

Therefore, while NGOs have used a broad range of different strategies in their capital market intervention, there has also been a focus on certain strategies over others. The analysis in Chapter 3 suggested that these were the most likely to cause problems for companies and their investors and suggests that NGOs have been adept at learning how to raise risks to them.

The section below considers whether any patterns underlying the evolution in these further strategies can be identified.

HAS NGO STRATEGY EVOLVED OVER TIME?

A qualitative analysis of the nature of first 10 NGO interventions indicates that four involved media-focused AGM disruption attempts of some kind. Examples include Surfers Against Sewage bringing a bag of sewage-related detritus to the 1990 AGM of South West Water, and PARTiZANS escorting Australian aborigines to RTZ's 1991 AGM to question the board about mining in sacred burial sites.

Conversely, the same analysis of the last 30 interventions[4] indicates that only three represent new[5] attempts to use an AGM to embarrass the company. This suggests a reduction from 40% of the first few interventions to 10% of approximately the last third of NGO interventions. Very broadly, representative examples of the latter period include the publication by Amnesty of a study linking human rights to corporate risk in 2002, and the collaboration between Oxfam, Christian Aid and VSO (also in 2002) to publish a set of company benchmarks enabling investors to compare pharmaceutical company performance concerning access to lifesaving drugs in the developing world. This indicates that NGOs have evolved from mainly confrontational media-focused activities at AGMs to more substantive interventions targeting issues that are more relevant to corporate strategy and SEE performance.

While this may have reduced the reputational risk, it has increased the risk that NGOs could change the way in which investors regard a particular company's prospects and lead to a change in investment allocation or voting decisions.

DOES THE RELATIVE SUCCESS IMPROVE OVER TIME?

The Table 5 is a chronological statistical analysis of the occurrence of *prima facie* success.

Success and possible success, combined, account for more than 55% (29.5% + 25.6%) of interventions, whereas only 20.5% (5.1% + 15.4%) were either unsuccessful or possibly unsuccessful. This indicates that overall, based on the success data, NGO capital market intervention has a reasonable probability of some success.

The reason why there are only four failures overall relates more to the simplistic classification of success in the chronological data. It does not necessarily suggest that NGOs have achieved broad and substantive campaign goals via NGO capital market interventions. It merely denotes that the capital market intervention appears to have contributed towards an outcome that furthered the overall aim of the intervention. A substantive evaluation of the extent of campaign success will be determined in the case studies (Chapter 5).

Regarding whether an increase in success can be discerned, 34.8% of successes occurred in the last year. Similarly, in absolute terms, there is a consistently positive increase in the number of successes occurring in each time period.

However, there was also a strong growth in the absolute number of interventions. Therefore, it is necessary to consider the relative intra-year success scores. Throughout the time period, the relative distribution of success per year remains relatively constant, suggesting that that the positive trend within success is due to the growth in NGO capital market intervention overall. Nevertheless,

Table 5 Chronological occurrence of success

Year * success? crosstabulation

Year		N	N?	?	Y?	Y	Total
1990	Count			1			1
	% within year (%)			100.0			100.0
	% within success? (%)			5.3			1.3
1991	Count		1	1	2	1	5
	% within year (%)		20.0	20.0	40.0	20.0	100.0
	% within success? (%)		8.3	5.3	10.0	4.3	6.4
1992	Count			2	2		4
	% within year (%)			50.0	50.0		100.0
	% within success? (%)			10.5	10.0		5.1
1993	Count					1	1
	% within year (%)					100.0	100.0
	% within success? (%)					4.3	1.3
1994	Count		2	1	2		5
	% within year (%)		40.0	20.0	40.0		100.0
	% within success? (%)		16.7	5.3	10.0		6.4
1995	Count					1	1
	% within year (%)					100.0	100.0
	% within success? (%)					4.3	1.3
1997	Count	1			1	1	3
	% within year (%)	33.3			33.3	33.3	100.0
	% within success? (%)	25.0			5.0	4.3	3.8
1998	Count	1	1	1		2	5
	% within year (%)	20.0	20.0	20.0		40.0	100.0
	% within success? (%)	25.0	8.3	5.3		8.7	6.4
1999	Count		2	2	2	2	8
	% within year (%)		25.0	25.0	25.0	25.0	100.0
	% within success? (%)		16.7	10.5	10.0	8.7	10.3
2000	Count			3	5	3	11
	% within year (%)			27.3	45.5	27.3	100.0
	% within success? (%)			15.8	25.0	13.0	14.1
2001	Count	1	3	4	4	4	16
	% within year (%)	6.3	18.8	25.0	25.0	25.0	100.0
	% within success? (%)	25.0	25.0	21.1	20.0	17.4	20.5
2002	Count	1	3	4	2	8	18
	% within year (%)	5.6	16.7	22.2	11.1	44.4	100.0
	% within success? (%)	25.0	25.0	21.1	10.0	34.8	23.1
Total	Count	4	12	19	20	23	78
	% within year (%)	5.1	15.4	24.4	25.6	29.5	100.0
	% within success? (%)	100.0	100.0	100.0	100.0	100.0	100.0

as argued above, the objectives of the NGO capital market intervention changed over the time period, with interventions becoming less focused on media attention and more on corporate strategy and performance. Arguably, it is easier to generate media coverage than to generate substantive changes in corporate strategy and performance. Therefore, in view of the more substantive nature of NGO objectives over the time period and the trend in success, it is reasonable to conclude that there has been an increase in the success of the interventions.

This conclusion may indicate that NGOs are learning from their previous interventions and further underlines the previous analysis above that came to similar findings. It may also indicate that the previously mentioned reform to the UK Pensions Act has indeed provided greater scope for NGO capital market intervention.

INITIAL LESSONS FOR COMPANIES AND INVESTORS

Are there any lessons for companies and investors regarding what kinds of campaigns are likely to raise greater risks than others? The best way of answering this question using the chronology is to single out which of the NGO strategies were most effective. The following are the attributes of the most successful campaigns:

Mechanism
❏ 34% of investor advocacy influence interventions were apparently successful whereas only 16.7% of economic influence interventions were apparently successful. This implies that the probability of success is almost twice as high for interventions using an investor advocacy influence mechanism; and
❏ an apparently successful intervention has a 69.9% chance of having involved a strategy of investor-advocacy influence and a 13% chance of having involved economic influence.

Route
❏ Overall, an indirect route was used in 83.3% of interventions and direct 16.7%; 25% of direct interventions were apparently unsuccessful, and only 8.7% apparently successful.

Nature of argument

❏ within all "apparently successful" interventions, there is a 69.6% probability that the intervention used a balance of "both moral- and business-case" arguments. This is significantly higher than purely "moral-case" arguments at only an 8.7% probability or "business-case" arguments at 21.7% probability; and

❏ similarly, there is a 50% chance that interventions adopting "both moral- and business-case" arguments will be "apparently successful". However, there is only a 17.2% chance that a predominantly "business-case" argument would be "apparently successful" and an 11.8% chance that a predominantly "moral" argument would be "apparently successful".

The above findings indicate that companies and their investors should consider the risks to be highest when the NGO capital market campaign adopts an indirect strategy of investor-advocacy influence, using a combination of moral- and business-case arguments. This is an important finding and will be revisited in Chapter 6.

SUMMARY

The chapter has analysed the empirical data of NGO capital market intervention between 1990 and 2002. In general, the analysis highlighted that NGO capital market intervention has increased and involved a broad range of strategies.

It has also been shown that an increase in the success of the interventions, coupled with evidence of a change towards strategies that are more likely to succeed, indicates that NGOs have learned from errors in previous interventions.

Finally, the analysis of success indicates that the risks to companies and their investors are highest when the campaign adopts an indirect strategy of investor advocacy influence using a combination of moral- and business-case arguments. The case studies in Chapter 5 will attempt to validate this finding. They will also seek to establish what companies and investors should do when targeted by such campaigns.

---

1 PIRC (1998, p 8) identifies that the resolution had been drafted following conversations with Amnesty International, Greenpeace and WWF-UK.

2 It should be noted that Mansley and Hildyard were both personally involved in this CM intervention.

3   A total of 39.9 million shares were voted in favour of the resolution, representing 10.5% of votes cast, and 24.9 million shares were voted as an abstention, representing 6.5% of votes cast.

4   The different numbers of interventions are chosen for comparison for two reasons: (1) the significantly higher number of interventions in the second period underlines the point that AGM-focused interventions have decreased; and (2) the higher number of interventions in the second period compensates for the fact that NGO CM intervention significantly increased in the latter years and, as AGMs are annual, a comparable number of years is required for fair comparison.

5   There were other NGO attempts to use the AGM. However, they were continuations of previous interventions – for example, the ongoing resolutions by Greenpeace and WWF-UK at BP's AGM.

5

Case Studies

The previous chapter analysed UK NGO capital market intervention (1990–2002) overall. This chapter takes a detailed look at four case studies selected from the chronology. The reason for including detailed case studies is to augment the above analysis of the implications of NGO capital market intervention strategy to companies and investors. Each case study includes a review of the degree to which the campaign objectives were achieved; the degree to which the achievement can be attributed to the capital market intervention; and an analysis of the efficiency and effectiveness with which the outcomes were generated. In addition to providing a record of the interventions, and insights into the specific cases, the main intention is to establish what specific lessons can be learned from each case for companies and investors.

In chronological order, the interventions chosen for case study review were as show in Table 6.

The structure of this chapter is to review the case studies in the order in which they occurred. The structure of the analysis was previously established in the scope and methodology (Chapter 1).

Where the intervention involved multiple objectives, the analysis is summarised at the end in a table. Where this is the case, the results of the analysis are presented in the following way:

❑ evidence that the NGO achieved desired outcome = Y
❑ evidence that the NGO partially achieved desired outcome = Y%
❑ insufficient evidence that the NGO achieved desired outcome = ?
❑ evidence that the NGO did not achieve desired outcome unsuccessful = N.

Table 6 NGO capital market intervention case studies

#	NGO	Intervention	Classification
20	People and Planet	Ethics for USS campaign	❏ Economic influence ❏ Indirect (orca) ❏ CM institutions ❏ Moral
33	WWF-UK (with WWF-US, the US Public Interest Research Group (PIRG) and Greenpeace)	BP and the Arctic Refuge 2002 resolution	❏ Economic influence and investor advocacy influence ❏ Indirect (orca) ❏ CM institutions ❏ Business case and moral case
34	Friends of the Earth	Capital punishment and Norwich Union Campaign	❏ Investor advocacy influence ❏ Indirect (orca) ❏ CM institutions ❏ Business case and moral case
63	Oxfam	GSK Cut the Cost campaign	❏ Investor advocacy influence ❏ Indirect (orca) ❏ CM institutions ❏ Business case and moral case

THE ETHICS FOR THE UNIVERSITIES SUPERANNUATION SCHEME CAMPAIGN

This case reviews People and Planet's Ethics for USS (see E-USS) campaign. It is different from the others presented later in the book because: (1) an NGO was established specifically for this intervention and (2) it is the only case where the members of the campaign group were recruited from the target entity.

People and Planet describes itself as "the largest student network in Britain campaigning to: end world poverty, defend human rights and protect the environment" (see People and Planet, 2003). Its mission, according to the same source, is "to educate and empower students to take effective action on the root causes of social and environmental injustice". People and Planet was originally called Third World First and was set up in 1969 to raise money for overseas aid. It is a relatively small NGO with around 10,000 active supporters, an annual income of some £600,000 and a staff of 25. In terms of the NGO's corporate campaigning position, it has adopted an orca stance.

People and Planet set up E-USS in September 1997. E-USS described itself as "the University staff campaign for ethical investment of our pension fund" (see E-USS, 2003) and aimed to "convince USS to adopt an ethical investment policy that is accountable to its members" (see Alexander, 2001).

Reference to the NGO capital market intervention chronology (Appendix 1) demonstrates that E-USS represents People and Planet's first and, for the time period in question, only significant attempt to use the capital market as a campaign tool. It is, however, noteworthy that the NGO established "Fair Share" in conjunction with other NGOs in 2003. This has plans to take the lessons learned during the E-USS campaign and lobby other pension schemes in a similar fashion. This is particularly noteworthy here, because pension schemes that are targeted by Fair Share should be able to learn from the response of the Universities Superannuation Scheme (USS) – the targeted financial institution in question here – when preparing their own response.

USS itself provides final-salary occupational pensions for academic and senior university administrative employees throughout the UK. Around the time the campaign was established, USS represented the second biggest pension fund in the UK with assets of nearly £20 billion under management, some 250 employees and more than 150,000 members. USS manages most pension-scheme money in house but also contracts out to external managers including Baillie Gifford, Capital, and Henderson Global Investors.

People and Planet appears to have singled out USS from other large financial institutions for three main reasons:

(1) *Scale*: USS is one of the largest occupational pension schemes with significant assets under management.
(2) *Stakeholder request*: People and Planet was motivated by members of USS to adopt their position on SRI.
(3) *Influence of their membership*: People and Planet is a student-based organisation. Consequently, the NGO had a greater

Table 7 A review of E-USS and People and Planet against ECOSOC criteria

ECOSOC requirement	E-USS and People and Planet
Must not be antithetical to the participatory democratic state	Complies
Should be non-profit-making	Complies
Should be non-violent and non-criminal	Complies
Must not be directed against a particular government	Complies

ability to influence the members of this scheme than any other large pension scheme because they include university lecturers.

Assessment of the capital market intervention(s)

NGO legitimacy

E-USS did not have ECOSOC consultative status, which is used here as a proxy for legitimacy. However, assessing it against the main components of the protocol for eligibility generates the analysis shown in Table 7.

As can be seen from the table, from a high-level perspective of legitimacy, it appears that E-USS complies with the criteria for ECOSOC consultative status. Consequently, from the perspective of this book, the NGO is regarded as legitimate.

Furthermore, as E-USS's membership is limited to members of the USS pension scheme, it is able to speak on behalf of a subset of USS members, which conveys a certain stakeholder legitimacy. Recognising this, USS formally recognised E-USS as a legitimate stakeholder.

Therefore, this NGO complies with the legitimacy proxy measures previously set out in Chapter 2.

Ex ante *effectiveness – viability and feasibility*

Overall, the aims of E-USS were highly ambitious in the sense that, at the time, there were very few pension funds making any claims to being socially responsible. However, at the outset of the campaign, E-USS advocated an exclusionary form of SRI to USS. In other words, they proposed that certain controversial corporate practices would be excluded from the investment portfolio. This was due to significant concerns among some E-USS members that the investment portfolio was undermining their research efforts. For example, "Tobacco is a very serious issue for a lot of our members – a lot of them do cancer research" (see Alexander, 2001). As highlighted in Chapter 3, such an approach ran counter to the Megarry Judgment and USS was therefore legally constrained from adopting this E-USS campaign suggestion. It is this case law that underlies USS's original response to E-USS that "the trustee company is legally prevented from instructing the managers to invest wholly or primarily on ethical or environmental considerations alone and has not done so" (see E-USS, 1999). Clearly, from an *ex ante* perspective, E-USS's advocating an illegal position cannot be considered to have been an effective approach.

In the light of the USS response regarding this legal limitation, E-USS was subsequently to adapt its investment policy recommendation and advocate an engagement approach (in other words, using the influence of share ownership to engage with investee companies and advocate good practice in relations to corporate governance and corporate responsibility). The key document was "Meeting the Responsibilities of Ownership – Our Proposal to USS" (see E-USS, 1999). This provided a detailed analysis of the legal and financial scope for USS defining and implementing an SRI policy. Financially, it argued:

> As we are not proposing that USS change its share portfolio, such a policy cannot negatively affect financial returns ... the growing practice of shareholder activism in the USA has, in recent years, had clearly beneficial results in terms of generating additional returns.

Legally, E-USS also now argued that an SRI investment policy was consistent with USS's legal responsibilities as articulated by the government's Goode Committee on Pension Law Reform (see Chapter 3). More specifically, the NGO highlighted the fact that a reform of the 1995 Pensions Act (see Chapter 4) would come into force the following year. As mentioned, this reform would require occupational pension funds to state whether or not they took social, environmental or ethical considerations into account in their investment decisions (HMSO, 1999, section 35(3)(f)). The fact that USS was to be legally compelled to make some kind of statement – and that it highlighted the scope for both integrated assessment and advocacy SRI policies – would have significantly increased the likelihood of the E-USS campaign's success. Consequently, this reform was a highly significant factor for the success of the E-USS campaign, since it changed the legal context within which the campaign was operating.

Other, lower-order, factors that increased the *ex ante* effectiveness of the E-USS campaign include:

- ❑ *Not calling for a boycott by potential members of the pension scheme*: This was appropriate, because USS has a degree of monopoly power – in general, academic and senior university administrative employees stand to lose financially if they elect to join an alternative to the USS pension scheme.
- ❑ *A highly targeted approach*: Following the "Meeting the Responsibilities of Ownership" document, E-USS began a targeted campaign, promoting its analysis to specific members of USS board and the university vice chancellors who played an important role in the governance of USS.
- ❑ *Seeking expert advice*: E-USS formed a steering committee from among its members. This included academics who, in addition to being members of USS, specialised in relevant fields. They also approached SRI practitioners for advice: "we are part of the UK Social Investment Forum, for example, and we've gotten some very, very useful advice from some well-connected people" (see Alexander, 2001).
- ❑ *Developing moral-case arguments*: E-USS used practical examples of the on-the-ground impact of companies in USS's portfolio to illustrate the moral case underlying its cause. For example, it highlighted allegations of involvement in defence exports to oppressive regimes by British Aerospace and Rolls-Royce.
- ❑ *A realistic request*: E-USS suggested that it should focus on SEE issues surrounding management policy rather than practice, and that "USS should keep its engagement activities to a manageable scale" (see E-USS, 1999).
- ❑ *Securing political support*: "socially responsible business behaviour by companies can have an enormous impact on the lives of

people in poorer countries... I welcome an opportunity to add the University Superannuation Scheme to the list of socially responsible investors" – Clare Short, Secretary of State for International Development (see Short, 1998, p 1). In addition, the Association of University Teachers, which is involved in the governance of the USS, agreed a motion endorsing E-USS campaign aims.

Therefore, in the context of the contemporary circumstances, from a perspective of *ex ante* effectiveness, the revised and updated E-USS campaign aims can be summarised as ambitious, yet both measured and realistic.

Ex post *effectiveness – implementation effectiveness*

USS was subsequently to announce a strengthening of its policy on SRI (see below). At that point, E-USS changed its strategy from one of promoting this change of policy to one of involving ongoing monitoring and review of its implementation by USS. This involved monitoring and review meetings, analysing USS's external communications on the issue and promoting specific engagement activity in support of USS's commitment.

The overall aims of the E-USS campaign broadly fell into three categories:

(1) *policy*: to encourage USS to produce a "positive" SRI policy position on active engagement;
(2) *transparency*: to encourage USS to publish what activity it has carried out in support of this engagement policy; and
(3) *monitor and evaluate*: to maintain an ongoing review of the degree to which USS was delivering on its policy commitments.

The analysis below reviews nine explicit and implicit E-USS campaign targets that cover these three areas. It assesses the actions taken by USS and analyses whether the campaign may have been responsible for generating this change.

The first E-USS aim was "to convince USS to adopt an ethical investment policy" (see Alexander, 2001). In response, USS issued a revised ethical policy statement saying that it would "strengthen its stance on socially responsible investment policies" (see USS, 1999). However, as previously mentioned, the SRI disclosure regulation came into force during the E-USS campaign, which is likely to have contributed towards E-USS's success. Nevertheless, when compared with other SIPs generated by the Pensions Act, the one produced by USS defines new standards of best practice (see later). E-USS can therefore justifiably claim to have influenced the generation of a strong SIP by USS, but it cannot claim to have achieved this entirely unaided.

The second E-USS aim was to promote "a policy of 'active investment' ". This would involve "USS using its influence as a major shareholder to encourage socially and environmentally responsible corporate behaviour" (see E-USS, 1999). For its part, the USS SIP committed it to "pursue a policy of more active engagement with companies" (see USS, 1999); to raise "ethical, environmental and social issues" (*ibid*) with all the companies in which it invests; to identify those companies that "do not meet best practice" on these issues "and may have an adverse financial impact on the value of the return on that investment"; to make "strong representations" in order to "seek a corporate policy change" and to closely monitor the results. Before the E-USS's campaign, USS's previous position on SRI had stated that it could not get involved in the operational decisions made on a day-to-day basis by the companies in which it invested. E-USS argued (see E-USS, 1999) that:

> although we have some sympathy for this position, an important distinction exists between day-to-day decision-taking and policy decision-making. Both for reasons of principle and of practice, we accept that the former must remain almost exclusively the concern of company management. Nevertheless we consider policy decisions, which can set the ethical and environmental standards of some of the world's largest corporations, to be a legitimate area of engagement for USS.

Therefore, that USS was to change this position following the E-USS campaign and require "FTSE100 companies ... to report and fully disclose their policies on and management of [corporate governance and SEE issues] at least once a year" (see USS, 1999) demonstrates the effectiveness of E-USS's argument.

The third E-USS aim was "For the ethical investment policy to be accountable to its members" (see Alexander, 2001). This would require USS (see E-USS, 1999) to:

> (1) post on the internet a detailed annual report outlining specific actions taken by USS to implement their policy… (2) provide scheme members with a full list of USS's 2,000 investments and (3) provide Scheme members with detailed information about the progress of USS's engagement with individual companies available on request.

In response, USS committed to "making more generally available some of the results of this policy, including an annual report" (see USS, 1999) and also to produce quarterly voting reports, which, since spring 2003, have contained reasonable detailed information. It also publishes the names of all of its investments on its Web site. However, it does not disclose the full detail of its engagement activity with individual companies due to a belief that this might affect its ability to enter into open debate with the company.

USS now meets the greater part of the E-USS transparency and accountability aims. However, E-USS has not achieved its third goal of USS providing details of progress on engagement with individual companies. Nevertheless, when compared with its occupational pension fund peer group, it is highly unusual to produce a report or to publish portfolio details on the Internet. Consequently, it is reasonable to conclude that there is evidence that E-USS partially achieved this desired outcome.

A fourth E-USS aim was that "USS would also need to employ experts in ethical investment analysis, and to provide existing staff with appropriate training" (see E-USS, 1999). USS subsequently recruited two new specialist staff to "step up our policy of active engagement. This will involve researching areas of social and environmental concern, and engaging with companies on these issues" (see USS, 1999). USS recognised that SRI had previously not been routinely undertaken: "To make socially responsible investment work for our members and the companies in which we invest, it needs to be part of our day to day business. This new appointment helps us to get to that position, bringing new insights and new networks to complement our expertise in fund management" (see USS, 1999). Using the recruitment practices of its pension peer group as a benchmark, at the time, it was uncommon for self-managed occupational pension schemes to appoint specialist staff on SRI. Consequently, this can be regarded as further evidence of E-USS success.

The fifth E-USS aim related to applying ongoing pressure on USS in relation to taking action on climate change. In attempting to achieve this aim, E-USS surveyed its members and presented the results to the USS with recommendations for action. USS was subsequently to commission and publish a discussion chapter on climate-change investment risk (see Mansley and Dlugolecki, 2001) and then to found the Institutional Investors' Group on Climate Change – a collaborative endeavour between institutional investors looking at, among other things, climate-change issues in investment, public policy and the property asset class. As E-USS recognised, when compared with other SEE issues at the time, a considerable amount of analysis into the impact of climate change on share price was available, and the subject was a prominent issue due to the climate-change negotiations in Kyoto. While USS chose to focus on the issue, there is insufficient independent evidence to conclude that it definitely chose to do so as a consequence of E-USS's campaign work. It could have simply been the clearest and most obvious place for the newly appointed SRI practitioners to start. Nevertheless, it is possible that the campaign played a role and this should not be entirely ruled out.

A sixth E-USS aim again related to applying ongoing pressure in a specific area. In particular, E-USS intended to promote engagement by USS with Balfour Beatty on the controversial Ilisu Dam (see Chapter 3). The voting record for the second quarter of 2002 discloses that, of the 11 resolutions at Balfour Beatty's AGM in 2002, USS voted in favour of 10 and abstained on one (see USS, 2002, p 9). While it does not explicitly say which resolution USS abstained on, the other resolutions were not controversial and involved standard AGM governance matters. Furthermore, as 40.9% of Balfour Beatty's investors abstained on this Friends of the Earth/Ilisu Dam campaign resolution, this is almost certainly the resolution on which USS abstained. That being the case, this resolution indicates that USS used its investor advocacy influence over Balfour Beatty in relation to the Ilisu Dam and that the

E-USS campaign was therefore probably successful in achieving this aim.

However, a seventh and related "ongoing pressure" E-USS aim was to promote USS engagement on BHP Billiton and Alcoa, in order to encourage them to uphold the World Commission on Dams Guidelines ("A group of aluminium producers, including two companies USS invests in, are involved in plans to build a series of 46 dams on the Tocantins and Araguaia river systems in the Amazon Basin" (see E-USS, 2003)). In a direct response, USS stated that it had explained to Ethics for USS that the USS scheme recognised that the construction of dams could have significant social and environmental impacts, but that it "had not been possible to prioritise this project because this issue did not affect the whole portfolio in the way that other issues and sectors do". So, while E-USS clearly failed to motivate the USS to engage with BHP Billiton and Alcoa on this issue, this does demonstrate that USS gave consideration to their request.

An eighth E-USS "ongoing pressure" aim was to promote USS divestment from the oil and gas sector. On this point, "It is clear from Ethics for USS's research that many USS members do not feel that it is in their interests for their pension fund to make a profit at the expense of the stability of the earth's climate" (see E-USS, 2000). It is notable that this was a return to its earlier "exclusionary" policy request that USS had already rejected on the grounds that it would have been inconsistent with its legal duties. It is therefore unsurprising that USS's March 2003 portfolio included three oil and gas multinationals in its top ten holdings (£598.6 million of BP shares, £309.5 million of Shell shares, and £96.7 million worth of BG Group). E-USS therefore clearly failed to meet this aim.

The ninth and final USS aim was to check that SRI principles were adopted by its external fund managers: "internal coherence would suggest that anything that their internal fund managers were doing on this would also be affecting their external fund managers as well" (see Alexander, 2001). In relation to this aim, USS subsequently disclosed the results of its "Learning Review" (see USS, 2003). This found that four of USS's seven fund managers had the basic foundations for corporate governance and corporate responsibility engagement in place. The external managers were also asked to outline their plans for further development of their approach to SRI both in response to this learning review and to the Institutional Shareholders' Committee's Principles on Engagement (see Chapter 3). USS also committed to:

> assess each manager's position again at the end of the scheme year, focusing on those managers and those issues where there is greatest opportunity for movement towards best practice... When managers are being considered for (re) appointment, performance in this area can be assessed (and compared) against the requirements of the SIP... A consistent finding was that this was the most thorough (in some cases, the first ever) evaluation that fund managers had experienced, either by clients or their agents (eg, investment consultants).

However, importantly, in 2003 USS ran a competition in conjunction with the *Financial Times* and the investment consultants Hewitt, Bacon and Woodrow. The competition was for proposals on a hypothetical portfolio of USS's money that was managed "as if the long term really mattered" and included engagement among the criteria for assessing the proposals. Schroders were to come second (to Henderson) in this competition, yet USS severed their fund management contract shortly after the competition. This suggests that, if the USS did assess each manager's position in relation to engagement, it did not play a significant role in the overall assessment.

So, as to whether the E-USS campaign was effective in achieving this aim, that it to USS checking what its external fund managers were doing in this area is a significant and positive outcome, as USS is a large institutional client with considerable leverage. Consequently, if its external fund managers believe that it is taking SRI issues seriously, they are likely to commit greater resources to this area. Indeed, before Schroders were dismissed, one of their SRI analysts stated that, "Representing many large institutional clients who have a strong interest in SRI has definitely increased the emphasis on SRI and its profile within Schroders" (see Stathers, 2003). However, there remain questions as to the extent to which this evaluation plays a significant role in the overall assessment of their external fund managers, as this information is not disclosed.

Table 8 summarises the above analysis in relation to the nine campaign aims that have been analysed. It uses the key introduced at the outset of this section.

Table 8 Overview of the effectiveness of E-USS capital market campaign

E-USS aim	USS action	Eval
To persuade USS to adopt an ethical investment policy	USS issued a revised ethical policy statement	Y
To get USS to encourage socially and environmentally responsible corporate behaviour	USS SIP committed itself to "pursue a policy of more active engagement with companies" (see USS, 1999)	Y
For the "ethical investment policy to be accountable to its members"	USS committed to making more generally available some of the results of this policy, including an annual report	Y%
For USS to employ experts in ethical investment analysis	USS recruited two new specialist staff	Y
To promote action by USS on climate change	Published a discussion chapter on climate change investment risk and founded the Institutional Investors' Group on Climate Change	
To promote engagement with Balfour Beatty on the Ilisu Dam	Probably withheld support from management on the vote	Y?
To promote engagement on BHP Billiton and Alcoa, re: the World Commission on Dams Guidelines	USS declined to engage	N
To promote divestment from the oil and gas sector	USS continues to invest in the sector	N
USS to check that SRI principles are adopted by its external fund managers	USS published a review of its external fund managers	Y?

As can be seen from the table, the above analysis of how effective the E-USS campaign was in its policy and transparency aims shows that it was highly effective: there is evidence that E-USS either achieved or partially achieved the desired outcome in respect of its initial objectives.

However, once USS committed to a positive SIP, the above *ex post* effectiveness analysis of E-USS's ongoing monitor-and-evaluate campaign targets demonstrates that, in many cases, there is either insufficient evidence that E-USS achieved its intended outcome, or evidence that it did not achieve its aim. It appears, therefore, that E-USS was less effective when monitoring and evaluating USS activity once it had made the commitment to an active engagement policy.

As highlighted in the *ex ante* review above, the fact that USS was to be compelled by regulation to make some kind of statement would have significantly increased the likelihood of success. While this renders assessing E-USS effectiveness difficult, it is possible to use the response to the regulation of other similar occupational pension funds that were not confronted by a campaign, as a benchmark against which to measure the *ex post* effectiveness of E-USS. To that end, most studies of UK occupational pension fund SRI policy and practice since the reform of the Pensions Act have singled out USS as a best-practice example:

❏ along with four other pension funds from the top 100, USS scored maximum marks in the FoE survey (see Friends of the Earth, 2001b);

❏ an example of "The Best We Found" (see Just Pensions, 2002); and

❏ "USS is without question the UK's leading pension fund in terms of socially responsible investment" (see TUC, 2003).

E-USS's initial effectiveness in delivering the policy change can be further substantiated by the following statements, which include comments made by interviewees:

❏ "People and Plant successfully lobbied the USS. Meeting the Responsibilities of Ownership is still one of the best things written in this area" (see Alam, 2001).

❏ "... without the Ethics for USS campaign, USS' SIP would not have been so strongly written" (see Stathers, 2003).

❏ "People and Planet succeeded in bringing pension fund managers to the table, and getting them to take members' social and environmental concerns seriously" (see Mansley, 2001).

❏ "People and Planet's Ethics for USS campaign has been an impressive campaign for socially responsible investment, particularly in its ability to mobilise pension fund members – the reverberations of this should spread across Europe and ultimately worldwide. More NGOs need to learn from People and Planet's experience" – Penny Shepherd, Chief Executive of UK Social Investment Forum (see People and Planet, 2003).

Therefore, by referring to other business-as-usual responses to the Pensions Act made by other occupational pension funds not targeted by NGO campaigns, it can be shown that the E-USS campaign made a significant difference to the extent to which USS embraced SRI.

It is also noteworthy that USS is now promoting SRI nationally and internationally. For example, in addition to the previously mentioned external fund manager review, it organised a high-profile conference at the Royal Institute of International Affairs reviewing the broader responsibility of investors in general. It also led the development of the Enhanced Analytics Initiative, which has had some significant success in encouraging brokers to increase their research on "extra-financial" issues – including SEE issues – that are important to a proper understanding of the long-term competitive positioning of the business.

In contrast, the contemporary role of E-USS has however been limited simply to monitoring USS. Indeed, with the establishment of Fair Share and the shift in emphasis away from USS and towards other pension schemes, there is evidence to suggest that E-USS (and, therefore, People and Planet) has decided that it does not have a significant ongoing monitoring and evaluating role.

It appears that USS now has a broader, better-resourced and better-informed SRI advocacy programme than E-USS. While this reduction of E-USS's relative influence may be seen by E-USS as a negative outcome, the fact that USS appears to have become a more influential (and arguably better-informed) advocate of SRI than E-USS is ultimately a positive outcome for the E-USS campaign.

In conclusion, from an *ex post* effectiveness perspective, after initially failing, E-USS was effective at generating a strong SRI engagement policy at USS. Consequently, People and Planet can justifiably claim to have "caused a £22 billion stock market fund to invest ethically" (see People and Planet, 2002, p 6) – although it was not the only "cause", and the phrase "investing ethically" is clearly open to interpretation. However, E-USS cannot claim to have been effective in relation to its ongoing monitor-and-evaluate objectives.

Efficiency

From the launch of the campaign, it took 27 months for USS to change its original SRI policy. This was partly due to the initial advocacy of an avoidance policy that failed for important legal reasons. Campaign research should have considered this legal

dimension so, to some extent, this duration was somewhat inefficient. However, the campaign did correct its initial error.

In terms of costs, the most significant to the campaign was a
half-time position, which "has been devoted to the campaign since
autumn of 1999" (see Alexander, 2001). In addition, an operating
budget of about £3,000 per annum was allocated to the campaign to
cover member mailings. Therefore, the overall cost of the ongoing
campaign to date is in the region of £60,000, which renders it
among the more resource-intensive NGO capital market interventions in the UK between 1990 and 2002.

In considering the benefit generated by the E-USS campaign (in
addition to the positive SRI policy adopted by USS), based on the
above *ex ante* and *ex post* analysis, the main direct benefit is the fact
that USS has become a strong advocate of SRI. In particular, it has
exerted some client influence over its external fund managers,
which collectively manage more than £220 billion. As this benefit
figure is a measure of the volume of assets rather than the economic value of the benefit, the cost-and-benefit figures are not
directly comparable. Even so, they are a useful measure and imply
a ratio for the campaign spend in excess of 3.5 million. Consequently, despite its being initially ineffective and inefficient, it is
reasonable to conclude that E-USS was efficient overall.

Capital market intervention model categorisation
According to the NGO capital market intervention model, E-USS
deployed an indirect investor advocacy strategy, aimed at capital
market institutions, using both business-case and moral-case arguments and having adopted an orca stance. A scaled polar diagram
is used in Figure 9 to depict a more nuanced classification:

The later polar diagram depicts the strategy undertaken by E-USS
in its capital market intervention. It demonstrates that, in addition
to the above classification, the NGO used some additional components: a limited economic-influence dimension (it promoted divestment as a sanction once engagement failed) and limited degree of
public-policy audience.

Lessons learned
The deductive analysis of the capital market campaign strategy
based on the model (Chapter 3) argued that the probability of

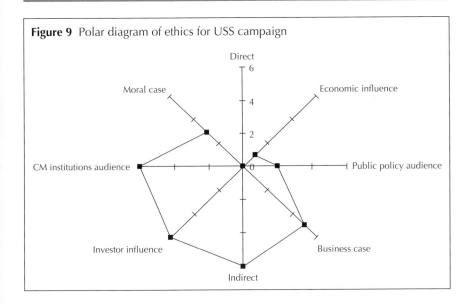

Figure 9 Polar diagram of ethics for USS campaign

success would be increased by adopting a strategy of investor-advocacy influence over one of economic influence. It also suggested that an indirect approach would be more likely to succeed than a direct. This case strongly supports both these hypotheses in that the initial investment policy recommendation of E-USS was an economic-influence strategy and failed. When it reformed its recommendation to become that of investor advocacy, it succeeded.

The deductive analysis also suggested that striking a balance between moral and financial arguments would be more likely to succeed. In adopting an indirect investor-advocacy influence using both business- and moral-case arguments, E-USS appears to have maximised the probability of success. As has been argued here, the E-USS campaign was highly effective (at changing USS's policy) and highly efficient, which would appear to support this hypothesis.

As the USS appears to have diffused the E-USS campaign with its response, it is particularly worth reviewing the main aspects of its response in order to establish the lessons for other pension schemes that are potential campaign targets (particularly, as mentioned, in the light of Fair Share). The key elements of USS response appear to have been:

(1) *Policy*: Developed a policy of active engagement and committed itself to using its influence as a major shareholder to

encourage socially and environmentally responsible corporate behaviour.

(2) *Reporting*: Made available some of the results of this policy, including an annual engagement report and a quarterly voting report.

(3) *Resources*: Recruited two new specialist staff to implement its policy of active engagement.

(4) *Voting integration*: Integrated the policy into its voting practices.

(5) *Performance evaluation*: Committed to consider performance in this area when (re)appointing fund managers.

(6) *Reputation*: Developed reputation for leadership by, for example, publishing a discussion chapter into climate-change investment risk and founding the Institutional Investors' Group on Climate Change.

Conclusion

It has been demonstrated that, after initially failing, the E-USS campaign to encourage the USS to adopt an SRI policy was ultimately effective. The above *ex ante* implementation-effectiveness analysis demonstrates that E-USS ultimately established ambitious yet realistic objectives, and the *ex post* effectiveness analysis demonstrates that it achieved the majority of its original policy targets.

Therefore, this case study has demonstrated that it is possible for NGO capital market intervention to be both effective and efficient. The empirical experience here also appears to confirm that the deductive capital market intervention theory appears to work in practice.

Importantly, this case also demonstrates that other investors seeking to reduce the risk of being targeted by campaigners should consider: developing an engagement policy; reporting on activity; investing in resources; integrating the policy into voting practices; evaluating performance and developing their reputation in this area.

WWF-UK'S ARCTIC REFUGE CAMPAIGN AGAINST BP PLC

The following case study reviews a shareholder resolution filed at BP's AGM by WWF-UK, WWF-US, US Public Interest Research Group (PIRG), and Greenpeace regarding exploration in the Arctic

National Wildlife Refuge (ANWR) and BP's climate change strategy. As the resolution bundled a number of various issues together, this case study particularly focuses on the ANWR/WWF component of the resolution as a discrete subset. The case differs from the others presented in this book in that it is the only detailed case study of an NGO shareholder resolution.

WWF was founded under Swiss law in Zurich on 11 September 1961. It was originally called the World Wildlife Fund, but changed its name in 1986 to World Wide Fund for Nature. It sets out its mission thus: "WWF takes action to: conserve endangered species; protect endangered spaces; [and] address global threats to the planet by seeking sustainable solutions for the benefit of people and nature" (see WWF, 2003).

The NGO had a global network of 52 offices working in more than 90 countries. In the 2001–2 financial year, the UK office generated £31 million in income and the WWF international network more than £200 million. WWF has 320,000 members in the UK and more than 5 million worldwide.

In terms of the "stance" that WWF takes towards business, its Business and Industry Policy (see WWF-UK, 1999b) states that the NGO's approach is one of "pragmatism, cooperation and partnership". This demonstrates that WWF generally adopts a dolphin stance. However, the policy also states, "The approach taken depends on a detailed assessment of the issue, audience and business. Use of the media is carefully considered, as are shareholder resolutions at annual general meetings and/or recourse to the legal system."[1]

The data list of capital market intervention chronology in Appendix 1 include 18 separate capital market interventions for WWF, rendering it a particularly active NGO in this area. The NGO's strategy refers to capital market campaigning as a "mechanism to achieve long-term change in business sustainability" (see WWF-UK, 2000h, p 17) and establishes a "Critical Indicator: Ethical Investment a key-influence on development pattern of key sectors". It argues that its capital market intervention is required due to the "lack of government willingness to regulate multinationals" (*ibid*) and describes its aims as being "to use the financial markets as a tool for change; to demonstrate that environmental sense makes good financial sense and to practise what we preach" (see

WWF-UK, 2000g, p 4). In 2001, WWF-UK became the first UK NGO to employ a full-time capital market campaigner (a sustainable-investment policy officer), indicating its resource commitment to this area.

Introduction to specific capital market campaign

This campaign targeted BP's potential involvement in the Arctic Refuge. This case study focuses on the effectiveness and efficiency of the shareholder resolution presented at BP's AGM in 2002. The main aim of WWF's capital market intervention was "to persuade BP Amoco to publicly withdraw its interest in developing the Arctic Refuge and publicly support permanent protection of the Refuge for its wilderness values" (see WWF-UK, 2000c).

The capital market intervention was one part of a broader campaign to protect the coastal plain of the ANWR, a wilderness covering 7.6 million hectares in northeast Alaska. The area being considered for drilling opportunities was the "1002 area".[2] This was the only protected part of Alaska's Arctic coastal plain, the remaining 95% being open for oil and gas drilling. Since the 1002 area was established, a heated debate has taken place regarding whether the Refuge should be opened up to drilling. In relatively recent times, President George W. Bush has argued that the Refuge should be exploited to reduce US dependency on foreign oil. Environmental organisations, including WWF, have argued that the Refuge is an important sanctuary for polar bears, musk oxen, caribou and migratory birds. Proponents of drilling say only a small fraction of ANWR would be needed for equipment and operations, leaving plenty of room for the wildlife. In particular, Arctic Power, the lobby group focused on opening up the Refuge, claims (see Arctic Power, 2003a) that:

> only the 1.5 million acre or 8% on the northern coast of ANWR is being considered for development. The remaining 17.5 million acres or 92% of ANWR will remain permanently closed to any kind of development. If oil is discovered, less than 2,000 acres of the over 1.5 million acres of the Coastal Plain would be affected.

Arctic Power also contends that caribou in other Alaskan drilling areas have not been harmed.

The indigenous people who have settled near the reserve are divided between those who see extra oil and gas investment as an opportunity for development, and those who regard it as a threat to their way of life. The Inupiat (an Inuit people) on the coast have traditionally depended on sea mammals rather than the 1002 area's wildlife. They support drilling for the direct economic benefit it would bring. But the economy of the Gwich'in (a Native American people) on the southern boundary is linked to the vast porcupine caribou herd in the Refuge. They oppose drilling because of its potential impact on the caribou.

WWF's broad ANWR campaign (see WWF-UK, 2000c) included:

> Continued direct negotiation with BP Amoco; concerted media activity to raise the profile of the Arctic Refuge in the UK; use of WWF activist network [including]... letters to politicians [and] petitions to the US government; partnerships with other NGOs...; and use [of] WWF-UK's shareholdings in BP Amoco to act as additional leverage.

This demonstrates that the capital market element under review here was established by the NGO as part of a broader ANWR campaign.

WWF's first capital market intervention in this area took place in 2000, when the NGO collaborated with Greenpeace. Greenpeace had filed a resolution that referred to the Arctic Refuge but focused mainly on the climate change impacts of oil and gas exploration and production. While WWF did not co-file this resolution, it did participate in its advocacy – for example, by placing an advertisement in the *Financial Times* that set out its rationale for BP not entering the Refuge. It also published "Challenging the Economic Myth: Oil & Gas in the Arctic Refuge, Alaska" (see WWF-UK, 2000d), distributed the chapter to large institutional shareholders, and voted in favour of the resolution using its own shares in BP.

During 2001 and 2002, along with other interested NGOs such as the US Public Interest Research Group and concerned investors, WWF participated in the drafting and co-filing of a resolution at BP's AGMs. It also approached institutional investors with large shareholdings in BP on a number of occasions in order to generate interest in and support for the resolution. WWF led the drafting of the 2002 resolution:

> "RESOLVED, shareholders instruct the company to prepare a report disclosing, as appropriate, how the company analyses and takes steps to control significant risks to shareholder value from operating in

environmentally or culturally sensitive areas, and lobbying for access to areas with a protected environmental status. These risks include operating, financial and reputation risks to the business in general, the ability to attract and retain high quality staff, and the impact on BP's effort in building its reputation as a good corporate citizen. The report should include a description of how the information therein affects BP's decision-making processes" (see BP, 2002).

In addition to submitting the resolution, the NGO also commissioned Innovest Strategic Value Advisors to prepare an analysis of the business case (see Innovest, 2002). This concluded that "performance around sensitive sites is a financial risk issue that warrants serious attention" (p 2). This report was used during dialogue with investors to back up the resolution's use of the influential Association of British Insurers disclosure guidelines (see Chapter 3).

As well as the specific business-case and reputational-risk arguments that were aimed at investors, WWF consistently argued a moral case for its preferred course of action by BP in the media. For example (see WWF-UK, 2000e):

> BP Amoco ... refuses to acknowledge publicly the damage that even exploratory drilling would do to the Refuge, let alone the impact of large-scale oil extraction. WWF believes that, as multinational oil companies already have access to 95% of Alaska's Arctic coastal plain, this last 5% should be left undisturbed. It is not only wildlife that could suffer as a result of oil drilling. The Gwich'in Athabascan people rely upon the caribou for their survival, and are therefore extremely vulnerable to the changes in migratory patterns that would be the result of oil extraction.

This statement is based on the potential for oil extraction to cause suffering to people and the environment rather than the economic costs of this outcome.

Assessment of the capital market intervention
NGO legitimacy
WWF has had ECOSOC General Consultative Status since 1996 and therefore complies with the proxy for NGO legitimacy set out above. With respect to transparency, WWF produces an audited report and accounts (in line with charity law), an annual review of

its activities, and an externally verified environmental report detailing its own resource consumption.

Regarding its internal consistency with its capital market intervention, it banks with the Co-operative Bank due to the bank's ethical stance and offers its staff the option of investing their pension in an ethical fund. The NGO also has an ethical-investment policy for its own reserves. At the time of the campaign, WWF's investment policy (see case study) approved ownership of shares in BP as a best-of-sector company,[3] so the shares were purchased to provide an investment return. Therefore, this specific campaign is also legitimised through its genuine investment ownership.

Ex ante *effectiveness – viability and feasibility*

The overall intention to prevent drilling in the 1002 area represented a highly ambitious campaign goal for WWF, as there were significant financial interests in support of opening up the Refuge for drilling. For example, a US geological survey estimated that with a market price of around US$24 per barrel, there was a 50% likelihood of recovering 5.3 billion barrels of oil from the ANWR, with up to 16 billion barrels being possible if prices were high enough (see Reuters, 2002) – that is, a 50% likelihood of US$127.2 billion dollars of oil at a US$24 market price. Revenues would have flowed to the government, state, local people, the companies involved, and their investors.

While the Refuge would be open to drilling by any oil and gas company approved by the US government, the NGO appears to have chosen to confront BP for the following reasons:

(1) BP was one of two oil companies that drilled exploratory wells in the area (Chevron being the other).
(2) WWF believed that a commitment from BP not to enter the Refuge would send a signal to the rest of the industry that the 1002 area was off limits, regardless of the US government's position on the area (see Wicks, 2002). WWF cites as evidence for this claim the view that BP was the most significant operator in the area and "the first mover on climate change – others follow their lead" (see Peck, 2002).

(3) BP was "furthest ahead on (biodiversity) thinking ... and we have been working with them for some time and feel it's time to challenge them to break the logjam on this issue" (see Peck, 2002).

(4) BP was "lobbying to go into the Arctic Refuge" (see Peck, 2002) through its membership of Arctic Power, an organisation that describes itself as "a grassroots, nonprofit citizen's organization with 10,000 members founded in April of 1992 to expedite congressional and presidential approval of oil exploration and production within the Coastal Plain of the Arctic National Wildlife Refuge" (see Arctic Power, 2003b). BP had also played host to delegations of Washington politicians and journalists visiting Alaska to see the coastal plain (see Banerjee, 2002, p 4).

BP was providing a considerable source of funds for Arctic Power, which was essentially the opposition to the NGO in this debate. Removing that funding would have weakened Arctic Power politically and financially – BP's fee was "at the top of the scale" for Arctic Power (*ibid*).

However, targeting BP generated a number of problems, not least of which was the general perception that the company led its sector on CSR – leadership that was recognised by the NGO in the resolution itself (see BP, 2002). In addition to the challenge presented by BP's expertise on environmental issues in the oil and gas sector, and the considerable financial resources allocated to its CSR work, this perception of sector leadership was broadly held and could have ultimately reduced support for the resolution. As one SRI analyst put it, "When NGOs focus on the leaders like BP... it is not very helpful for us because BP is already doing more than any other oil company" (see Johnston, 2001).

In addition to the perceived CSR strength of BP, there is flaw in the logic supporting the overall aim of the capital market intervention (see Wicks, 2002). The flaw stems from the NGO's rationale that a commitment from BP not to enter the Arctic Refuge would send a signal to the rest of the industry that the 1002 area was completely off limits, regardless of its legal status. Even if such a statement from BP was feasible, it is highly unlikely that it would have secured the protection of the Refuge should the government open the area for exploration. An oil- and gas-industry-wide *voluntary* commitment not to go into a legally accessible area would have been unprecedented.[4] Furthermore, ExxonMobil operated in Alaska and was considered a strong contender for potential exploration leases in the area. Exxon was already regarded by environmentalists as a pariah not only because of the *Exxon Valdez* disaster in 1989 but also because it did not follow BP's commitments on climate change. This demonstrates Exxon's reluctance to respond to signals from the industry and highlights the flaw in the logic.

This flaw represents a significant weakness in the stated aims of the capital market intervention. It also hints at further possible internal reasons for challenging BP: confrontation by an NGO of a large multinational generally creates considerable media coverage. This would have been useful for the campaign to preserve the status of the refuge.

Regarding the *ex ante* strengths of the capital market intervention, as can be seen above, the NGO used both moral and financial arguments to further its aims. As argued in Chapter 3, this should have increased the effectiveness of the investor-focused campaign. From the perspective of maximising potential votes in favour of the resolution, an additional strength of the resolution itself was that it asked for a report into how the company managed the risk to shareholder value from operating in environmentally or culturally sensitive areas, and lobbying for access to areas with a protected environmental status, rather than asking directly for a commitment not to enter the Refuge – WWF's overall campaign goal. The reason why this represents a strength relates to the controversial nature of the business case for not drilling in the Refuge. If investors' financial analysis of the costs in terms of reputational risk to the brand and so forth was lower than the potential benefit to BP from extracting "up to 16 billion barrels" of oil, then a resolution focus on a commitment not to drill would have generated less support than a request for a report into how the company analyses the risk to shareholder value.

In respect of this focus on a business rationale, a city editor was to comment, "It is rather smart of the environmental lobbyists to focus their arguments on shareholder value. After all, BP has gone out of its way to trumpet its green credentials and its desire to be regarded as a good corporate citizen" (see Kahn, 2002, p 57).

An insight into the resolution drafters' analysis of this point can be discerned from the following memo from Walden Asset Management (2001, p 2), which was involved in the drafting:

> The reason the resolution is framed as a request for a report is twofold. One, we know that a resolution of this sort gets more votes from concerned investors cautious about the financial impact of an outright ban on drilling in the Refuge. Second, however a resolution is framed, it engages the company in a serious debate about its plans – a public debate in which a whole range of arguments can be raised. We believe this resolution still sends a strong message of concern to BP.

In summary, therefore, both the resolutions focus on shareholder value and its request for a report rather than not drilling. This increased the feasibility of generating significant interest from mainstream investors in this issue.

Ex post *effectiveness – implementation effectiveness*
The analysis below details the explicit and implicit intervention targets and assesses what related actions the target company took.

WWF's first aim was "To persuade BP Amoco to publicly withdraw its interest in developing the Arctic Refuge and publicly support permanent protection of the Refuge for its wilderness values" (see WWF-UK, 2000c). BP's response to the resolution included the following statement:

> The company's position on the Arctic National Wildlife Refuge (ANWR) has been principled and remains unchanged. It is that the American people should decide ... whether or not they wish to open the Refuge for exploration. Our decision would then be made in light of the economic, environmental and social risks and in light of ANWR's attractiveness within a global portfolio of opportunities.

While BP does state that any decision to enter into ANWR would consider "environmental and social risks" it did not make a statement to the effect that WWF intended and, in respect of this target, the campaign failed.

WWF's second aim was to persuade BP to "prepare a report disclosing, as appropriate, how the company analyses and takes steps to control significant risks to shareholder value from operating in environmentally or culturally sensitive areas, and lobbying for access to areas with a protected environmental status" (see BP, 2002).

In its formal response to the resolution, which was supported by new material on its website, BP sets out how it is dealing with the issues raised by the resolution. BP's response to resolution 14 states that:

> the board opposes Resolution 14 for the reasons given below and for those set out following the text of the resolution: Our business systems and processes throughout the company are designed to address and manage appropriately technical, competitive, commercial and political risks as well as environmental and social risks... BP supports the work IUCN[5] (The World Conservation Union) is doing to develop more common environmental definitions... In particular, if we decide to explore or develop in IUCN category I-IV designated sites where development is permitted, we will, where we have operational control and are legally and commercially able to do so, include in the annual Environmental and Social Review descriptions of risk assessments carried out. These will include discussion of:
>
> (a) issues and risks identified, both technical and values based
> (b) consequent environmental, economic and social impacts and benefits
> (c) stakeholder dialogue undertaken to inform and be informed
> (d) actions taken to mitigate risk.

The new material published by BP included a position statement on sensitive sites that stated that "exploring for and developing new oil and gas reserves can have environmental and social impacts on a variety of scales... Our approach to assessing new areas takes... an integrated approach to the consideration of environmental, social and economic issues."

As to whether BP's above response meets the aims of WWF's campaign, when taken in conjunction with supporting text published elsewhere, represented significant new disclosure on how the company analyses and takes steps to control significant risks to shareholder value from operating in environmentally or culturally sensitive areas. Furthermore, the company made two new specific commitments that strengthened its approach to biodiversity: first, that it supported the work of IUCN in developing more common environmental definitions of sensitive sites and, second, that if it decided to explore or develop in IUCN category I–IV designated sites it would include in the annual Environmental and Social Review descriptions of risk assessments carried out.

However, BP did not contend with the "lobbying for access to" element of the resolution in this response but did make a number of statements elsewhere on the issue – some of these conflicted, which enabled WWF to claim (see WWF-UK, 2002c) that BP was being duplicitous:

> They [BP] say "We have sought to play a positive role in that debate" (13 March 2002) and yet in the same week in a speech at Stanford, Lord Browne stated BP "should take no part in the debate" (11 March 2002). These statements cannot both be true and yet come within days of each other.

So, regarding this second aim, there is only some evidence that WWF was successful in achieving this aim.

The third aim of the campaign was to generate a significant vote in favour of the resolution. Shareholders owning 59% of BP's stock voted, with 9.7% of these backing the resolution. This was the third year that NGOs had filed resolutions that mentioned ANWR (the first two focused principally on climate change). The year 2000 resolution received a 13.5% vote in favour and the year 2001 received 13%. While 9.7% represented shareholders with over £8 billion of BP stock (and a reasonably high percentage when compared with similar resolutions filed at other companies), compared with previous years, this lower vote may be regarded as a failure. However, when including abstentions, a total of 14.9% of BP still withheld support from the company – despite a strong response to the resolution – which, it could be argued, represents a considerable success for the campaigners.

A fourth apparent aim of the campaign was to promote investor dialogue on biodiversity issues. BP held several meetings with investors regarding the resolution in advance of the AGM. The Association of British Insurers also hosted a debate that was attended by a significant number of large institutional investors. Such dialogue on biodiversity was almost entirely absent before the resolution and it is reasonable to conclude, therefore, that it would not have taken place otherwise. Therefore, the campaign succeeded in relation to this aim.

A fifth campaign aim was to persuade BP to disclose a policy in relation to biodiversity. As mentioned above, BP published a new position statement on sensitive sites that included an analysis of its impact on biodiversity. In advance of the resolution, BP did not have such a policy statement. That it published one concurrent with its response to the resolution demonstrates that it did so as a consequence of the resolution itself and, therefore, this campaign aim was successfully achieved.

A sixth aim was to persuade BP to pull out of Arctic Power. As the shareholder resolution put it: "BP states that it does not advocate opening the Refuge for development. However, the company is a financial contributor to the advocacy group Arctic Power, which is lobbying the U.S. Congress to open the region for drilling." After the AGM, BP pulled out of Arctic Power – which the *New York Times* described as "a major lobbying group spearheading the campaign to open the Arctic National Wildlife Refuge in Alaska to oil drilling". It quoted a BP spokesman as saying "we are no longer going to be involved in ANWR debate... When and if the American people decide ANWR should be opened, we will consider it based on its commercial and competitive attributes." This represented a significant campaign success for the NGO.

A seventh aim was to persuade investors that biodiversity issues are relevant to investment decisions. BP partially acknowledged the shareholder-value case made by the resolution, stating that:

> managing risks is fundamentally important both to good corporate citizenship and to the preservation and enhancement of shareholder value... Our business systems and processes throughout the company are designed to address and manage appropriately, technical, competitive, commercial and political risks as well as environmental and social risks.

Separately, in advance of the AGM, a spokesperson for Friends Ivory & Sime, one of BP's largest investors, was quoted as saying, "We consider these issues to be very significant in terms of shareholder value and we believe the resolution has considerable merit" (see Jones, 2002, p 22). Furthermore, as previously mentioned, Société Générale Global Research was later to conduct an assessment of BP's exposure to political risks (see Ennis, 2002, p 11). This included "environmental sensitivity", and cited the opposition to drilling in the ANWR as an example. Subsequently, institutional investors such as Insight Investment and Foreign and Colonial were to publish analysis into the shareholder-value ramifications of biodiversity in the extractive sectors. This therefore indicates that the resolution has successfully catalysed a broader debate about the risks to business operations from operating in environmentally sensitive sites.

In the longer term, if analysis of oil and gas companies' performance in relation to how they manage their biodiversity impacts and risks were to become more broadly integrated into institutional investors' analysis, then (as argued in Chapter 3) the cost of capital-pricing signals will promote better practices by those companies in relation to biodiversity management.

The eighth aim was to generate sufficient media coverage for the campaign in order to secure protection for the ANWR. The resolution was covered by a large number of mainstream newspapers including, the *Independent, Guardian, Financial Times, Evening Standard, Daily Mail, New York Times* and *Wall Street Journal*. The *New York Times* in particular noted that BP's withdrawal from Arctic Power came "just as the Republicans, who back drilling in the area, [were] about to regain control of the Senate, giving proponents their best chance in years to pass legislation opening the area along Alaska's Beaufort Sea coast to oil exploration", implying that the withdrawal would make it harder for the ANWR to be opened to drilling.

It is similarly noteworthy that Reuters (see Chatterjee, 2002) linked the resolution to the Senate vote thus:

> The resolution came just before US President George W. Bush suffered a major energy-policy defeat with a Senate vote on his administration's plan to give oil companies access to the Arctic National Wildlife Refuge in Alaska. Bush, a former Texas oilman, made drilling in the refuge the centrepiece of his proposed US energy policy but failed to gain the 60 votes necessary to end the debate and allow drilling to go ahead.

The refuge remains the subject of intense discussion, but at the time of writing it remains closed to oil extraction. While this suggests that the campaign was successful in achieving this aim, the debate to open up the refuge is highly controversial and has been raging for a number of decades. In the context of this much broader debate it is extremely difficult to assess the extent to which the campaign's successful attraction of media coverage to its issue secured the protection of the Refuge. Nevertheless, the withdrawal of BP from

Arctic Power was significantly due to the campaign and is likely to have badly damaged, the financial resources of the campaign to open up the refuge and to BP's broader political support for it. Therefore, it is reasonable to conclude that the resolution played an important role in the overall debate.

Table 9 summarises the above analysis regarding the campaign. The later analysis demonstrates that the resolution failed to generate a statement from BP publicly withdrawing its interest in developing the Arctic Refuge, and failed to generate a vote in favour of the resolution. However, the analysis also demonstrates that the resolution catalysed a number of changes in BP prior to the resolution vote at the AGM. This may have been the reason why more support from institutional investors was not forthcoming. In particular, the resolution generated considerable change in BP's biodiversity policy, systems and disclosure. It also promoted a new discussion among capital market institutions on the issue and appears to have persuaded a significant number of investors that there was a shareholder value argument in support of establishing biodiversity risk management systems by extractive companies.

Furthermore, while the resolution may not have reduced the likelihood of BP's entering the Refuge if the US government is to ever allow such a thing, it may have reduced the possibility that the Refuge would be opened at all. Despite at least three opportunities for the US Senate to open the Refuge since the resolution, the area retains its protected status.

From the perspective of the NGO's broader campaign to protect the Arctic Refuge, there are two significant outcomes from the capital market intervention: first, it generated directly attributable success both in the form of BP's withdrawal from Arctic Power and a commitment from BP to play no further part in the debate, which may have contributed to the protection of the reserve itself; and, second, the resolution created a considerable quantity of media interest. Therefore, from this perspective, this capital market intervention was *ex post* effective.

Chapter 3 argued that it is misleading to judge the ultimate success or failure of resolutions just by reference to the AGM vote on the day. Judging the outcome of this case study based simply on the vote would have entirely obscured the main outcomes from the

Table 9 An analysis of the 2002 WWF-UK BP plc capital market intervention

WWF aim	BP action	Eval
To persuade BP Amoco to publicly withdraw its interest in developing the Arctic Refuge	BP did not formally withdraw its interest in developing the Arctic Refuge	N
To persuade BP to "prepare a report disclosing, (1) how it analyses and controls significant risks to shareholder value from operating in environmentally or culturally sensitive areas, and (2) lobbying for access to areas with a protected environmental status"	BP published its formal response to the resolution and placed new material on its Web site dealing with the issues raised by the resolution. The material, though, did not substantively deal with WWF's second point re lobbying	Y%
To generate a significant vote in favour of the resolution	Shareholders owning 59% of BP's stock voted, with 9.7% of these backing the resolution, and a total of 14.9% withholding support from the management	Y?
To promote investor dialogue on biodiversity issues	Several meetings with investors regarding the resolution took place in advance of the AGM	Y
To persuade BP to disclose a policy in relation to biodiversity	BP published a new position statement on sensitive sites, which included analysis of its impact on biodiversity	Y
To persuade BP to pull out of Arctic Power	BP pulled out of Arctic Power	Y
To persuade investors that biodiversity issues are relevant to investment decisions (implied target)	BP acknowledged the shareholder value case made by the resolution. Since this time, a few institutional investors including, in particular, F&C and Insight Investment, have published reports on the issue	Y
To generate media coverage for the broader campaign to secure protection for the ANWR	The resolution was covered by a large number of mainstream newspapers and it appears likely that it played a significant political role, although this is hard to assess	Y?

resolution. This confirms the fallacy of judging a shareholder resolution outcome based simply on the level of votes.

Efficiency
WWF's main additional costs from the 2001 capital market intervention were the Innovest research, and the staff time in coordinating the

resolution and broader media work.[6] WWF worked in a coalition on the campaign, so many costs in terms of time and resources in preparing the resolution were carried externally. The main combined costs to the NGO of this resolution would have been in the order of £25,000. The costs incurred by BP in defending itself from the resolution are estimated to have been some £5 million (see Kirk, 2002). It is instructive to consider that the relative costs are different by many orders of magnitude, with BP's costs some 200 times higher.

Regarding the investment assets influenced by WWF, 7% voted against company management (representing shareholders with £8 billion of BP stock), which means that the cost/investor influence ratio was 320,000. However, in practice, the actual ratio is likely to be much higher as there were investors who intentionally abstained due to some sympathy[7] with the filer's issue, and other investors who supported company management only after discussion of the issues it raised.

The above *ex post* analysis demonstrates that the intervention appears to have generated considerable success. While it is difficult to assign economic values to the outcomes, based on the outcomes themselves, and the relative distribution of costs, it is reasonable to conclude that this was an efficient capital market intervention.

Broader equity considerations
The most significant equity benefits and burdens relate to the degree to which the resolution played a role in maintaining the protected status of the Refuge itself. If the resolution did play a role, then the Gwich'in people, for example, benefited from the prevention of potential damage to the porcupine caribou herd, whereas the Inupiat did not derive their sought-after economic benefits of development.

Regarding the unintended consequences of the capital market intervention, one of the main outcomes was BP's improved policy, procedures and reporting systems on biodiversity and socially and environmentally sensitive sites. While this was an intended outcome, if the 1002 area is opened to drilling, and BP secures a lease, this suite of new and improved biodiversity documents will better prepare it for a more robust defence of a decision to enter the 1002 area (or, for that matter, any other protected area).

Capital market intervention model categorisation
The NGO capital market intervention model has four main components. The following classifies this intervention using these components:

(1) *Mechanism of company influence*: The intervention uses the rights associated with share ownership to raise concerns with the company and is therefore "investor advocacy influence".
(2) *Route of influence*: The NGO approached institutional investors via the AGM resolution and through a number of communications leading up to the event. It is therefore classified as "indirect". As the resolution involved challenges to institutional investors, the stance is classified as orca.
(3) *Primary audience*: The broader context of this intervention was public policy on ANWR – so, therefore, public policy to some degree. However, the resolution primarily targeted a company and it's investors, therefore the main "audience" is "capital market institutions".
(4) *Nature of argument*: As shown above, WWF used both moral- and business-case arguments.

In the light of the above detailed analysis, the overall tabular classification in the chronology in Appendix 1 is accurate. However, a scaled polar diagram is used in Figure 10 to depict a more nuanced classification incorporating the relative emphasis of the other tactics discussed above.

Figure 10 demonstrates that, in addition to the tabular classification in the chronology, this capital market intervention involved a degree of direct influence (the NGO used, in part, its own reserves to file the resolution). It also shows that the public-policy audience was a target of the campaign. While the main audience for the capital market intervention itself was capital market institutions, underlying this was the intention to influence the broader public-policy debate on the legal status of ANWR.

Lessons learned
From a campaign-effectiveness perspective, the discussion in Chapter 3 suggested that the probability of NGO campaign's success would be increased by adopting an investor-advocacy

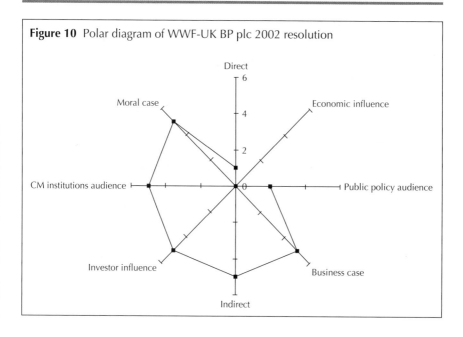

Figure 10 Polar diagram of WWF-UK BP plc 2002 resolution

influence rather than an economic-influence mechanism; co-opting FIs' influence through an indirect approach; and striking a balance between moral and financial arguments. In this case, the NGO adopted an indirect investor-advocacy strategy using both financial and moral arguments that theoretically should have increased its probability of success. While this NGO capital market intervention did not achieve all its stated targets, it has been effective in generating change efficiently. Consequently, the empirical experience with this case supports the above analysis. This suggests that, where campaigners adopt such a strategy, they are more likely to raise risks to companies and their investors and they therefore should be particularly careful to plan an effective response to the campaigners.

With the previous USS case study, an institutional investor was the target entity and lessons for other investors were distilled from the case. Here the target entity is a listed company and, similarly, lessons for other companies can be distilled.

The main lesson originates from the proactive and detailed response that BP gave to the resolution. In providing the new position statement and biodiversity policy, and committing to report on their risk assessments, they were able to demonstrate to the satisfaction of the vast majority of their shareholders that their detailed technical knowledge of the issue and their risk management systems were sufficient to manage the issues that the campaigners wished to highlight. In essence, BP used the resolution as an opportunity to showcase its approach, stating that:

> managing risks is fundamentally important both to good corporate citizenship and to the preservation and enhancement of shareholder value... Our business systems and processes throughout the company are designed to address and manage appropriately technical, competitive, commercial and political risks as well as environmental and social risks.

In addition to the lessons regarding need to develop internal competency and policy statements on these potentially quite technical issues, the specific risk management elements that can be replicated by other companies include a commitment to reporting on full risk assessments, including:

❑ which issues and risks were identified, both technical and values based;
❑ consequent environmental, economic and social impacts and benefits;
❑ stakeholder dialogue undertaken to inform and be informed; and
❑ actions taken to mitigate risk.

While these are perhaps most directly relevant to companies operating in environmentally or socially sensitive sites, the general principles can also be applied at a project or business unit level by companies in other sectors.

Arguably, the most significant problem that BP faced as a result of this resolution was the accusation of duplicity arising from its inconsistent position in relation to Arctic Power (from which it later withdrew). This suggests that companies should also ensure that they have a consistent and coherent approach to "responsible lobbying" and review the policy positions of the aims of the various trade associations and political activities that they fund. While corporate membership does not imply endorsement of every detailed aim and position statement, the central aims of the organisation being funded should not be contrary to the corporation's public positions in this area, and may raise risk by association.

Regarding the lessons from the way in which BP managed the shareholder resolution, fundamentally, BP did not dismiss the issue out of hand and engaged thoughtfully and sensibly in the debate. This enabled it to demonstrate that it fully understood and acknowledged the environmental and social problems that can arise from the oil and gas business, and had sufficient technical expertise to defend its position. BP also proactively organised a series of consultation meetings with large institutional investors – both before and after its formal response to the resolution – in order to listen to their issues and respond.

Conclusion

This case has highlighted the fact that NGOs can deploy effective and efficient indirect strategies of investor-advocacy influence and use a capital market campaign as part of a broader campaign to generate significant media coverage on politically relevant issues. It has also confirmed the importance of judging the success of a resolution by measuring outcomes as well as votes at the AGM.

Regarding the lessons for companies, where they are involved in potentially controversial activities it is sensible to develop internal competency on the issue and produce a policy statement. In addition, some development to enterprise risk management systems may be required in order to incorporate environmental, economic and social impacts and benefits and stakeholder dialogue procedures. A commitment to reporting to stakeholders on the risk assessments and ensuring that the company has a consistent and coherent approach to "responsible lobbying" is also recommended. Finally, in relation to shareholder resolutions, it is important to participate thoughtfully and sensibly in the debate and consult broadly with large institutional investors in order to seek out and attend to their views.

"CAPITAL PUNISHMENT": FRIENDS OF THE EARTH'S CAMPAIGN AGAINST NORWICH UNION

This case reviews the Friends of the Earth (FoE) "Capital Punishment" campaign, which targeted insurance companies – particularly Norwich Union – in order "to demand greener investment policies" (see Friends of the Earth, 2000b, p 1). This case is also similar to the Ethics for USS case study in that it involves the targeting of an individual investment institution in an attempt to encourage it to promote responsible fund-management practices and the lessons learned are therefore compared for consistency.

FoE describes its vision as "a world where everyone's needs are met in a way which values our quality of life and safeguards the future of the environment" (see Friends of the Earth, 2002, p 3). Its mission is to work "for a world where environmental protection, social justice and economic welfare for all people go hand in hand". Internationally, FoE has a million supporters and claims to be the "largest international network of environmental groups in the world, represented in 68 countries". More than 90% of its income derives from individual donations (see Friends of the Earth, 2002, pp 11–16).

FoE has a series of active corporate campaigns and has established an overall strategy in this area. Its rationale for this work states that "economic power is shifting from the general public to the boardrooms" and that "multinationals trade-off the policies of one nation against another – resulting in erosion of standards, damage to wildlife and loss of jobs" (see Friends of the Earth, 2003b). Regarding the NGO's corporate campaigning stance, it is mainly orca, although it has also adopted shark and dolphin stances from time to time.[8]

Reference to the NGO capital market intervention chronology (Appendix 1) demonstrates that FoE appears to have participated in at least 16 capital market interventions between 1990 and 2002. According to the chronology, its first, in 1991, was an attempt to stop Fisons extracting peat from Sites of Special Scientific Interest (Intervention 6).

Background to the campaign

In January of 2000, Friends of the Earth published "Capital Punishment: UK Insurance Companies and the Environment", which intended to "stimulate debate around the environmental consequences of the investment strategies of institutional investors" (see Friends of the Earth, 2000a, p 4). This report focused on the Top 14 insurance companies and reviewed their investments in companies that FoE believed to be causing significant environmental damage, including Chevron, Elf Aquataine, Exxon, Glaxo Wellcome, ICI, Monsanto, Rio Tinto, UPM Kymmene and Zeneca. The report claimed that the insurance companies "have the leverage and moral responsibility to change those companies' behaviour". More generally, it suggested that the financial sector had:

> a vital role to play in promoting sustainable development: it could potentially bring massive leverage to bear on other economic players to encourage them to integrate environmental and social with economic aims. There are powerful moral and economic reasons why it must now do so.

In terms of these moral end economic reasons, financially, it argued that, due to the impacts of climate change, insurance companies in particular would suffer losses from an increase in weather-related claims caused, in part, by the very activities that its fund-management arms were supporting through their investments. Morally, it argued that:

> institutional investors have a moral responsibility not to fund the destruction of the environment and the exploitation of people... Most insurance companies shun on moral grounds investment in perfectly legal businesses such as strip clubs, the production of hardcore pornography, or the export of torture equipment. Likewise it is not only illegality that would make heroin dealing or protection rackets unacceptable to them and their shareholders.

However, the report did not provide evidence in support of its claim that most insurance companies made investment decisions on purely moral grounds – a point that is reviewed further later in this case study.

Following its "Capital Punishment" report, FoE distributed an information pack to its "Campaign Express" network for use between March and June 2000. It was "targeting pension companies and the Norwich Union, demanding greener investment policies" (see Friends of the Earth, 2000b, p 1).

Assessment of the capital market campaign
NGO legitimacy
FoE has had ECOSOC Roster Consultative Status since 1972. Consequently, FoE meets the criteria being used here as a proxy for legitimacy.

Ex ante *effectiveness – viability and feasibility*
The "Capital Punishment" report concluded (*ibid*, p 73) with the following recommendation:

> Insurance companies should urgently conceive strategies to use their considerable influence to hasten the changes that are required to create truly sustainable businesses. This must be done through systematically rewarding environmentally successful companies while penalising those who persist with unsustainable practices.

This can be achieved through:

(1) asset management to encourage leading-edge sustainable business practice, including through (a) direct dialogue to improve performance of better companies and (b) withdrawal of investment from the non-compliant and worst companies.
(2) direct advocacy for tougher public policy and legal measures (such as mandatory corporate environmental reporting and more realistic official greenhouse gas emission reduction targets).

The first of the two recommendations is particularly important in terms of assessing the viability and feasibility of the campaign, because it represents an NGO calling for a highly controversial action. It also contradicts other statements in the report.

Regarding the controversy surrounding the proposed investment policy, withholding investment capital from the environmentally worst-performing companies was likely to run against significant resistance: if the most environmentally damaging companies also happened to be good financial investments, then the insurance company was highly unlikely to *voluntarily* prohibit such investments in its own account due to the implications for its own profitability.

Furthermore, the asset-management function of the insurance company also manages money for other external institutional clients (such as pension schemes). Unless these clients had specified that they wanted to avoid environmentally damaging companies (and were in a position to do so – see Chapter 3), then FoE's recommendation could well have led the fund manager to breach the fiduciary duty that it owed its clients.[9] As a consequence, the divestment aspect of FoE's asset recommendation was likely to fail on both financial and legal grounds and is therefore *ex ante* ineffective.

However, the same financial and fiduciary conflict does not arise with the engagement aspect of the asset-management recommendation. Nevertheless, FoE's recommendation here does fall foul of the earlier-mentioned contradiction: FoE's proposed investment-policy conclusion includes the "withdrawal of investment from the non-compliant and worst companies". Yet elsewhere the report is critical of such an approach: "By screening all such companies out of their portfolios, how do ethical funds exert influence for change?" (*ibid*, p 8). The implication of this statement is that fund managers should adopt an active "engagement" approach in order to "get the attention of major corporate players". Yet FoE's recommendation of withdrawal of investment from the non-compliant and worst companies would mean the loss of share-ownership rights required for engagement, and a reduction of influence over the very companies they are most concerned with. While divestment can be a coherent part of an engagement strategy, its appropriate place is at the end of an engagement process and it indicates a failure of the engagement process. That FoE did not set out a coherent way of integrating divestment and engagement represents a logical discontinuity in the report and means that the combined aims were not collectively viable or feasible – and were therefore *ex ante* ineffective.

However, based on interviews with FoE staff, it appears that, initially, the main purpose of the report was to convince members of the FoE network that this was an important area of campaigning (see McLaren, 2001):

> ["Capital Punishment"] was very much our base marker to establish the legitimacy for a campaign in this area. So our interest wasn't so much – surprisingly – to expect to move particular companies through that report itself but to say here is the evidence as to why FoE wants to engage with this sector... this is a legitimate target for campaigning. On the back of that we wanted to be able to produce a briefing sheet for our members ... about ethical investment or the influence of the investment community.

As to whether the report was likely to be effective in achieving these internal aims, it included a number of company case studies that graphically highlighted the environmental damage caused by the FoE pariah companies. It also detailed the holdings of the top 14 insurance organisations in those companies and contained some discussion of what their moral obligations were in relation to those companies. It is unlikely that its members would have been aware of the limitations and contradictions inherent within FoE's proposed investment policy. Therefore, from an *ex ante* perspective, FoE members would have been persuaded by "Capital Punishment" and agreed that FoE should increase its capital market campaigning work.

A second medium-term aim of the report's analysis of insurance companies' investment holdings was to assess which companies FoE should confront in a campaign: "The analysis also gave us a company amongst the insurance industry which had the largest investments amongst the listed companies we had selected, and this insurance company therefore became the focal company of the campaign" (*ibid*).

The target selected by FoE was Norwich Union. On the face of it, this appears to have been an illogical choice, as an analysis of the shareholdings detailed in the report indicates that both Prudential Assurance and Standard Life would have been more influential campaign targets. Both Prudential Assurance and Standard Life are ranked in the report (by long-term business – p 77) first and second ahead of CGU and Norwich Union Life and Pensions, which were third and fourth respectively. Similarly, both Prudential and Standard Life did not perform as well as Norwich Union in FoE's own evaluation of their "commitment to sustainable development" (see Friends of the Earth, 2000a, p 78). Moreover, in 85% of cases either Standard Life or Prudential owned more shares in FoE target companies than Norwich Union. Finally, for half the companies in question, the shares owned by Norwich Union were in passive index-tracking funds where, Norwich Union would not have had the ability to adhere to the FoE recommendation to divest.

However, this apparent anomaly between chosen target and published analysis strongly indicates that FoE considered the merger between CGU and Norwich Union (which became public knowledge shortly after the time of the publication of "Capital Punishment"). This merger produced a new entity – CGNU (now Aviva) – with £200 billion funds under management, substantially more than the Prudential, the previous frontrunner in the FoE report. Furthermore, the new group would have then engaged in establishing group-wide policy, providing an opportunity for FoE to influence this policy. Finally, CGU had developed a reputation for being at the forefront of the debate on environmental management for financial institutions. For example, it had founded and chaired the first Financial Organisations Reporting Guidelines on the Environment (FORGE). These three factors combined to make the new entity a logical campaign target from FoE's perspective, so this choice of target was *ex ante* effective.

In terms of the scale of FoE's ambition to confront this new entity, at the time only Friends Ivory & Sime, Henderson/NPI and Jupiter had invested significantly in the kinds of activities that FoE was promoting. Consequently, if one interprets the "Capital Punishment" conclusion as being in favour of engagement across all the assets managed by a fund manager, FoE's ambition was significant but realistic in that there were precedents among its peers that it could point to.

In conclusion, therefore, from a viability and feasibility perspective, the report was effective with regard to its internal aims but ineffective in respect of its specific investment-policy recommendations. Nevertheless, the decision to target Norwich Union was appropriate and increased the viability at that time.

Ex post *effectiveness – implementation effectiveness*
As highlighted above, FoE's internal targets for the "Capital Punishment" report were to establish legitimacy for campaigns on investment; produce a briefing sheet for members and activists about the influence of the investment community; and establish a specific target for an investment campaign. Following the report, FoE did achieve these aims and was therefore effective at achieving these internal targets.

FoE also achieved extensive coverage in the financial press and general media with the campaign. So, in a general sense, the NGO's campaign was successful in that broader campaign messages reached audiences that FoE would not usually have been able to address.

However, the report's explicit and more substantive external aims related to changing investment practices of the insurance companies. Therefore, to be able to draw comprehensive conclusions concerning implementation effectiveness, it is important to examine whether there is any evidence that the report has brought about those changes. As mentioned, while 14 insurance companies were included in the report, FoE mainly targeted the investment practices of Norwich Union. Therefore, in order to assess the degree to which the report changed investment practices, the analysis will focus on the extent to which Norwich Union's investment practices changed as a consequence of the report.

Following the merger, CGNU announced that it would establish an ethical unit, and recruited seven people from Henderson's SRI team. In line with industry SRI best practice, Morley Asset Management[10] made a commitment to engage on social, ethical and environmental issues on all the funds it had under management. It was also to establish a range of sustainability funds within Morley's overall product range. It was also later to announce that it would be using its voting influence across all its funds to promote better reporting of corporate social responsibility performance. Specifically, if an FTSE company was not disclosing sufficient information on its environmental and social performance, Morley would vote against the adoption of an FTSE100 company's annual report and accounts at the AGM. Morley also now produces periodic reports that provide some insight into the work that has taken place (but fall some way short of the kind of disclosure necessary to fully evaluate the effectiveness of its engagement activity).

As the asset management company would now be promoting sustainability improvements within investee companies, this change represented a significant part of the outcome that FoE was seeking to achieve through its campaign. However, CGNU's investment policy did not involve withholding investment capital from the environmentally worst companies, which was (somewhat inconsistently) advocated in FoE's conclusion. While the SRI team was later to establish investment products that adopted this kind of approach, this accounted for only a small percentage of the overall assets under management, not the fund manager-wide approach sought by FoE.

Nevertheless, CGNU's announcement did represent a change in its engagement practices. So the main implementation effectiveness question is, to what degree was this change a consequence of the FoE report?

FoE is absolutely clear that it believes that the change was as a response to its report: Tony Juniper, its then policy and campaigns director, stated that "socially responsible investment has now gone mainstream. Financial companies who continue to ignore ethical or environmental concerns will lose customers to those who don't. In responding to our campaign for greener investment policies, CGNU has gained a competitive advantage."

Clearly, though, it would have been in FoE's organisational interests to demonstrate that it could be effective. Perhaps for similar reasons, CGNU rejects the claim suggestion that its change was entirely a response to FoE's campaign: "the 'Capital Punishment' campaign certainly raised awareness... but the fact is that Morley was already... thinking about hiring us before the report was published" (see Johnston, 2001).

Regarding whether any CGNU change was as a result of the "Capital Punishment" campaign, other non-FoE and non-CGNU interviewees have voiced doubts at the extent of change. For example, one stated (unattributably) that: "I thought Friends of the Earth attack on the insurance industry was very poor, frankly – I thought it was ill presented, poorly argued and really off the mark. Having said that, it does seem to have had an impact in certain insurance-based investors." Similarly, another stated (again unattributably) that "I don't think that [FoE] can claim that they achieved [the change at CGNU] alone. However, I am willing to agree that they contributed to the debate."

A combined view, therefore, appears to be that the campaign was not well constructed, and that, while FoE cannot claim sole success for generating the change in CGNU, they can claim to have increased the pressure on CGNU to respond in the way that it did.

Therefore, on the basis of the available information, from an implementation perspective, this campaign was effective in relation to its internal targets, highly effective at raising the profile of SRI issues in the investment community, but only reasonably effective in relation to its investment-policy targets. In relation to these investment-policy targets, measuring its effectiveness is significantly limited by the contradictory nature of the proposed policy itself.

Efficiency
The report's main initial focus was research and internal advocacy. It is estimated that the report would have cost in the region of £10,000. The additional cost of the Norwich Union campaign to

FoE would have been about two weeks of staff time and the production and mailing costs associated with the Campaign Express leaflet. The additional costs of the Norwich Union component of the campaign are estimated to have been £5,000.

Regarding the assets affected by the NU policy change, the engagement commitment across the (then) £200 billion of assets under management implies a cost/investor influence ratio of 13 million. The campaign also generated considerable media coverage for FoE and its issues, which, from the NGO's perspective, has significant value.

Therefore, from the NGO campaign perspective, the campaign appears to have been an efficient allocation of its resources.

Capital market intervention model categorisation
This NGO capital market intervention is classified against the four main components of the model as follows:

(1) *Mechanism of company influence*: While its recommendation is somewhat contradictory, the "Capital Punishment" report attempted to exert "economic" and "investor advocacy" influence.
(2) *Route of influence*: The NGO sought to mobilise the shares of institutional investors and is therefore classified as "indirect". The NGO scrutinised the relative performance of different insurance companies and attacked selected targets. This is classified as orca.
(3) *Primary audience*: "CM Institutions".
(4) *Nature of argument*: The NGO used both business- and moral-case arguments (see above).

In the light of this detailed analysis, the overall tabular classification in the chronology in Appendix 1 can be confirmed as accurate. The scaled polar diagram in Figure 11 is used here to depict a more nuanced classification.

Figure 11 indicates that the report was also intended to address, to some degree, the public-policy audience. As identified in the *ex ante* effectiveness analysis above, the reason for this is that the report called for investors to advocate "tougher public policy and legal measures such as mandatory corporate environmental reporting and more realistic official greenhouse gas emission reduction targets". While this was not the subsequent focus of the campaign,

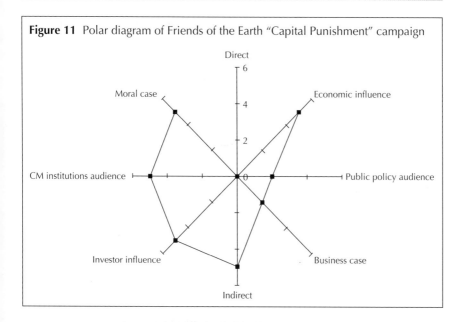

Figure 11 Polar diagram of Friends of the Earth "Capital Punishment" campaign

it does represent an attempt to use investors to change public policy.

Lessons learned

According to the above analysis, there was likely to be a significant limitation associated with FoE's economic-influence advocacy in that it was contradictory and potentially unlawful.

In practice, the fund-manager-wide action taken by CGNU was investor advocacy influence, not economic influence. This reinforces the suggestion in Chapter 3 that the likelihood of success is increased when an NGO adopts a strategy of investor-advocacy-influence rather than one of economic influence.

From the NGO perspective, there are two main lessons that can be discerned from this case: first, it is necessary to carefully construct investment-policy recommendations that are legally viable; and, second, strategy recommendations should be consistent and not contradictory.

Whether the NGO created the change in its target entity is not quite as clear as with the USS case study previously presented in this chapter. Nevertheless, the target entity appears to have responded in a similar way and the campaigners no longer target the investment company. Therefore, in many ways, the lessons for other investors seeking to reduce NGO campaign risks are very similar:

(1) *Policy*: Developed a policy of active engagement and committed itself to using its influence as a shareholder to encourage environmentally and socially responsible corporate behaviour.
(2) *Reporting*: Issued periodic reports providing a high-level overview of what activity had been undertaken.
(3) *Resources*: Recruited seven people to set up an SRI team.
(4) *Voting integration*: Integrated environmental and social issues into its voting practices.
(5) *Reputation*: Developed a reputation for leadership in SRI by providing a range of sustainability funds.

Conclusion

Regarding the efficiency and effectiveness of this intervention, this study has demonstrated that it is possible for an NGO to generate significant media interest and succeed at changing investment practices – despite having been ineffective in respect of its specific investment policy recommendations.

However, in the light of changes that took place in CGU prior to the campaign, the extent of FoE's influence should be considered questionable. Overall, its implementation effectiveness for its investment policy was limited by the poorly constructed nature of the proposed policy.

Regarding the lessons learned by investors aiming to reduce the risks arising from NGO capital market campaigns, this case supports the findings of the USS study. In particular, it again appears that such investors should: develop an engagement policy; report on the activity associated with this policy; invest in resources to implement it; integrate the policy into voting practices and seek to develop a reputation in this area.

"CUT THE COST": OXFAM'S CAMPAIGN AGAINST GLAXOSMITHKLINE PLC

This case reviews the "Cut the Cost" capital market intervention by Oxfam, which focused on the difficulties of access to medicines in developing countries. The target entity in this case is a company, and it therefore has similarities with the WWF/BP/ANWR case study. However, in this case, Oxfam made a direct approach to investors outside of the context of a formal shareholder resolution at the AGM. Therefore, this case assesses whether risks to companies can be generated by an NGO outside of the formal context of an AGM.

Oxfam was founded in 1942 as the Oxford Committee for Famine Relief and was one of a number of groups dealing with social and development problems created by the Allies' naval blockade of Nazi-occupied Greece. Since then, the organisation has updated its mission: "Oxfam works with others to overcome poverty and suffering" (see Oxfam, 2003c).

Oxfam has approximately 23,000 volunteers as well as 1,300 staff in the UK. Its fundraising income for the 2001–2 financial year was £124.3 million, with a further £11 million from trading activities. There were 68 policy staff and an overall strategy for engaging with the private sector has been developed (see Oxfam, 2002b, p 26).

Oxfam's corporate sector work includes campaigns aimed at supporting coffee farmers, strengthening the rules on arms exports and making progress in cutting the cost of medicines by changing global patent rules (see Oxfam, 2003a, p 36). The NGO mainly applies a dolphin stance in its dialogue with business, although, as demonstrated by this case, it adopts an orca stance when it believes the situation warrants it.

Reference to the NGO capital market intervention chronology (Appendix 1) demonstrates that Oxfam participated in at least five capital market interventions between 1990 and 2002. Oxfam has not deployed a capital market intervention strategy as often as some environmental NGOs (eg, Forum for the Future and WWF), but it has used such a strategy more than most development NGOs.

Background to the campaign

The Oxfam "Cut the Cost" campaign was intended to encourage the "the world's pharmaceutical companies to do more to improve access to medicines in poor countries" (see Oxfam, 2001a, p 1). Oxfam published a briefing paper that targeted investors and called on them to use their influence to encourage GSK (in particular) to develop a policy setting out how it would meet its commitment to "maximising affordable access... within the first three months of the company's existence" (*ibid*). This paper was launched at a briefing for City investors on 14 February 2001, with the intention of mobilising the support of large institutional investors for its campaign.

Oxfam was more concerned with the humanitarian consequences of pricing drugs out of the reach of people in developing countries. Moreover, at the City briefing it highlighted the risks to reputation arising from GSK's position and its involvement with the South African Pharmaceutical Manufacturers Association in a case against the South African government, regarding the right to import cheaper medicines. Oxfam also criticised GSK for appearing to defend patents on AIDS drugs in Ghana and Uganda.

It should be noted that the pharmaceutical companies were previously aware of the problems surrounding access in developing countries and had taken some steps to address the matter. For example, GSK has offered antiretrovirals on a not-for-profit basis for mother-to-child transmission since 1997, and had worked with UNAIDS to distribute medication (see GSK, 2001, p 2). However, Oxfam believed these steps were insufficient to fulfil its responsibility in relation to the issue.

Assessment of the capital market campaign
NGO legitimacy
Oxfam has had ECOSOC Special Consultative Status since 1973. Therefore, it complies with the criteria for establishing NGO legitimacy set out previously.

Oxfam also has a "Statement of Legitimacy and Accountability" (see Oxfam, 2003b), which claims a sound basis for the organisation's legitimacy in "speaking out on issues such as world poverty". This refers to 50 years of practical humanitarian work, giving it "vast experience, respected by the international community, southern and northern governments, other charities and people on the ground". Oxfam also conducted a stakeholder survey, which gathered views from different groups of stakeholders (internationally and in the UK) on its performance: "a key mechanism which supports Oxfam's accountability" (*ibid*).

Ex ante *effectiveness – viability and feasibility*
At the outset, GSK was a strategically astute campaign target for the campaigners for five principal reasons:

(1) It was newly formed from a merger of Glaxo Wellcome (GW) and SmithKlineBeecham (SKB) and was consequently receiving a considerable degree of media and investor attention.
(2) The newly combined entity was establishing group-wide policy. This provided Oxfam with an opportunity to exert influence.
(3) The component parts of the group had previously reported total sales of US$27.2 billion, including pharmaceutical sales of US$22.2 billion, giving it around a 7% share of the global market (see Oxfam, 2001a, p 10). This market share rendered the company highly influential in its sector.
(4) The CEO had previously voiced his "commitment to maximising affordable access to medicines in the developing world" (*ibid*, p 8). Oxfam may have discerned an opportunity to use GSK to establish a new norm for the industry in relation to this issue.
(5) It was the largest UK company in the sector with a market capitalisation in the order of £110 billion. As a consequence, it was likely to have been a significant shareholding for many UK institutional investors – Oxfam's target audience.

The previously mentioned briefing for City investors targeted SRI investors. It was hosted by Friends Ivory & Sime and included Co-operative Insurance Society, Henderson, Hermes, Jupiter, Methodist Central Finance Board, Morley and the Universities Superannuation Scheme among the audience. As outlined in Chapter 3, this was likely to enhance Oxfam's chances of success, as the SRI investment sector should have been predisposed to the issue.

However, there were two underlying limiting factors – "parallel importing" and "reference pricing" – both of which significantly reduced the likelihood of success for Oxfam's proposed solution of charging a cost price in developing countries. Parallel importing involved the country arbitrage opportunities that could lead to the smuggling of medication back into developed countries. Oxfam's approach to this problem involved more stringent policing, tougher penalties and specific labelling. It also cited evidence from existing restrictions on parallel importing of branded products that allowed prices of patent-protected products to vary substantially among developed countries (see Oxfam, 2001b, p 2).

Reference pricing involves developed countries using the developing country's cost price as a reference point in negotiating their own contracts. Oxfam's approach here required the political will of developed countries' governments to refuse to use such negotiating tactics. It cited the UK government as an example of a country that had made such a commitment. That Oxfam recognised the limiting factors in relation to its proposal, and provided counterarguments, would have reduced the extent to which these factors represented a limitation.

Furthermore, rather than concentrate on the limitations of its suggested alternative, Oxfam focused on the potential impacts on the company from the status quo. Using both the business and moral case, Oxfam (2001a, p 5) argued:

> Pharmaceutical companies face a major reputation risk if they do not do more to promote access to life-saving drugs in the developing world. This is particularly important at a time of unprecedented scrutiny of the industry's record in this field. The withdrawal of public support could lead the industry to suffer the same problems of staff recruitment and retention suffered by companies charged with complicity in human rights abuses or environmental damage. Perhaps more significantly it carries with it the threat of more stringent government regulation... [It] is both ethically correct and in the company's self interest to ensure that those who own and control medical knowledge use all means at their disposal to stop preventable diseases from killing millions of people every year, particularly if they are using their exclusive marketing position to prevent others from developing the same knowledge.

In respect of the above business-case arguments, the most significant was the potential for more stringent government legislation. This referred, in particular, to the potential for change in the framework for intellectual-property rights. Pharmaceutical companies invest billions of pounds in research and development, and depend on protection from intellectual-property rights to secure future revenue streams from this investment. Such an argument, if plausible, would have been of significant interest to investors.

In conclusion, from a perspective of viability and feasibility effectiveness, this capital market intervention may be characterised as highly effective: it was focused, clearly defined, used well structured moral- and business-case arguments, and fostered relationships with carefully targeted institutional investors.

Ex post effectiveness – implementation effectiveness
Following the campaign's launch, Jean-Pierre Garnier, chief executive of GSK, reportedly undertook to "make the issue a priority" (see *Financial Times*, 2001a, p 12) and subsequently published a policy on access to drugs (see GSK, 2001) that was cautiously welcomed by Oxfam. Similarly, on 19 April 2001, the South African Pharmaceutical Manufacturers Association abandoned its case against the South African government. For GSK, this was a "significant event... amount[ing] to a recognition that their legal battle in South Africa was a public relations disaster" (see *Financial Times*, 2001b, p 19).

From the point of view of the effectiveness of the implementation of the NGO capital market intervention, it is necessary to establish the degree to which this increased access to medication. GSK's subsequent CSR report highlighted "increased shipments of Combivir[11] to the developing world from 2.2 million tablets in 2001 to nearly 6 million tablets in 2002" (GSK, 2003, p 3). This increase approximately equates to an additional 2 million daily doses, which implies that a further 5,500 people per annum, approximately, have access to "affordable" Combivir. This confirms that access to medication increased. While this increase is significant, in view of the fact that 29.4 million people are thought to be suffering from AIDS in Sub-Saharan Africa alone (see UNAIDS/WHO, 2002, p 6), this increase in access is clearly sufficient to make only a small difference to the overall problem of AIDS.

As to whether the NGO's capital market intervention contributed to this increased access, Friends Ivory & Sime had "emphasised how important it [was] for GSK to protect its intellectual property rights... Failure to be seen to respond adequately to global concerns about the negative effects of the new... intellectual property regime could undermine the public case for patent protection" (see Mackenzie, 2001). This confirms that investors had been persuaded by Oxfam's arguments and had raised concerns regarding the reputational risks.

Much more significantly, the target company confirmed that it had been influenced by the concerns of such investors: "Jean-Pierre

Garnier, chief executive of GlaxoSmithKline, one of the pharmaceutical companies that led the industry's retreat from the case, which had become a public relations catastrophe, said he had been influenced by concerns from investors, shareholders and the public about access to medicines" (see *Financial Times*, 2001, p 9). This indicates that Oxfam had successfully mobilised investor interest, and that this investor interest contributed to the change of GSK's policy.

Sophia Tickell, Oxfam's senior policy adviser on the public sector, later commented, "We knew that if we could persuade investors of our arguments, this would have a powerful impact on the companies as [investors] are more influential [with companies] than non-governmental organisations" (see EIRIS, 2002b, p 3). This highlights the fact that Oxfam had made a strategic decision to attempt to harness investor-advocacy influence in the belief that it would magnify its own influence.

Interviewees highlighted this case as a good example of NGO capital market intervention. For instance Green (2001) says in an interview, "Oxfam was a really classy departure for a development NGO when it launched its campaign against GSK. To launch a campaign with a City seminar is a first... That launch was really interesting because it represented a real departure from a more activist-based campaign and gone straight for the jugular... I've never seen a development NGO campaign on the front page of [the *Financial Times*] 'Companies and Markets' before. And I think the other NGOs should be looking at it." This comment by a campaigner from another NGO demonstrates the degree to which this capital market intervention was regarded by Oxfam's NGO peers as containing dimensions that could be usefully replicated by other NGOs in their own campaigns.

Oxfam followed its "Cut the Cost" campaign with a broader initiative calling on the pharmaceutical sector in general to be more socially responsible when dealing with the developing world, and for investors to be active in changing their policies. Oxfam, Save the Children and VSO jointly developed a standard for assessing pharmaceutical companies in responding to health problems in the developing world (see Oxfam, Save the Children and Voluntary Service Overseas, 2002). The document proposed a set of benchmarks to assist investors in assessing the social responsibility of pharmaceutical companies and surveyed GSK, Abbott, AstraZeneca, Aventis, Bayer, Boehringer Ingelheim, Bristol-Myers Squibb (BMS), Hoffmann-La Roche, Merck, Novartis and Pfizer. The benchmarks relate to company policies and practices in pricing, patents, joint public–private initiatives, research and development and appropriate use of medicines. In launching this report, Oxfam stated (see Manifest, 2002):

> Twenty six people die every minute from infectious diseases. These deaths are avoidable. Drugs companies can and should do more. Investors too have a vital role to play, since how they invest their money can have a positive influence on people's lives. There is a direct link between the City investor and an HIV-positive baby in Zambia.

This follow-up campaign is highly relevant, because it represents a significant outcome for the "Cut the Cost" campaign. This is because two institutional investors – FIS (later to become F&C) and USS – developed it into a broad collaborative investor initiative on access to drugs. This initiative was to become formalised as the Pharmaceutical Shareowners Group (PSG) "with more than £454bn of assets" and comprising "six investment houses: Co-operative Insurance, Henderson Global Investors, Insight Investment Management, ISIS Asset Management, Jupiter Asset Management, Morley Fund Management and Schroders ... [and] one pension fund: Universities Superannuation Scheme" (see Gimbel, 2003, p 2). The purpose of this collaborative endeavour was to benchmark all companies in the sector in order to assist management, investors and analysts to evaluate how pharmaceutical companies were responding to the risks related to the public health crisis in emerging markets (see USS, 2003a, p 1). Arguably, the PSG has had the effect of institutionalising the analysis and review of Oxfam's original issue within the capital market itself – a significant campaign outcome that further demonstrates the considerable *ex post* effectiveness of the original capital market intervention.

In conclusion, from a perspective of implementation effectiveness, this capital market intervention can be shown to have been highly successful: it achieved its original campaign targets in a few months and was able to mobilise considerable investor-advocacy influence outside the context of an AGM. It is particularly noteworthy that the target company's CEO confirmed that he had changed its policy in response to the campaign and concerns from investors, and that the shipment of antiretroviral drugs significantly increased (albeit not in line with the scale of the issue). Finally, the subsequent establishment of the PSG demonstrates that investors have formalised the ongoing monitoring and measurement of the issue, which represents a significant campaign influence multiplier outcome for the initial Oxfam campaign.

Efficiency

Most of the costs to the company associated with the campaign relate to GSK's loss of profit from developing countries (estimated to have been less than 1% of overall profitability). However, these costs need to be juxtaposed against the benefits to the industry from having reduced the risks to the system of global intellectual property rights.

In terms of the costs to the NGO, it is estimated that the costs were about four months of Oxfam staff time, plus the costs of literature production and dissemination. The total cost to the NGO is an estimated £13,000.

However, in respect of unintended consequences, questions remain regarding the costs of this campaign on Oxfam's broader campaign against the World Trade Organisation rules on patents ("Trade Related Aspects of Intellectual Property Rights" or "Trips"). "Trips" enables companies to set prices over a 20-year period at the level necessary to make profitable returns on investment by ensuring that others cannot copy the product and sell it at a much lower price. While it contains provisions for developing generic drugs for those in patent for countries to use in times of "national crisis", Oxfam believed that the structure of the "Trips" system created further problems surrounding access to drugs in developing countries. Ironically, Oxfam's success with GSK may have made its long-term objective harder to attain: while the GSK campaign generated widespread publicity, it may have reduced Oxfam's longer-term ability to generate public outrage on a scale sufficient to reform "Trips".

Nevertheless, as mentioned, the capital market intervention appears to have contributed to 5,500 more people in developing countries having greater access to antiretroviral medication in

2002 – with further increases expected in subsequent years. The previous annual cost of a course of Combivir in Africa was around £10,000. Consequently, a proxy for the value of the increase in access can be calculated and is in the order of £55 million. As cost price is about 10% of the original cost, this means that the campaign benefit was some £50 million, which, when compared with Oxfam's campaign spend, represents a campaign cost/benefit multiplier in excess of 3,800.

As to the cost/investor-influence ratio, the campaign has resulted in the managers of more than £450 billion of capital expressing formal concern about the issue and institutionalising its ongoing monitoring and measurement. Assuming half of the assets under management by these fund managers are in equities, this suggests that the cost/investor-influence ratio is in excess of 17 million. Consequently, as well as being highly effective, this NGO capital market intervention was also highly efficient.

Capital market intervention model categorisation
This NGO capital market intervention is classified against the four main components of the model as follows:

(1) *Mechanism of company influence*: Oxfam targeted investors' influence, which is classified here as "investor-advocacy influence".
(2) *Route of influence*: The NGO did not purchase shares in GSK, seeking instead to mobilise the shares of institutional investors. This is therefore classified as "indirect". That it lobbied selected investors denotes the stance as orca.
(3) *Primary audience*: While the subtext of Oxfam's overall campaign was changing public policy on intellectual-property rights, the primary audience for this capital market intervention was "capital market institutions".
(4) *Nature of argument*: The NGO used both business- and moral-case arguments.

In the light of this detailed analysis, the overall tabular classification in the chronology in Appendix 1 can be confirmed as accurate. The scaled polar diagram in Figure 12 is used here to depict a more nuanced classification.

Figure 12 is intended to show that, in addition to the above classification, the public-policy audience was, to a lesser extent, a capital

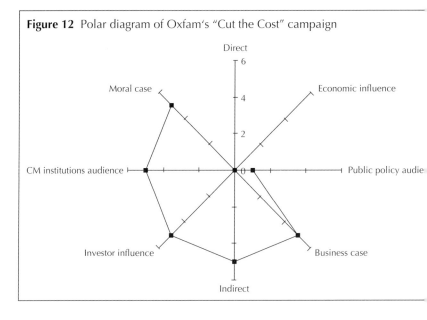

Figure 12 Polar diagram of Oxfam's "Cut the Cost" campaign

market intervention audience. This reflects the fact that underlying the intervention was the intention to reform the Trips system.

Lessons learned

From the perspective of campaign effectiveness, the analysis in Chapter 3 suggests that, in general, the probability of success of any NGO capital market intervention would be increased by: (1) adopting an "investor-advocacy influence" rather than a "capital-redistribution" mechanism; (2) co-opting FIs' influence "indirectly"; and (3) striking a balance between moral and financial arguments. In this case, the NGO capital market intervention used just such a strategy and was highly effective.

The NGO allocated significant resources to the campaign, provided well-researched business-case arguments based on clear ethical principles, and focused public attention through a concerted media campaign. It disseminated its case to carefully targeted socially responsible investors and can be shown to have influenced their views. Furthermore, Oxfam advocated a solution that was not antithetical to GSK's business – that is to say, had Oxfam called for intellectual-property rights to be overturned, it is likely that investor interest would have been far less forthcoming.

This case also demonstrates that an indirect strategy of investor-advocacy influence can succeed outside the formal procedures surrounding an AGM, and suggests that campaign risks to companies are by no means limited to the AGM. Significantly, the establishment of the PSG demonstrates that there are circumstances in which the ongoing monitoring and measurement of an NGO issue can be formalised by investors – with potential implications for the cost of capital.

Oxfam also conducted an internal review of the campaign in order to ascertain what other opportunities may arise from capital market campaigning (see Buckley, 2002). It strongly recommended increased use of the capital market for other campaigns. However, it also highlighted limitations (p 42):

> SRI has not demonstrated that it can or should replace legislation... While it remains tempting to see SRI and market-based approaches as a powerful way to limit the effects of corporate ethics/harm issues, NGOs and civil society should also look at ways that this can enter onto legislative agendas.

This suggests that Oxfam does not regard the ongoing monitoring and measurement of an NGO issue by investors as a sufficient replacement for regulation on corporate-responsibility issues.

Nevertheless, from the perspective of companies and investors concerned about the risks of capital market campaigning, it is particularly noteworthy that the NGO concluded that it will use the capital market in its future campaigns and has promoted the benefits of such campaigns to other NGOs.

In terms of the lessons for companies seeking to reduce the risk from capital market campaigns, as with BP's response, GSK engaged proactively in the debate and did not dismiss the issue out of hand. GSK also developed a detailed response to the campaign claims, and redeveloped a corporate policy in relation to the issue. Similarly, GSK also included a section in subsequent reports on corporate social responsibility that covered the extent to which the new policy was being implemented.

Furthermore, just as BP experienced problems with its membership of a lobbying group, GSK experienced similar problems with its membership of the South African Pharmaceutical Manufacturers Association – and this association's case against the South African government. This problematic relationship highlights the risks of association and underscores the earlier suggestion that companies should ensure that they review the policy and positions of the various trade bodies that they are members of. In this instance, if GSK did give consideration to the brand risks before becoming involved in the campaign against the South African government, it appears that it significantly underestimated the risks.

Conclusion

This case study has again demonstrated that it is possible for NGO capital market campaigns to be both a highly effective and a highly efficient form of NGO campaigning. Oxfam's intervention has been shown to have contributed to a significant increase in access to medication, worth in the order of £50 million. The intervention also subsequently influenced the capital market to integrate the ongoing monitoring and analysis of the issue in the form of the PSG. To the extent that the PSG is effective, Oxfam's intervention can be said to have institutionalised the concern into the capital market.

Regarding lessons learned, this case has also highlighted the importance for NGO capital market campaigns, which seek to harness investor advocacy influence, not to advocate a course of action that is antithetical to the target company's business.

From a target company's perspective, this case suggests that companies seeking to reduce capital market campaign risk should: consider the risks that they are exposed to from such campaigns; engage proactively in the debate on the issue; develop a corporate policy; report on performance against the policy; and ensure that they review the policy and positions of their various trade bodies in order to ensure consistency with the company's own policy.

1   This reference to "selective lobbying" and the adoption of different approaches where an assessment deems it appropriate – including shareholder resolutions – demonstrates why it is necessary to classify each CM invervention individually rather than at the level of the NGO.
2   Defined by section 1002 of the Alaska National Interest Land Conservations Act of 1980.
3   WWF subsequently divested in autumn 2002, citing ongoing concerns with BP regarding the Arctic Refuge and health-and-safety problems in Alaska.
4   The closest similar case would be the Antarctic. However, this is protected under a government-ratified Antarctic Treaty, rather than an industry voluntary agreement.
5   IUCN – the World Conservation Union – defines a protected area as "an area of land and/or sea especially dedicated to the protection and maintenance of biological diversity, and of natural and associated cultural resources, and managed through legal or other effective

means". IUCN categorises protected areas by management objective and has identified six distinct categories of protected areas.

6   The total costs of the broader campaign to protect the ANWR are considered to have been costs that would have been incurred in the absence of the CM intervention and are therefore not incorporated here.

7   As noted, Sparkes states, "Abstentions should usually be read as shareholders who sympathise with the resolution but don't want to go the whole hog" (2002, p 39).

8   As noted in Chapter 2, this demonstrated one of the limitations of Elkington's model in that it attempted to categorise an NGO into one taxon.

9   In addition to being an insurance provider, Norwich Union also managed a number of occupational pension funds. The Megarry judgement prevented the trustees of these pension funds from divesting from (as FoE describes them) the "non-compliant and worst companies" on purely ethical grounds (see Chapter 3).

10 Morley Asset Management was previously the fund manager of CGU – the acquiring group – and was combined with the fund-management function of Norwich Union following the merger.

11 An antiretroviral drug used in the treatment of patients with AIDS.

6

Analysis and Critical Questions

The case studies in Chapter 5 consider two important questions. The first is whether or not NGO capital market campaigns can be both effective and an efficient use of NGO resources. If the answer to this question is yes, then it increases the likelihood that NGOs will continue to use the capital markets to exert pressure on companies, indicating that capital market campaigning represents a general risk that companies and investors need to actively manage. The second question is what lessons can be learned for companies and their investors when managing the risks arising from these campaigns.

IS NGO CAPITAL MARKET CAMPAIGNING EFFECTIVE AND EFFICIENT?

In order to address the above question systematically, this section is divided into two parts. The first compares and contrasts the relative success, effectiveness and efficiency of each of the above four case studies. The second part considers the lessons regarding the risks arising to companies and investors from capital market campaigns.

Table 10 summarises the outcomes from the four capital market campaigns presented in Chapter 5.

The table shows that the four campaigns reviewed here were ultimately effective in achieving their campaign goals, ranging from encouraging a very large pension fund to adopt and implement an engagement policy, through to convincing a pharmaceutical company to supply mediation in developing countries at cost.

Table 10 Overall comparison of campaign case studies

#	NGO	Intervention	Implementation effectiveness
20	People and Planet/Ethics for USS	Ethics for USS campaign	After initially failing, the E-USS campaign was highly effective, and led to a robust SRI engagement policy at the USS. However, E-USS has not been effective in relation monitoring and evaluating USS' implementation of this policy
33	WWF-UK	BP and the Arctic Refuge 2002 resolution	The resolution contributed directly to BP's withdrawal from Arctic Power and secured a commitment from BP to play no further part in the debate regarding whether or not to open the Arctic Refuge for oil drilling. These outcomes may have contributed to the protection of the Arctic Refuge, which, at the time of writing, remains closed to drilling. The resolution also generated a considerable amount of media interest
34	Friends of the Earth	"Capital Punishment" and Norwich Union Campaign	This campaign was effective in relation to its internal target to develop FoE's own investment policy. However, it was only marginally effective in relation to promoting the targets within the investment-policy. This was because the effectiveness of the campaign was limited by the poorly constructed nature of the proposed policy itself, which was somewhat contradictory. Nevertheless the campaign very effectively raised the profile of SRI issues by generating considerable media interest
63	Oxfam	GSK "Cut the Cost"	This capital market intervention was a highly effective campaign: it achieved its original campaign target to increase access to medication in developing countries by getting GSK to charge at cost, and was able to mobilise considerable investor influence

This indicates that there are circumstances in which NGO capital market campaigns can be a highly effective tool for campaigners.

While this helps us to address the question as to whether capital market campaigning is effective, and demonstrates that there are clear risks for companies and investors, it does not address how efficient such tactics can be. This is an important question because effective but expensive forms of campaigning are less likely to be used by NGOs given their limited financial resources. Therefore, the efficiency evaluation gives a sense of the frequency with which investors and companies may be exposed to risks from capital market campaigns.

As noted in the introduction, measuring NGO campaigns is a complex business as NGOs focus on issues that are both difficult to measure, and often outside their exclusive control. In examining efficiency we are looking at the relationship between the outcomes generated by the campaign and the inputs or resources the NGO allocated to it. In only one of the case studies – the Oxfam Cut the Cost campaign – was it possible to put a clear financial measure on the outcomes of the campaign and measure its efficiency. This was because the target of the campaign was the cost of something, which is both inherently measurable and directly comparable to the costs of the campaign. For the other campaigns, we must develop a proxy for efficiency. The proxy chosen for this purpose is the ratio of the cost of the campaign to the total funds under management (FUM) influenced by the campaign. In using FUM as the measure of influence, it follows the shareholder-activism convention used by the City itself and has the benefit of allowing relative comparisons between campaigns. It should be noted, however, that this ratio does not measure campaign outcomes, and in order to use it as a measure of efficiency we must assume that the higher the assets influenced, the more effective the campaign. To allow comparisons between the campaigns, we must also assume that the benefit to society of each campaign is equivalent.

The ratio of campaign cost to assets influenced is presented in Table 11.

The table shows that, on average, the capital market campaigns covered in the case studies cost approximately £28,250 and influenced £163 billion. While these financial figures are significant, £160 billion represents well under 10% of the value of the FTSE All Share, which does indicate that there are limitations on the degree to which NGOs can secure the influence of capital market. By this measure, the least efficient campaign was run by WWF on the

Table 11 Case study Cost*Assets Influenced analysis

Case	Cost (£)	Assets influenced (£)	Cost-AI ratio
WWF–ANWR	25,000	8,000,000,000	320,000
E-USS	60,000	220,000,000,000	3,666,667
FoE	15,000	200,000,000,000	13,333,333
Oxfam	13,000	225,000,000,000	17,307,692
Averages	28,250	163,250,000,000	8,656,923

Arctic Refuge, and the most efficient was Oxfam's Cut the Cost campaign. Based on the above figures it is still not possible to conclude that the Oxfam campaign was highly efficient, nor is to possible to say that the WWF campaign was highly inefficient. This would require figures for equivalently effective non-capital market forms of NGO campaigning, which are of course not available. Nevertheless, as all of the campaigns were effective and the sums in question relatively modest, it could be argued that all of the campaigns were efficient. As a result, it does seem reasonable to suggest that is some circumstances the capital market can be a very efficient campaign tool.

As noted at the outset of the case study, the Oxfam campaign was conducted outside of the formal proceedings of an AGM, whereas WWF used a shareholder resolution. That the Cost*Asset Influenced ratio is so much greater for Oxfam than for WWF may suggest that, in the UK, it is more efficient for campaigns to be conducted outside of the AGM because the resources required to file shareholder resolutions are significantly higher.

Returning to the above point regarding the clear measure on the outcomes of the campaign on the Oxfam "Cut the Cost" campaign against GSK, the financial benefit was calculated to be in the order of £50 million. When compared with Oxfam's campaign spend, this represented a direct cost/benefit ratio of more than 3,800, which is likely to be very favourable from the NGO perspective and suggests that the capital market can be a highly efficient form of campaigning.

Drawing together the overall analysis of capital market campaign effectiveness and efficiency, the case studies do indicate that this kind of campaigning can be a highly efficient and effective mechanism for targeting companies or investors. This is an important conclusion for this book and confirms that companies and investors are exposed to significant risks from NGO capital market campaigns, which need to be managed.

OTHER FINDINGS

The interviewees made a number of general comments relating to the length of time that NGOs have understood the potential for such campaigns, and their relative sophistication when conducting them. In particular, a number of campaigners commented that NGOs' understanding of capital market intervention was increasing. Such comments originated from the following NGOs:

❑ Greenpeace: "It has only been relatively recently that [NGO capital market intervention] has been seen to be so successful in the US. They've got their heads around how it works and what you need to do. We've gone through the protesting and disrupting AGMs and begun to realise that the power is passing from the hands of governments into companies and, therefore, if companies aren't going to be regulated by governments they have to be regulated by their investors. So now we need not to alienate investors but to approach them and talk to them and get them to regulate the company" (see Tunmore, 2001).[1]

❑ WWF-UK: "NGOs are getting better at understanding capital markets and shareholder meetings and how the whole system works" (see Jones, 2001).

❑ Friends of the Earth: "NGOs are really only just beginning to focus on this area and employ staff whose full-time focus is SRI ... It has probably been a usable lever for longer than we have realised" (see McLaren, 2001).

This was consistent with the view from interviewees working for capital market institutions that had been targeted by the NGOs. Specific comments in relation to the claim that their knowledge of the capital market was increasing include the following:

❑ USS: "The much greater professionalism of the NGOs in ... targeting fund managers and investors ... there is a spectrum – obviously – but there is a very savvy part of that spectrum" (see Thamotheram, 2001).

❑ PIRC: "I think that within Greenpeace, FoE and WWF it is now understood as something you do alongside your government lobbying and consumer campaigns as a campaign tactic" (see Bell, 2001).

However, there was some evidence from the case studies that NGOs have made strategic mistakes. In particular, People and Planet's "Ethics for the Universities Superannuation Scheme" campaign initially advocated an avoidance form of SRI to USS that ran counter to the trustees' fiduciary duties. Similarly, the Friends of the Earth "Capital Punishment" report (see Friends of the Earth, 2000a) suggested withholding investment capital from the "environmentally" worst companies and implied that this should be done even where these companies were profitable investments, contravening the fiduciary responsibility of fund managers. Rather than implying that NGOs have a general tendency to make such mistakes, it perhaps indicates that in their enthusiasm to hold investors to account, campaigners can overlook the constraints imposed by fiduciary duties when engaging with fund managers. This conclusion regarding a potential lack of detailed understanding of the constraints on investors was reflected in some of the comments by interviewees:

❑ "There is a general lack of sophisticated understanding of how the capital markets work ... At least we have got to the stage where NGOs are developing a vocabulary that investors understand" (see Bell, 2001).
❑ "A lot of older people in the NGO world don't know the financial world and don't know how to deal with analysts" (see Elkington, 2000).
❑ "There is still a lot of learning in terms of understanding how financial markets operate and targeting your campaign accurately" (see Mansley, 2001).

Nevertheless, both E-USS and Friends of the Earth came to recognise the shortcomings of their policy and update them accordingly. So, overall, it appears that NGOs have some gaps in their understanding of the machinery of the capital market, but that this understanding is improving. This finding is supported by the analysis of the chronology in Chapter 4, which found that capital market campaigns were achieving more substantive successes over time. Despite a few potential gaps in understanding, as has been shown, there are a number of instances where capital market campaigners have been highly effective in achieving their campaign goals via the capital market, so the current level of understanding is sufficient for their purposes. It is fair to assume that this understanding will continue to increase, so it is possible that NGOs could become even more effective at capital market campaigning. It is noteworthy in this regard that NGO learning networks have emerged that seek to help other campaigners understand how best to conduct such campaigns. For instance, following a number of campaigns focussed on the capital markets, The Corner House produced the previously mentioned "The Campaigners' Guide to the Financial Markets: Effective Lobbying of Companies and Financial Institutions" (see Hildyard and Mansley, 2001). Similarly, following its successful Ethics for USS intervention, People and Planet (see the case study in Chapter 5) helped to establish Fair Share – an NGO network that attempts to take the lessons learned during the E-USS model and apply them to other pension schemes. There should be little room, therefore, for complacency by companies and investors regarding the risks that they face from NGO capital market campaigns.

LESSONS FOR COMPANIES AND INVESTORS

What practical measures to reduce the risks posed by NGO capital market campaigns might companies and investors undertake?

One response is to do nothing different but to instead rely on a public relations exercise to deflect or neutralise the NGO campaign. This is, perhaps surprisingly, a common strategy. However, rather than representing a considered company response, it may reflect the fact that companies first became aware of the NGO campaign via negative publicity, and therefore leave the response to a public relations team rather than dealing with the substantive criticism. There are a range of strategies than have been used ranging from press briefings, and engaging proactively in the debate, through to more aggressive or underhand approaches by, for example, financing carefully chosen, supposedly "independent" spokespeople to act on their behalf, and seeking to damage the personal reputations of the individuals involved in the campaign. While more aggressive tactics may help over the short term, they can significantly increase the risk to companies over the long term. If and when concerted subversion actions are discovered, such as during the tobacco litigation in the US, then they actually serve to increase the risks to companies by tarnishing the companies reputation and helping the campaigners achieve even higher levels of media coverage. Furthermore, where NGOs suspect that such tactics are being used, this can lead to a re-doubling of efforts and an increase in resources allocated to the campaign.

So, perhaps the most obvious answer to what companies and investors can do is that they should seek to avoid situations where campaigners can target them for socially, environmentally or ethically questionable behaviour by not undertaking these activities in the first place. However, the world is not quite so black and white, as different individuals can hold quite different views on what is acceptable. Furthermore, the campaign can be targeting unconsidered unintended consequences that arise from otherwise well-intentioned corporate activity, therefore, a more sophisticated response than just endeavouring "do the right thing" is required.

In recent times, a great deal of corporate resource has gone into the establishment and maintenance of CSR teams. This is in part because companies now recognise that they will be better able to defend themselves from NGO campaigning if they can demonstrate that they have considered the issue at hand and developed an understanding of whether and how it relates to their business. Companies also recognise that it helps to publish information setting out how they are performing in relation to the issue. CSR departments can help by identifying the issue, establishing policy, shaping corporate strategy, measuring and reporting on performance, and proactively engaging with stakeholders in order to mitigate the risk of campaigns. This is re-enforced by the WWF/BP/ANWR case and the Oxfam/GSK/"Cut the Cost" campaign case studies, which show that it is possible for companies to reduce capital market campaign risk by engaging proactively in the debate; developing a detailed response to the campaign claims; developing corporate policy on the issue; and commit to reporting on performance in relation to this policy.

In addition, some of the risk management elements adopted by BP are a useful model for other companies. BP committed to

reporting on the project risk assessments, including: which technical and values-based risks were identified; what the environmental, economic and social impacts and benefits would be; the
stakeholder dialogue process; and which actions would be taken to
mitigate the risks to the company and its stakeholders. These measures help the company to better understand the concerns of their
stakeholders and earn their trust.

Both BP and GSK also found themselves involved in controversial lobbying activities. This suggested that it is also sensible to
ensure that the company has a consistent and coherent approach to
"responsible lobbying".[2]

It may be helpful to put these company recommendations into a
broader risk management framework. Such a framework would
focus on reducing the risk of NGO campaigning overall, therefore
automatically including those campaigns arising via the capital
market. Using the framework presented in Lam (2003), a typical
enterprise risk management process incorporates an iterative
process of *risk identification, risk scoring, critical risk analysis* (where
the scale of the risks are assessed) and development of an *action plan*
(where the plan for mitigating and managing the risk is defined),
and the allocation of responsibility for delivery within the plan. The
discussion below explains how NGO campaign risks could be integrated into such a framework, in order to help manage the risks
from capital market campaigns that are the focus of this book.

First of all, the risk identification process should seek to identify
potential NGO campaigns – or, perhaps, "civil regulation risk".
One way of doing so, although by no means the only way, is
through attempting to answer the following three questions:

(1) What are the SEE impacts of this business? For example, how
do we treat our employees, suppliers, customers, regulators, or
local community stakeholders, and how does our business
impact on the environment?
(2) What could these stakeholders reasonably expect the business
to be doing about them?
(3) Is there a gap between stakeholder expectation and corporate
practice?

Where companies have CSR teams in place – as is increasingly
common – expertise from within this team should be brought into

this risk-identification process. Such teams may also have expertise in stakeholder engagement,[3] which can be an enormous help in identifying their concerns and expectations. In so doing, the company becomes better informed as to what the gaps might be, which adds depth to the risk-identification process.

Once the SEE risks have been identified, the next phase is that of risk scoring. The general focus here is on considering the frequency with which the risk may occur, and the consequences on the business should it do so. When assessing the financial implications for the business, it may be helpful to conduct a scenario-planning exercise that envisages a highly effective NGO campaign. In the context of capital market campaigns, as highlighted in Chapter 4, companies and their investors should consider the risks to be highest when the NGOs adopt an indirect strategy of investor-advocacy influence, using a combination of moral- and business-case arguments.

In the final action phase of the risk management project, plans should be developed for mitigating and managing the SEE risks that have been identified, with ownership of the plan then being allocated within the organisation. The key question at this stage is what actions, if any, should be taken to close the gap between stakeholder expectations on the key SEE issues and the company's or investor's performance in relation to the issue? It is at this phase where the key lessons from the case studies identified earlier come into play.

Again, where a CSR department exists, then it should be involved in the development of corporate policy on the SEE issue and the plan to manage and mitigate it. However, it is likely that there is a considerable amount of relevant expertise outside of this department, so judgement regarding which teams should work on which policies needs to be exercised. It may also be that the responsibility for the delivery of the management plan should be allocated outside of the CSR team. For example, the management of the sales and marketing division should be responsible, in the first instance, for implementing a bank's attempts to reduce the mis-selling of financial services. Similarly, for a large construction company, responsibility for managing the safety of employees could be best delivered by site managers. Finally, avoidance of sweatshop labour by a retailer could be best led by the purchasing department. The ultimate step of the plan is to ensure that it is being implemented, by monitoring and reviewing ongoing performance in a systematic way. This requires periodic reviews – or audits – to ensure that the policy is being delivered, and this is appropriately conducted by the CSR department, perhaps in conjunction with the internal audit function. For very large organisations with particularly acute SEE risks, it may be sensible to seek an independent audit. Lastly, the findings of this audit may have implications for the future development of corporate policy, which closes the virtuous circle that CSR management systems are intended to harness. Developing the system in this way should help to reduce the risk of any NGO targeting the campaigns, regardless of whether the NGO chooses to use the capital market or not.

Turning now to the lessons from this research for investors, the Ethics for USS campaign and the Friends of the Earth "Capital Punishment" campaigns provided a series of useful learning points. The actions taken by investors to respond to these campaigns included: developing a policy of engagement that commits the investment institution to using its influence to support and promote socially and environmentally responsible corporate behaviour; integrating the policy into voting and investment practices; recruiting staff with the skills to implement the policy of active engagement; making available the actions taken to implement this policy, and report periodically on the outcomes in terms of corporate change achieved; committing to the consideration of performance in this area when (re)appointing fund managers (relevant only where the institutional investor appoints external fund managers, as with the USS study); and developing a public profile for work in this area.

It is also worth returning to the Collevecchio Declaration (the full text of which is included in Appendix 2), since it represents the most important combined NGO statement of the changes that social and environmental campaigners would like to see. The Declaration requires investors to make commitments to:

(1) sustainability;
(2) "do no harm";
(3) responsibility;
(4) accountability;
(5) transparency; and
(6) sustainable markets and governance.

Despite the somewhat aspirational tone of the declaration, it provides a useful insight into the broader collective aims of capital market campaigners, and offers guidance to investors regarding the issues that NGOs are likely to engage with them on that are seeking to reduce the risk that they will be targeted by such campaigns – see Panel 4.

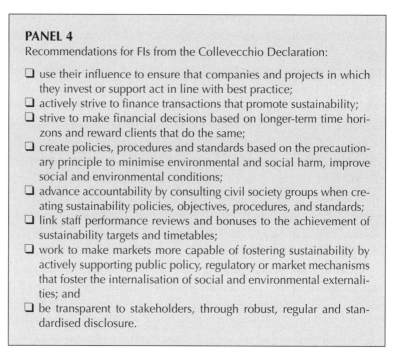

PANEL 4
Recommendations for FIs from the Collevecchio Declaration:

❑ use their influence to ensure that companies and projects in which they invest or support act in line with best practice;
❑ actively strive to finance transactions that promote sustainability;
❑ strive to make financial decisions based on longer-term time horizons and reward clients that do the same;
❑ create policies, procedures and standards based on the precautionary principle to minimise environmental and social harm, improve social and environmental conditions;
❑ advance accountability by consulting civil society groups when creating sustainability policies, objectives, procedures, and standards;
❑ link staff performance reviews and bonuses to the achievement of sustainability targets and timetables;
❑ work to make markets more capable of fostering sustainability by actively supporting public policy, regulatory or market mechanisms that foster the internalisation of social and environmental externalities; and
❑ be transparent to stakeholders, through robust, regular and standardised disclosure.

The Collevecchio Declaration recommendations in Panel 4 resonate very closely with the findings from the case-study analysis above. In particular, the recommendations that they re-emphasise are: the development of a policy of engagement; integrating the policy into voting and investment practices; securing the skills to implement the policy; and reporting to stakeholders on the outcomes. However, they do go beyond this in a number of areas. The question institutional investors need to consider is how they would respond effectively to all of these recommendations, should they be challenged by NGOs. This will require careful consideration of the implications of the recommendations and the development of corporate policy in relation to them.

1   In addition to acknowledging an increased understanding of the CM, Tunmore's point reinforces the analysis in Chapter 4 regarding the claim that "NGOs have changed from mainly confrontational media-focused activities at AGMs to focus more on substantive interventions that target corporate strategy".

2   There are two useful reports for companies thinking through this aspect of the recommendations. First, Accountability has produced "Towards Responsible Lobbying: Leadership and Public Policy" (2005); and, second, the Institute of Business Ethics has produced "The Ethics of Influence: political donations and lobbying" (2005); see References for further information.

3   See Andriof *et al* (2003), for a detailed description of the background to and challenges of stakeholder engagement.

7

Conclusion

Capital markets exert influence over companies via two principal mechanisms: economic influence via a company's cost of capital, and investor-advocacy influence via the rights associated with share ownership. Throughout this book, and particularly within the case studies, we have seen how NGOs have sought to harness this influence to change corporate practice. We have also seen some NGOs focusing on the capital market in an attempt to change the system itself. Many of these campaigns have been effective. It has been shown that they have the potential to affect a company's cost of capital (see, eg, the cases of Monsanto, Shell and Exxon Mobil in Chapter 3) and mobilise significant support from investors (see, eg, the discussion on the Balfour Beatty and BP shareholder resolutions in Chapter 4).

The fact that capital market campaigns are effective is a centrally important conclusion for this book, as it confirms that companies and investors can be exposed to significant risks from NGO capital market campaigns. That there are institutional investors willing to respond to these campaigners may also say something about the culture within the City – despite a common perception to the contrary, not all capitalists focus on making money, regardless of the costs. It appears that capitalism can have a conscience.

NGOs derive legitimacy for these kinds of campaigns mainly from their welfare-oriented role in society. More specifically, when NGOs act as a civil regulator of unethical corporate practices, they help to maintain trust in the market and therefore help maintain the market itself. Consequently, NGO capital market intervention that aims to enhance welfare (and operates within the boundaries of the law) can be both legitimate and in the long-term collective interests of companies and their shareholders.

Over the past few decades, NGO capital market intervention has increased – there was quite literally an order of magnitude more campaigning during 2002 than in 1990, and relatively constant growth throughout the time period. In view of the fact that this campaigning helps maintain the market, its growth should be broadly welcomed.

The historical turning point in UK NGO capital market campaigning appears to have been during the mid 1990's, which witnessed a combination of successful campaigns. In particular, the international environment and development NGO coalition to stop Asea Brown Boveri (ABB plc) constructing the Bakun hydroelectric, and the intervention by PIRC in conjunction with Greenpeace, Amnesty International and WWF-UK surrounding Shell's disposal of the Brent Spar storage buoy and its human rights record in Nigeria. To date, most such NGO campaigns have been mainly this kind of short-term instrumental use of the capital market in support of specific corporate campaigns.

This book has also shown that there has been an increase in the success of NGO capital market campaigns, and a marked change of NGO strategy towards those that are more likely to succeed – namely campaigns that adopts an indirect strategy of investor-advocacy influence, using a combination of moral- and business-case arguments. It appears, therefore, that NGOs have learned from errors in previous interventions, and that the risk of being targeted by an effective campaign has significantly increased.

As to what the future may have in store, it is not yet clear whether the significant growth in these kinds of campaigns will continue to the point where they become a standard part of all NGOs corporate campaigning. However, it is clear that a large group of NGOs is increasingly active in this area. Furthermore, once an NGO has attempted such a strategy, only rarely does it stop, so the number of these campaigns can be expected to further increase.

Might the nature of these campaigns continue to shift in some way? As mentioned above, NGO capital market campaigning is mainly short-term instrumental use of capital market influence for corporate campaigning rather than an attempt to change the structure of the capital market. This research has found very few examples of NGOs running campaigns to change government policy in relation to capital markets. Even where an NGO appears to believe that the capital market is systematically undermining the achievement of its long-term objectives, it tends not to have a detailed alternative public-policy agenda that would reform or replace the functions of the capital market (exceptions include the New Economics Foundation and Centre for Tomorrow's Company). In view of the vociferous nature of some NGO criticism of "capitalism", this is an interesting omission. Therefore, it is possible that we may see more attempts to change the structure of the capital market in order that it might promote more sustainable business activities. This may include, for example, increased calls by NGOs for governments to take measures that force investors to undertake a responsible ownership role and engage with the companies that they own on issues of corporate responsibility. It may also involve NGOs lobbying for the government to correct the long-term market failures arising from the capital market's promotion of unsustainable patterns of growth. This could involve campaigns for policies that internalise companies' environmental and social costs on to company balance sheets, in order that the market incorporates companies' full social and environmental costs in its valuation.

In terms of other changes to the nature of these NGO campaigns, the emerging UK experience with shareholder resolutions – some of which can be shown to have achieved considerable success – indicates that we may see more UK NGOs filing such resolutions, despite the significantly increased resources required. To some extent, this would reflect the US experience, where a few hundred resolutions are now routinely filed on these issues each year. Nevertheless, there are some cultural differences that reduce the likelihood of the UK ever experiencing quite such significant levels of shareholder resolutions. For example, in the UK active shareholders tends to prefer to resolve the issue through a discussion without filing a shareholder resolution, whereas in the US filing a resolution is often the way of beginning a discussion.

Regarding the lessons for companies, the most important conclusion is that companies fare better when they deal with the strategic and operational implications arising from the NGO criticism, rather than simply concentrating on the communications style of a response. Perhaps because companies often first encounter such campaigns via the media, they tend to have had a communications-led response, rather than dealing with the implications for broader company strategy. This research clearly indicates that companies should have an organisation-wide approach to considering the risks that they are exposed to from NGO capital market campaigns. Having identified the issues, they will need to engage proactively in a debate by developing a corporate policy in relation to these issues, reporting on performance against each policy and ensure that they review their policies and positions of the various trade bodies of which they are members in order to ensure consistency with the company's own policy. This work programme could be an ongoing part of a company's enterprise risk management programme, with implications for the corporate risk function. In order to develop an integrated strategic response to the threat of NGO campaigning, the programme should also include, in particular, expertise from within the CSR team. There are also certain implications for Investor Relations teams – they may wish to identify which of their investors have a predisposition towards these issues, and then enter into a proactive programme of discussion with them on the identified issues in order to secure their support.

Similar to the implications for companies, investors may also wish to prepare for the possible impact of NGO capital market intervention. The case study analysis suggests that investors seeking to reduce capital market campaign risk should: develop a responsible engagement policy; report on the activity associated with this policy; invest in resources to implement it; integrate the policy into voting practices; and seek to develop a reputation in this area. There are also more general implications from the Collevecchio Declaration, which investors may wish to consider and develop their policy in relation to.

Fundamentally, if companies and investors are to avoid being targeted by NGO campaigns, then they need to put in place measures to ensure that they meet the reasonable expectations of stakeholders. However, this will be a significant ongoing challenge – particularly when the interests and views of different stakeholder groups collide. As a consequence, directors must juggle a broad range of commercial, social, political, environmental, ethical and economic issues.

From the perspective of makers of public policy, a number of issues arise because of the effectiveness of this capital market campaigning. Where, the campaigns are effective and legitimate, they enhance welfare and do not present a problem. Indeed, as argued above, they can be in the long-term collective interests of companies and their shareholders, and should therefore be encouraged. Conversely, where NGO capital market campaigns are effective but illegitimate, they undermine welfare. While the vast majority of UK capital market intervention to date appears to have been welfare-enhancing, the threats of violence seen during the Huntingdon Life Sciences case (Chapter 2) raise significant cause for concern. Unless the government devises ways of preventing illegitimate and welfare-undermining use of capital market, we are likely to see more of this type of campaigning by extreme pressure groups. Therein lies the future challenge to policy makers: encouraging NGOs with welfare-enhancing objectives to play a full role in a civil economy, while preventing those that undermine welfare from so doing.

Appendix 1

The NGO Capital Market Intervention Chronology

Table A overleaf summarises the main NGO capital market (CM) interventions between 1990 and 2002 inclusive. The chronology maps the decisions taken by each NGO in relation to the four main dimensions of the NGO CM intervention model: mechanism of influence; route of influence (including "stance" when indirect); primary audience; and nature of argument (detailed in Chapter 3 above). It also includes a *prima facie* categorisation of the perceived success of the intervention where "success" is defined as some of the campaign objectives have been met (Key: apparently successful = Y; possibly successful = Y?; unsure one way or another = ?; possibly unsuccessful = N?; apparently unsuccessful = N):

Table A

	Date	NGO(s)	Aim	Nature of CM intervention	Classification	Success
1	Apr 1990	Surfers Against Sewage (SAS)	Change South West Water's sewage disposal policy	Brought a bag of sewage-related detritus to the 1990 AGM and questioned the board about its policy in relation to marine dumping of sewage	Investor advocacy Direct CM institutions Moral	?
2	1991–ongoing	Campaign Against the Arms Trade	"Name and shame" local authority pension funds with defence company holdings	Clean investment campaign launched	Economic Indirect (shark) CM institutions Moral	Y
3	Mar 1991	Minewatch	Prevent Hanson from developing mineral deposits in Navajo reserves	Purchased shares in order to enable four Navajo Native Americans to attend AGM	Investor advocacy Direct CM institutions Moral	N?
4	Apr 1991	Greenpeace	Stop ICI manufacturing ozone-depleting chemicals	Disrupted AGM	Investor advocacy Direct CM institutions Moral	?
5	1991	Forests Monitor	Persuade James Latham plc (one of Britain's largest timber merchants) to source sustainable timber	Wrote to investors encouraging them to put pressure on the board	Investor advocacy Indirect (orca) CM institutions Moral	Y?
6	1991	Friends of the Earth	Stop Fisons extracting peat from sites of special scientific interest	Attempted to file resolution	Investor advocacy Indirect (orca) CM institutions Business and moral	Y?

	Date	Organisation	Goal	Action	Classification	Outcome
7	April 1992	Surfers Against Sewage	Change South West Water's sewage disposal policy	Presentation at AGM on the environmental performance of South West Water plc	Investor advocacy Indirect (dolphin) CM institutions Moral	?
8	1992	RSPB	Stop Fisons extracting peat from Sites of Special Scientific Interest	RSPB criticise Fisons in the FT for peat extraction from SSSIs; targets shareholders	Investor advocacy Indirect (dolphin) CM institutions Business and moral	Y?
9	1992	WWF-UK	Improve MFI Environmental Policy	Provided critique of MFI environmental policy; support from NPI	Investor advocacy Indirect (dolphin) CM institutions Moral	Y?
10	1992	PARTiZANS	Prevent RTZ from mining in sacred land	Took Australian Aborigines and others to AGM	Investor advocacy Direct CM institutions Moral	?
11	1993	NGO coalition	Stop Barito Pacific illegally logging	Wrote to investors asking them not to invest in the new issue. Subsequently named investors in the media	Economic Indirect (orca) CM institutions Business and moral	Y
12	1994	Greenpeace	Promote emissions reduction by National Power/ Powergen	Published report at flotation showing that companies would be loss if environmental costs included	Economic Indirect (orca) CM institutions Business	?
13	1994/95	Greenpeace	Reduce EVCs dioxin emissions	Produced "sell" broker analysis on the basis that PVC carried high-risk exposure due to health impacts	Economic Indirect (orca) CM institutions Business	N?

Table A (continued)

Date	NGO(s)	Aim	Nature of CM intervention	Classification	Success
14 Oct 1994	World Rainforest Movement	Reduce demand for illegal timber	Encouraged investors to question the existence of approved forest-management plans	Economic Indirect (orca) CM institutions Business and moral	N?
15 Nov 1994	Business in the Environment	"Raise awareness of environmental issues among the financial community"	Commissioned Extel survey: "City Analysts and the the Environment – a survey of environmental attitudes in the City of London"	Economic Indirect (dolphin) CM institutions	Y?
16 1994–5	Greenpeace	Reduce climate change emissions	Published financial research suggesting reallocating holdings from oil and gas to solar	Economic Indirect (orca) CM institutions Business	Y?
17 1995–7	NGO coalition	Stop Asea Brown Boveri (ABB) and Ekran Berhad from building Bakun Dam	Broad-ranging campaign including joint letter with some ABB investors ABB president successfully encouraging withdrawal from Bakum Dam	Investor advocacy Indirect (dolphin) CM institutions Business and moral	Y
18 1997	PIRC (in conjunction with Greenpeace, Amnesty and WWF-UK)	"The directors [of Shell] are requested to designate responsibility for the implementation of environmental and corporate responsibility policies to a named …"	Shareholder resolution at AGM	Investor advocacy Indirect (orca) CM institutions Business and Moral	Y

		director; publish a report to shareholders on the implementation of such policies in relation to the company's operations in Nigeria" (see PIRC, 1998, p 8)			
19 1997	WWF-UK	To invest its own reserves so that "the principle of sustainable development is promoted" (see WWF-UK,1997, p 1)	Published ethical investment policy	Economic and investor advocacy Direct CM institutions Business and moral	Y?
20 Sep 1997	Ethics for USS	"[C]onvince USS to adopt an ethical investment policy its members" (see Alexander 2001)	Campaign against the Universities Superannuation Scheme (USS) "negative" position on SRI (see Chapter 5)	Economic Indirect (orca) CM institutions Moral	N (NB See intervention no 31 below)
21 Sep 1998	WWF International	Reduce investment in unsustainable forestry	Launched "Forests for Life" campaign (see WWF International, 1998)	Economic Indirect (dolphin) CM institutions Business	N?
22 Oct 1998	Traidcraft Exchange	Explore potential for NGO and ethical investment funds collaboration (see Traidcraft Exchange, 1998)	Ran seminar hosted by Friends Provident looking into this question	Investor advocacy Indirect (dolphin) CM institutions Moral	Y

Table A (continued)

Date	NGO(s)	Aim	Nature of CM intervention	Classification	Success
23 Oct 1998	UKSIF, in conjunction with WWF-UK and FoE	Persuade Treasury to require independent financial advicers to ask clients about ethical concerns	Responded to "Financial Services and Markets Bill Consultation Document". Argued that regulated persons be required to "ask consumers whether they have any ethical, soical or environment concerns which they wish to have taken into account" (see WWF-UK, 1998b, p 3)	Economic Direct Public Policy Audience Business and moral	N
24 Nov 1998	Friends of the Earth	Question the extent to which ethical investment funds "can shift the behaviour of the large corporate powerhouses" (see UKSIF, 1998, p 1)	Spoke at UK Social Investment Forum AGM (see UKSIF, 1998, pp 2–4)	Economic and investor advocacy Indirect (orca) CM institutions Business and moral	Y
25 1998	Forum for the Future	"[C]atalyse the incorporation of environmental considerations into … investment analysis" (see Suranyi, 1999, p (i))	Launched Capital Futures Project to build dialogue with the city	Economic investor advocacy Indirect (dolphin) CM institutions Business	?
26 Jan 1999	WWF-UK	Promote investment in more sustainable companies for and raise funds conservation work	Launched the NPI/WWF investment fund (see WWF-UK, 1999a)	Economic and investor advocacy Indirect (dolphin) CM institutions Business	?

No	Date	Organization	Aim	Description	Categories	Marker
27	1999	Forum for the Future	"[C]atalyse the incorporation of environmental considerations into … investment analysis" (see Suranyi, 1999, p (i))	Published first Capital Futures Project Report: "Blind to Sustainability? Stock Markets and the Environment"	Economic and investor advocacy / Indirect (dolphin) / CM institutions / Moral	?
28	1999	War on Want	Promote good labour standards	Launched "Invest in Freedom" campaign aimed at union members requesting support for the promotion of ILO Core Labour Standards by their occupational pension fund (see War on Want, 1991, p 1)	Investor advocacy / Indirect (orca) / CM institutions / Moral	N?
29	1999	Account-Ability	Promote an inclusive approach to corporate management including engagement with all stakeholders	AA 1000 promoted by Account-Ability as "provid[ing] all parties focusing upon corporate responsibility – ethical investors, political consumers, engaged employees, regulatory bodies, activist groups – with a powerful new perspective and toolkit" (see Account-ability, 2003)	Investor advocacy / Indirect (dolphin) / CM institutions / Business	N?
30	Feb 1999	UKSIF in conjunction with Traidcraft Exchange, Friends of the Earth, War on Want and WWWF-UK	Promote that "statement-of-investment principles" disclose the degree to which SRI is incorporated	Responded to the DSS "Strengthening the pensions Framework" consultation (see WWF-UK, 1999c, p 2)	Economic and investor advocacy / Indirect (dolphin) / Public Policy / Business and moral	Y?

Table A (continued)

Date	NGO(s)	Aim	Nature of CM intervention	Classification	Success
31 Oct 1999	Ethics for USS	EUSS updated its aim to call for responsible ownership	Produced a report "Meeting the Responsibilities of Ownership" (see E-USS, 1999)	Investor advocacy Indirect (orca) CM institutions Business and moral	Y?
32 1999–2000	Greenpeace and WWF-UK (see below)	To persuade BP to: 1. Stop the expenditure of any funds for the development of Northstar project; 2. Make capital freed up by the cancellation of Northstar available to BP Solar	Submitted a resolution to BP's AGM in 2000	Investor advocacy Indirect (orca) CM institutions Business and moral	Y?
33 1999–2002	WWF-UK and Greenpeace (see above)	"To persuade BP Amoco to publicly withdraw its interest in developing the Arctic Refuge" (WWF-UK, 2000)	Filed a resolution at BP's AGM in 2000, 2001 and 2002. Commissioned "Brand Risk and Sustainability – is shareholder value at risk in the new BP?" (see Innovest, 2002)	Economic and investor advocacy Indirect (orca) CM institutions Business and moral	Y?
34 Jan 2000	Friends of the Earth (UK)	To "stimulate debate around the environmental consequences of the investment strategies of institutional investors" (see Friends of the Earth, 2000a, p 4)	Published "Capital Punishment", which reviewed the holdings of the fund-management arms of the top 15 insurance companies in controversial companies	Investor advocacy Indirect (orca) CM institutions Business and moral	Y?

35	Feb 2000	Just Pensions – an NGO coalition	"The project's objective is to bring about changes in business practices that will benefit the poor" (see Traidcraft Exchange/War on Want, 2000, p 1)	Applied to National Lottery for £140k to launch Just Pensions. Intended to "produce guidance materials for pension fund trustees, fund managers and pension funds" advisers on development-related issues and their links with investment" (see Traidcraft Exchange/War on Want, 2000, p 1)	Investor advocacy Indirect (dolphin) CM institutions Business and moral	Y
36	Mar to Jun 2000	Friends of the Earth	"Targeting pension companies and the Norwich Union, demanding greener investment policies" (see Friends of the Earth, 2000b, p 1)	Distributed an information pack to its Campaign Express Network to persuade Norwich Union to adopt an SRI engagement policy	Investor advocacy Indirect (orca) CM institutions Business and moral	?
37	Jun 2000	WWF-UK, Traidcraft, War on Want	Mandatory reporting of SEE issues in the Company Law Review	Co-signed letter with FIs to DTI Company Law Review	Investor advocacy Indirect (dolphin) Public policy Business and moral	?
38	Jul 2000	Amnesty International	"[P]ension fund trustees to adopt Statements of Investment Principles (SIPs) that included consideration of social environmental and ethical issues" (see Amnesty International, 2000a, p 1)	Produced "Human Rights Guidelines for Pension Fund Trustees to educate trustees about forms of SRI, particularly engagement policies" (see Amnesty International, 2000b, p 1) and an 'Individual Action' campaign" (Amnesty International, 2000a, p 1)	Investor advocacy influence Direct CM institutions Business and moral	Y

Table A (continued)

Date	NGO(s)	Aim	Nature of CM intervention	Classification	Success
39 Jul 2000	WWF-UK	Pressure pension fund managers to adopt positive SIPS	Promoted model letter to its members	Investor advocacy Direct CM institutions Business and moral	Y?
40 3 Jul 2000	WWF-UK in conjunction with Traidcraft, Amnesty International, Forum for the Future and Friends of the Earth	Promote mandatory reporting of CSR information by listed companies and to promote the adoption of positive statements of investment principles	Co-signed letter to top 100 UK pension schemes asking them "to engage in the DTI Company Law Review consultation process and support a mandatory requirement for companies to report on their environmental and social performance"	Investor advocacy Indirect (shark) Both public policy and CM institutions Business	Y?
41 Nov 2000	WWF-UK	Promote mandatory reporting of CSR information	Argued at All-Party Parliamentary Group on SRI that "access to comparable and reliable environmental and social performance information is currently a problem for investors" (see UKSIF, 2000)	Investor advocacy influence Direct Public policy Business case	?
42 2000	Forum for the Future	To review "state of the art thinking on understanding how sustainability issues affect a company ... [and] opportunities	Published "Background Briefing: Capital Markets, the Financial Services Sector and Sustainability" (see Pearce, 2000)	Economic and investor advocacy Indirect (dolphin) CM institutions Business	Y?

43	2000	WWF-UK in conjunction with the Alliance of Religions and Conservation	for financial institutions" (see Pearce, 2000, p 1) Help faith groups "implement their beliefs through their investments"	Established the International Interfaith Investment Group (3iG). Published "A Capital Solution: Faith Finance and Concern for a Living Planet" (see Triolo et al, 2000)	Economic and investor advocacy / Indirect (dolphin) / CM institutions / Business and moral — Y?
44	2000–1	NGO coalition	Balfour Beatty and Ilisu Dam	Submitted resolution to 2001 AGM. Published an alternative annual report, "2000: Balfour Beatty's annus horribilus". Used Turnbull listing requirements (see Chapter 3) to suggest that investors ask for reassurances that any reputational risks are justified financially. Targeted socially responsible investors (2001, p 2). Critical of some SRIs	Investor advocacy / Indirect (orca) / CM institutions / Business and moral — Y
45	2001	Forum for the Future	To "help financial institutions become leading participants in the move to a sustainable, wealth-creating economy" (see Forum for the Future, 2001, p 1)	Launched the Centre for Sustainable Investment.	Economic and investor advocacy / Indirect (dolphin) / CM institutions / Business — ?

Table A (continued)

Date	NGO(s)	Aim	Nature of CM intervention	Classification	Success
46 Mar 2001	Friends of the Earth	Prevent Shell from exploring for gas in Kirthar National Park, Pakistan	Encouraged investors in Shell to raise concerns regarding allegations that Shell intended to explore for gas in the Kirthar National Park	Investor advocacy Indirect (dolphin) CM institutions Business and moral	Y?
47 Apr 2001	WWF-UK	Promote inclusion of SEE issues by venture capital	Commissioned Ecsponent to conduct a review of the British Venture Capital Association. Published "BVCA Environmental Investment Survey Report" (see Spark, 2001, p 15)	Investor advocacy influence Indirect (orca) CM institutions Business	N?
48 May 2001	Friends of the Earth	Review the environmental and financial issues within Asia Pulp and Paper (APP)	Produced a report into the problems associated with APP (see Matthew and Willem van Gelder, 2001, p 6)	Economic Indirect (orca) CM institutions Business	Y?
49 May 2001	Just Pensions	Provide "practical guidance to pension fund trustees and fund managers on how to address . . . . development issues in their approach to socially responsible investment" (see Just Pensions, 2001a, pp 2–3)	Published "Socially Responsible Investment and International Development: A Guide for Trustees and Fund Managers" (Just Pensions, 2001a, p 3)	Investor advocacy Indirect (dolphin) CM institutions Business and moral	Y

50 2001	WWF-UK	Identify best practice and to promote the business case for sustainability through the use of concrete examples (see WWF-UK and Cable and Wireless, 2001, p 2)	Published "To Whose Profit? Building a Business Case for Sustainability" (see *ibid*)	Economic Indirect (dolphin) CM institutions Business	N?
50 2001	Centre for Tomorrow's Company	Promote investment based on a long-term view of shareholder-value generation	Published "Twenty-first Century Investment, an agenda for change" (Goyder, 2001)	Economic Indirect (dolphin) CM institutions Business	?
52 2001–2	Corner House	Motivate other NGOs to engage in CM campaigning	Published "The Campaigner's Guide to the Financial Markets"	Investor advocacy Indirect (orca) CM institutions Business	Y?
53 2001	Friends of the Earth	Promote best-practice "statements of investment principles"	Published "Top 100 Pension Funds – How Ethical Are They?"	Economic and investor advocacy Indirect (orca) CM institutions Business and moral	Y

Table A (continued)

Date	NGO(s)	Aim	Nature of CM intervention	Classification	Success
54 2001	Christian Aid	Demonstrate how oil was fuelling the civil war in Sudan and to promote divestment	Published "The Scorched Earth: Oil and War in Sudan" (2001). Encouraged "BP and other foreign and institutional investors in Petrochina, a subsidiary of CNPC, [to] divest their holdings" (see Christian Aid, 2001, p 2). Submitted resolution to BP's AGM	Investor advocacy Indirect (orca) CM institutions Moral	N?
55 2001	WWF-UK	Reduce investment in unsustainable forestry practices	ISIS join WWF's 95 + Group as the first financial services company to do so (see ISIS, 2003).	Investor advocacy influence Indirect (dolphin) CM institutions Business	Y
56 May 2001	Institute for Public Policy Research (IPPR)	Investigate the role of assets in individual and collective welfare	IPPR launched "The Centre for Asset-based Welfare" (see IPPR, 2003)	Economic Indirect (dolphin) Public policy Business and moral	?.
57 2001	Business in the Environment	Overall objective defined as "to raise awareness of environmental issues amongst the financial community" (follow-up to 1994 survey – see Business in the Environment, 1994)	Published "Investing in the Future" (see UKSIF, 2001, p 4)	Economic Indirect (dolphin) Investor audience Business	?.

58 2001	Free Tibet/ Tear Fund	Persuade BP to divest holding in Petrochina	Filed a resolution at the 2002 AGM calling on BP to divest its holding	Investor advocacy Indirect (orca) CM institutions Moral	N
59 Dec 2001	The Burma Campaign	Promote the withdrawal from Burma by multinational companies	Organised briefing for SRI funds from Harn Yawnghwe, director of Euro-Burma Office, Brussels, adviser to Burmese government in exile, as a briefing for institutional investors	Economic advocacy Indirect (orca) CM institutions Moral	Y?
60 Dec 2001	WWF-UK and Carbon Disclosure Project	To "(a) help investors better understand climate change in the context of their portfolios; and (b) help the corporate community provide better quality information to shareholders on climate change related risks" (see Carbon Disclosure Project, 2001)	WWF is main funder of CDP at launch and a member of CDP's advisory board	Investor advocacy influence Indirect (dolphin) CM institutions Business	Y

Table A (continued)

Date	NGO(s)	Aim	Nature of CM intervention	Classification	Success
61 Jan 2002	Amnesty UK + IBLF (with support from ISIS and Insight Investment)	Raise companies' awareness of the human rights contexts of their activities and to encourage them to develop appropriate practices and procedures	Published "Business and Human Rights: A Geography. of Corporate Risk" (Amnesty International, 2002)	Investor advocacy influence Indirect (dolphin) CM institutions Business	Y
62 2002	War on Want	Reduce the negative affects of globalisation on the working poor	Relaunched the "Invest in Freedom" campaign. Focused on "encouraging the 10 million people who are occupational pension scheme members to find out where their money is invested" (see EIRIS, 2002c, p 2)	Investor advocacy influence Indirect (orca) CM institutions Moral	?
63 Feb 2002	Oxfam	Encourage "the world's pharmaceutical companies to do more to improve access to medicines in poor countries" (see Oxfam, 2001b, p 1)	Launched a "Cut the Cost" campaign at a briefing for City investors	Investor advocacy influence Indirect (orca) CM institutions Business and moral	Y

64 2002	Transparency International	Promote the transparency of facilitation payments by multinationals to governments for large-scale investment projects	Secured ISIS Asset Management membership of Transparency International UK's Corporate Supporters' Forum.Collaborated in the development of *Business Principles for Countering Bribery*	Investor advocacy Indirect (dolphin) CM institutions Business	Y
65 Apr 2002	New Economics Foundation	Promote improved ethical standards in the SRI industry	Published "An Ethical Door Policy: How to Avoid the Erosion of Ethics in SRI" (see UKSIF, 2002b)	Investor advocacy and Economic influence Direct CM institutions Moral case	N?
66 Jul 2002	Forum for the Future	Examine the evidence for a business case for socially responsible investment	Published a report "Sustainability Pays" (2002) in collaboration with PIRC and CIS (see Forum for the Future, PIRC, and the Co-operative Insurance Society, 2002)	Economic and investor advocacy Indirect (dolphin) CM institutions Business	Y?
67 Jul 2002	Just Pensions	Ascertain impact of amendment to 1995 Pensions Act on SRI (see Just Pensions, 2002).	Published "Socially Responsible Investment and International Development. Do UK Pension Funds Invest Responsibly? A survey of current practice on Socially Responsible Investment"	Investor advocacy influence Indirect (orca) CM institutions Business and moral	Y

Table A (continued)

Date	NGO(s)	Aim	Nature of CM intervention	Classification	Success
68 2002	War on Want and Communication Workers Union	Encourage fund trustees managing pensions for staff at BT and Consignia to engage with holdings to improve working conditions in the developing world	"The campaign will concentrate on engaging with companies to improve workers' rights in the developing world, such as eradicating child labour and forced work, and ensuring the right to join a trade union" (see EIRIS, 2002c, p 2)	Investor advocacy influence Indirect (orca) CM institutions Moral	Y?
69 Jul 2002	Friends of the Earth	Persuade the FSA to impose sanctions on Xstrata	Produced an analysis of climate risks and the degree to which the Xstrata share prospectus neglected to include sufficient information in this area. Submitted to the FSA in support of their argument	Investor advocacy Indirect (dolphin) Public policy Business	N
70 Aug 2002	Forum for the Future	To "examine the role of the UK financial services sector in promoting sustainable development, compile a compendium of best practice ... lessons for future	Published "The London Principles of Sustainable Finance", commissioned by the Department for the Environment, Food and Rural Affairs (Defra) and funded by the Corporation of London	Economic and investor advocacy Indirect (dolphin) Public policy and CM institutions Business	Y

		innovation and . . . [provide] mechanisms to ensure continual progress" (see Pearce and Mills, 2002)	The prime minister launched the document at the World Summit on Sustainable August 2002		
71 2002	Friends of the Earth	Change the FSA listing requirements	Used Xstrata case study to encourage the FSA to review the listing rules to ensure that they fully reflect the changing needs of investors with regard to social and environmental issues	Investor advocacy influence Indirect (dolphin) Public policy Business	N?
72 Sep 2002	Forum for the Future	Promote engagement on SEE issues by mainstream investors	Published "Engaging the Mainstream with Sustainability – a survey of investor engagement on corporate social, ethical and environmental performance" (see Pearce and Ganzi, 2002)	Investor advocacy Direct Investor audience Business	?

Table A (continued)

Date	NGO(s)	Aim	Nature of CM intervention	Classification	Success
73 2002	Oxfam	A fair price for developing country coffee producers	Launched "What's that in your coffee?" campaign and published "Mugged: Poverty in your coffee cup" and "called on investors to engage with the world's biggest coffee marketing firms – Nestlé, Kraft, Procter & Gamble and Sarah Lee – to improve their supply chain management and pricing policies." (see EIRIS, 2002c, p 2)	Investor advocacy Indirect (dolphin) CM institutions Business	N?
74 Sep 2002	Traidcraft plc	Raise approximately £3 million of additional capital	Issued share prospectus inviting further investments	Economic Direct CM institutions Business and moral	Y
75 2002	Oxfam, Save the Children and Voluntary Services	Encourage drugs companies to do more to improve access to lifesaving medicines	Published "Beyond Philanthropy" (see Oxfam, Save the Children and Voluntary Service Overseas, 2002) which included	Investor advocacy Indirect (dolphin) CM institutions Business and moral	Y

76 Nov 2002	Overseas (VSO) Forum for the Future	Strengthen the SRI SIP policy requirement in the reform of the 1995 Pensions Act	a set of benchmarks for investors Published "Government's Business" (see Forum for the Future, 2002c) which, among a series of recommendations, urges the government to require pension fund trustees to report to members on how they implement any SRI policies	Investor advocacy influence Direct Public policy Business and moral	?
77 Nov 2002	Just Pensions	To "contribute towards the Millennium Development Goals by improving the social and environmental impact of foreign trade and investment in developing countries" (see UKSIF, 2002c, p 4)	Funding for second stage secured from DFID (see UKSIF, 2002c, p 4)	Investor advocacy influence Indirect (dolphin) Investor audience Business and moral	Y

Table A (continued)

Date	NGO(s)	Aim	Nature of CM intervention	Classification	Success
78 Dec 2002	The Corporate Responsibility Coalition (CORE)	To improve the environmental, social and economic performance of companies by requiring greater disclosure and accountability to stakeholders	CORE called on ethical investors to help it promote legislation for a legal requirement for UK companies to report on their SEE performance	Investor advocacy influence Indirect (orca) Public policy Business and moral	?

Appendix 2

The Collevecchio Declaration

As mentioned in Chapter 1, the Collevecchio Declaration is the most important collective contemporary statement of the changes that social and environmental capital market campaigners would like to see. It has been endorsed by more than 100 NGOs worldwide, including: Greenpeace Italy; WWF national offices in Italy and the UK; Friends of the Earth national offices in Brazil, Germany, El Salvador, Australia, Canada, Czech Republic, Lithuania, Switzerland; and the Sierra Club in the USA. The text of the declaration follows.

* * *

THE COLLEVECCHIO DECLARATION ON FINANCIAL INSTITUTIONS AND SUSTAINABILITY

Financial institutions (FIs) such as banks and asset managers can and must play a positive role in advancing environmental and social sustainability. This declaration calls on FIs to embrace six main principles, which reflect civil society's expectations of the role and responsibilities of the financial services sector in fostering sustainability. The following civil society organizations call on FIs to embrace the following principles, and take immediate steps to implement them as a way for FIs to retain their social license to operate.

The role and responsibility of financial institutions
The financial sector's role of facilitating and managing capital is important; and finance, like communications or technology, is not inherently at odds with sustainability.

However, in the current context of globalisation, FIs play key roles in channeling financial flows, creating financial markets and influencing international policies in ways that are too often unaccountable to citizens, and harmful to the environment, human rights, and social equity.

Although the most well-known cases of resource misallocation in the financial sector have been associated with the high tech and telecom bubbles, FIs have played a role in irresponsibly channeling money to unethical companies, corrupt governments, and egregious projects. In the Global South, FIs' increasing role in development finance has meant that FIs bear significant responsibility for international financial crises, and the crushing burden of developing country debt. However, most FIs do not accept responsibility for the environmental and social harm that may be created by their transactions, even though they may be eager to take credit for the economic development and benefits derived from their services. And relatively few FIs, in their role as creditors, analysts, underwriters, advisers, or investors effectively use their power to deliberately channel finance into sustainable enterprises, or encourage their clients to embrace sustainability.

Similarly, the vast majority of FIs do not play a proactive role in creating financial markets that value communities and the environment. As companies FIs concentrate on maximising shareholder value, while as financiers they seek to maximise profit; this dual role means that FIs have played a key role in creating financial markets that predominantly value short-term returns. These brief time horizons provide strong incentives for companies to put short-term profits before longer-term sustainability goals, such as social stability and ecological health.

Finally, through the work of international public policy bodies such as the Bretton Woods institutions, the power of FIs has increasingly expanded as countries have deregulated, liberalised, and privatised their economies and financial markets. Financial institutions have not only actively promoted these policies and processes, they have benefited from them through increased profit and influence.

In too many cases, FIs unfairly benefit from their power at the expense of communities and the environment. For example, during financial crises, FIs have charged indebted countries high risk premiums while at the same time relying on public bail-outs. They have spoken out against innovative solutions to the debt crisis, such as the sovereign-debt restructuring processes proposed by civil society groups and now being discussed in the International Monetary Fund. And their voice has been absent in efforts to address tax havens, a problem that blocks progress towards equity and sustainability.

As a result, civil society is increasingly questioning FIs' accountability and responsibility, and challenging FIs' social license to operate. As major actors in the global economy, FIs should embrace a commitment to sustainability that reflects best practice from the corporate social responsibility movement, while recognising that voluntary measures alone are not sufficient, and that they must support regulations that will help the sector advance sustainability.

Commitments to six principles

Acknowledging that FIs, like all corporations, exist as creations of society to act in the public interest, FIs should promote the restoration and protection of the environment, and promote universal human rights and social justice. These principles should be inherent in the way that they offer financial products and services, and conduct their businesses.

Finance and commerce has been at the center of a historic detachment between the world's natural resource base, production and consumption. As we reach the boundaries of the ecological limits upon which all commerce relies, the financial sector should take its share of responsibility for reversing the effects this detachment has produced. Thus, an appropriate goal of FIs should be the advancement of environmental protection and social justice rather than solely the maximisation of economic growth and/or financial return. To achieve this goal, FIs should embrace the following six principles:

Commitment to sustainability

FIs must expand their missions from ones that prioritise profit maximisation to a vision of social and environmental sustainability. A commitment to sustainability would require FIs to fully integrate the consideration of ecological limits, social equity and economic justice into corporate strategies and core business areas (including credit, investing, underwriting, advising), to put sustainability objectives on an equal footing to shareholder maximisation and client satisfaction, and to actively strive to finance transactions that promote sustainability.

Commitment to "Do No Harm"
FIs should commit to do no harm by preventing and minimising the environmentally and/or socially detrimental impacts of their portfolios and their operations. FIs should create policies, procedures and standards based on the Precautionary Principle to minimise environmental and social harm, improve social and environmental conditions where they and their clients operate, and avoid involvement in transactions that undermine sustainability.

Commitment to responsibility
FIs should bear full responsibility for the environmental and social impacts of their transactions. FIs must also pay their full and fair share of the risks they accept and create. This includes financial risks, as well as social and environmental costs that are borne by communities.

Commitment to accountability
FIs must be accountable to their stakeholders, particularly those that are affected by the activities and side effects of companies they finance. Accountability means that stakeholders must have an influential voice in financial decisions that affect the quality of their environments and their lives – both through ensuring that stakeholders rights are protected by law, and through practices and procedures voluntarily adopted by the FI.

Commitment to transparency
FIs must be transparent to stakeholders, not only through robust, regular and standardised disclosure, but also through being responsive to stakeholder needs for specialised information on FIs' policies, procedures and transactions. Commercial confidentiality should not be used as an excuse deny stakeholders information.

Commitment to sustainable markets and governance
FIs should ensure that markets are more capable of fostering sustainability by actively supporting public policy, regulatory and/or

market mechanisms which facilitate sustainability and that foster the full cost accounting of social and environmental externalities.

IMMEDIATE STEPS (2003)

Committed FIs can demonstrate their commitment to these six principles by working with civil society to take the following immediate steps:

Commitment to sustainability

Measurement of environmental and social impacts

FIs should measure the environmental and social impacts of their portfolios in core business areas, including lending, investing, underwriting and advising.

Continuous improvement based on environmental and social impacts of portfolios

Although some FIs embrace the concept of continuously improving their management systems, all FIs must assess the sustainability challenges and issues facing their portfolios; and create objectives, strategies, timetables and performance indicators to increase the sustainability profile of their portfolios.

Fostering sustainability

FIs must actively seek to shift their businesses to proactively sustainable practices which improve environmental and social conditions. This might include, for example, reducing the carbon footprint of their portfolios by shifting investments from fossil fuel to renewables; or the capitalisation of sustainable enterprises. FIs should use their influence to ensure that companies and projects in which they invest or support act in line with best practice. FI should set clear timetables for improving their clients' sustainability performance, and if necessary, withdraw their support of non-performing clients.

Implementation and capacity building

FIs should take all necessary steps to ensure that staff are trained and capacity is built to ensure that sustainability objectives are met and that procedures, policies and standards are implemented. Staff performance reviews and bonuses should be linked to the achievement of sustainability targets and timetables.

Commitment to "Do No Harm"

Sustainability procedures

On the basis of the Precautionary Principle, FIs should create transactions-based procedures that screen and categorise potential deals on the basis of environmental and social sensitivity. Based on a transaction's sensitivity, the FI should perform appropriate levels of due diligence, stakeholder consultation, and assessment. FIs should also create processes for influencing, legally enforcing and monitoring sensitive transactions.

Sustainability standards

FIs should adopt internationally recognised, sector-specific, best practice standards that can be the basis for financing or refusing to finance a transaction (eg, World Commission on Dams guidelines, Forest Stewardship Council standards).

Banks should also establish supplementary sectoral standards with stakeholder input and guidance. Some such standards exist already for the forests sector and others are being developed for other issues/sectors such as Minerals and Dams projects. These standards will vary, but should as a minimum cover issues such as: respect for international conventions, no-go zones, gender equity issues, supply chain issues, human rights, etc.

Commitment to responsibility

Bear full responsibility for the impacts of transactions

FIs must pay for their full and fair share of risks that they accept and create. This means FIs should not help engineer country bail-out packages that aggravate the debt burden of developing countries. It also means that FIs should bear full responsibility for the environmental and social costs that are created by their transactions but borne by communities. This includes using their influence and resources to address the needs of communities whose livelihoods and ways of life are compromised by the adverse environmental or social impacts of their transactions.

Recognise their role in developing country debt crisis

FIs should recognise that the ability of countries to service external debt depends on the maintenance of social and ecological systems, and that developing country debt burdens are socially, environmentally, and economically unsustainable. FIs should refrain from lobbying against innovative solutions to the developing country debt crisis, and support calls for significant debt relief/cancellation.

Commitment to accountability
Public consultation
FIs can advance accountability by consulting civil society groups when creating sustainability policies, objectives, procedures, and standards. FIs should incorporate the views of stakeholders affected by their credit, lending, underwriting or advisory functions. This includes respecting the right of affected communities to "say no" to a transaction.

Stakeholder rights
FIs must also support regulatory efforts that increase the rights of stakeholders in having a more influential voice in the governance of FIs and their transactions.

Commitment to transparency
Corporate sustainability reporting
FIs should publish annual sustainability reports according to an internationally recognised reporting format supported by civil society. FIs should further include disclosure on the sustainability profile of the FI's portfolio, a breakdown of core business activity by sector and region, and the implementation of the FI's sustainability policies and objectives.

Information disclosure
There should be an assumption in favour of disclosure of information. Particularly for completed transactions, but also for those in the pipeline, FIs should publicly provide information on companies and significant transactions in a timely manner, and not hide behind the excuse of business confidentiality.

Commitment to sustainable markets and governance
Public policy and regulation
FIs must recognise the role that governments must play in setting the market frameworks within which companies and FIs function.

FIs should work to make markets are more capable of fostering sustainability by actively supporting public policy, regulatory or market mechanisms that foster the internalisation of social and environmental externalities.

Financial practices
FIs should avoid and discourage inappropriate use of tax havens or currency speculation that are unfair and that create instability. FIs should also strive to make financial decisions based on longer-term time horizons and reward clients that do the same.

Appendix 3

The "Equator Principles"

The Equator Principles (EP) are an industry approach for financial institutions in determining, assessing and managing environmental & social risk in project financing. They represent an attempt by FIs to offer a coherent response to the challenges to them on SEE issues by NGOs. EP simultaneously provides a framework for banks when assessing controversial projects for loans, and guidance for joint ventures that are seeking project finance from banks.

As mentioned in Chapter 1, a group of 10 banks published the Equator Principles (EP) in June 2003. At the time of writing, 33 FIs have signed up, collectively representing roughly three-quarters of the project finance loan market. The text of EP follows.

* * *

PREAMBLE

Project financing plays an important role in financing development throughout the world. In providing financing, particularly in emerging markets, project financiers often encounter environmental and social policy issues. We recognize that our role as financiers affords us significant opportunities to promote responsible environmental stewardship and socially responsible development.

In adopting these principles, we seek to ensure that the projects we finance are developed in a manner that is socially responsible and reflect sound environmental management practices.

We believe that adoption of and adherence to these principles offers significant benefits to ourselves, our customers and other stakeholders. These principles will foster our ability to document and manage our risk exposures to environmental and social matters associated with the projects we finance, thereby allowing us to engage proactively with our stakeholders on environmental and social policy issues. Adherence to these principles will allow us to work with our customers in their management of environmental and social policy issues relating to their investments in the emerging markets.

These principles are intended to serve as a common baseline and framework for the implementation of our individual, internal environmental and social procedures and standards for our project financing activities across all industry sectors globally.

In adopting these principles, we undertake to review carefully all proposals for which our customers request project financing. We will not provide loans directly to projects where the borrower will not or is unable to comply with our environmental and social policies and processes.

STATEMENT OF PRINCIPLES

We will only provide loans directly to projects in the following circumstances:

(1) We have categorised the risk of a project in accordance with internal guidelines based upon the environmental and social screening criteria of the IFC as described in the attachment to these Principles.

(2) For all Category A and Category B projects, the borrower has completed an Environmental Assessment (EA), the preparation of which is consistent with the outcome of our categorisation process and addresses to our satisfaction key environmental and social issues identified during the categorisation process.

(3) In the context of the business of the project, as applicable, the EA report has addressed:
  (a) assessment of the baseline environmental and social conditions;
  (b) requirements under host country laws and regulations, applicable international treaties and agreements;
  (c) sustainable development and use of renewable natural resources;
  (d) protection of human health, cultural properties, and biodiversity, including endangered species and sensitive ecosystems;
  (e) use of dangerous substances;

(f)   major hazards;

(g)   occupational health and safety;

(h)   fire prevention and life safety;

(i)   socioeconomic impacts;

(j)   land acquisition and land use;

(k)   involuntary resettlement;

(l)   impacts on indigenous peoples and communities;

(m) cumulative impacts of existing projects, the proposed project, and anticipated future projects;

(n)   participation of affected parties in the design, review and implementation of the project;

(o)   consideration of feasible environmentally and socially preferable alternatives;

(p)   efficient production, delivery and use of energy;

(q)   pollution prevention and waste minimization, pollution controls (liquid effluents and air emissions) and solid and chemical waste management.

Note: In each case, the EA will have addressed compliance with applicable host country laws, regulations and permits required by the project. Also, reference will have been made to the minimum standards applicable under the World Bank and IFC Pollution Prevention and Abatement Guidelines and, for projects located in low and middle income countries as defined by the World Bank Development Indicators Database, the EA will have further taken into account the then applicable IFC Safeguard Policies (Exhibit II). In each case, the EA will have addressed, to our satisfaction, the project's overall compliance with (or justified deviations from) the respective above-referenced Guidelines and Safeguard Policies.

(4) For all Category A projects, and as considered appropriate for Category B projects, the borrower or third party expert has prepared an Environmental Management Plan (EMP) which draws on the conclusions of the EA. The EMP has addressed mitigation, action plans, monitoring, management of risk and schedules.

(5) For all Category A projects and, as considered appropriate for Category B projects, we are satisfied that the borrower or third party expert has consulted, in a structured and culturally appropriate way, with project affected groups, including indigenous peoples and local NGOs. The EA, or a summary

thereof, has been made available to the public for a reasonable minimum period in local language and in a culturally appropriate manner. The EA and the EMP will take account of such consultations, and for Category A Projects, will be subject to independent expert review.

(6) The borrower has covenanted to:
   (a) comply with the EMP in the construction and operation of the project;
   (b) provide regular reports, prepared by in-house staff or third party experts, on compliance with the EMP; and
   (c) where applicable, decommission the facilities in accordance with an agreed Decommissioning Plan.

(7) As necessary, lenders have appointed an independent environmental expert to provide additional monitoring and reporting services.

(8) In circumstances where a borrower is not in compliance with its environmental and social covenants, such that any debt financing would be in default, we will engage the borrower in its efforts to seek solutions to bring it back into compliance with its covenants.

(9) These principles apply to projects with a total capital cost of US$50 million or more.

The adopting institutions view these principles as a framework for developing individual, internal practices and policies. As with all internal policies, these principles do not create any rights in, or liability to, any person, public or private. Banks are adopting and implementing these principles voluntarily and independently, without reliance on or recourse to IFC or the World Bank.

Environmental and social screening process (exhibit I of the equator principles)

Environmental screening of each proposed project shall be undertaken to determine the appropriate extent and type of EA. Proposed projects will be classified into one of three categories, depending on the type, location, sensitivity, and scale of the project and the nature and magnitude of its potential environmental and social impacts.

Category A: A proposed project is classified as Category A if it is likely to have significant adverse environmental impacts that are sensitive, diverse, or unprecedented. A potential impact is considered "sensitive" if it may be irreversible (eg, lead to loss of a major natural habitat) or affect vulnerable groups or ethnic minorities, involve involuntary displacement or resettlement, or affect significant cultural heritage sites. These impacts may affect an area broader than the sites or facilities subject to physical works. EA for a Category A project examines the project's potential negative and positive environmental impacts, compares them with those of feasible alternatives (including, the "without project" situation), and recommends any measures needed to prevent, minimize, mitigate, or compensate for adverse impacts and improve environmental performance. A full environmental assessment is required which is normally an Environmental Impact Assessment (EIA).

Category B: A proposed project is classified as Category B if its potential adverse environmental impacts on human populations or environmentally important areas-including wetlands, forests, grasslands, and other natural habitats-are less adverse than those of Category A projects. These impacts are site-specific; few if any of them are irreversible; and in most cases mitigatory measures can be designed more readily than for Category A projects. The scope of EA for a Category B project may vary from project to project, but it is narrower than that of Category A EA. Like Category A EA, it examines the project's potential negative and positive environmental impacts and recommends any measures needed to prevent, minimize, mitigate, or compensate for adverse impacts and improve environmental performance.

Category C: A proposed project is classified as Category C if it is likely to have minimal or no adverse environmental impacts. Beyond screening, no further EA action is required for a Category C project.

Exhibit II: IFC safeguard policies
As of 4 June 2003, the following is a list of IFC Safeguard Policies:
Environmental Assessment
OP4.01 (October 1998)
Natural Habitats
OP4.04 (November 1998)
Pest Management
OP4.09 (November 1998)

Forestry
OP4.36 (November 1998)
Safety of Dams
OP4.37 (September 1996)
Indigenous Peoples
OD4.20 (September 1991)
Involuntary Resettlement
OP4.30 (June 1990)
Cultural Property
OPN11.03 (September 1986)
Child and Forced Labor
Policy Statement (March 1998)
International Waterways
OP7.50 (November 1998)*

World bank and IFC specific guidelines (exhibit III of the equator principles)

As of 4 June 2003, IFC is using two sets of guidelines for its projects.

(1) IFC is using all the environmental guidelines contained in the World Bank Pollution Prevention and Abatement Handbook (PPAH). This Handbook went into official use on July 1, 1998.

(2) IFC is also using a series of environmental, health and safety guidelines that were written by IFC staff in 1991–1993 and for which there are no parallel guidelines in the Pollution Prevention and Abatement Handbook. Ultimately new guidelines, incorporating the concepts of cleaner production and environmental management systems, will be written to replace this series of IFC guidelines. When completed these new guidelines will also be included in the Pollution Prevention and Abatement Handbook.

Where no sector specific guideline exists for a particular project then the World Bank General Environmental Guidelines and the

*Note: The principal requirements relate to the role of IFC as a multi-lateral agency and notification requirements between riparian states which are generally outside the remit of private sector operators or funders. It is referenced for the sake of completeness. The substantive elements of good practice with respect to environmental and social aspects therein are fully covered by OP4.01.

IFC General Health and Safety Guideline will be applied, with modifications as necessary to suit the project.*

The list below includes both the World Bank Guidelines and the IFC Guidelines.

World Bank Guidelines

(1) Aluminum Manufacturing
(2) Base Metal and Iron Ore Mining
(3) Breweries
(4) Cement Manufacturing
(5) Chlor-Alkali Plants
(6) Coal Mining and Production
(7) Coke Manufacturing
(8) Copper Smelting
(9) Dairy Industry
(10) Dye Manufacturing
(11) Electronics Manufacturing
(12) Electroplating Industry
(13) Foundries
(14) Fruit and Vegetable Processing
(15) General Environmental Guidelines
(16) Glass Manufacturing
(17) Industrial Estates
(18) Iron and Steel Manufacturing
(19) Lead and Zinc Smelting
(20) Meat Processing and Rendering
(21) Mini Steel Mills
(22) Mixed Fertilizer Plants
(23) Monitoring
(24) Nickel Smelting and Refining
(25) Nitrogenous Fertilizer Plants
(26) Oil and Gas Development (Onshore)
(27) Pesticides Formulation
(28) Pesticides Manufacturing
(29) Petrochemicals Manufacturing

*Exception (the following are World Bank Guidelines not contained in the PPAH and currently in use).

(30) Petroleum Refining

(31) Pharmaceutical Manufacturing

(32) Phosphate Fertilizer Plants

(33) Printing Industry

(34) Pulp and Paper Mills

(35) Sugar Manufacturing

(36) Tanning and Leather Finishing

(37) Textiles Industry

(38) Thermal Power Guidelines for New Plants

(39) Thermal Power Rehabilitation of Existing Plants

(40) Vegetable Oil Processing

(41) Wood Preserving Industry

IFC Guidelines

(1) Airports

(2) Ceramic Tile Manufacturing

(3) Construction Materials Plants

(4) Electric Power Transmission and Distribution

(5) Fish Processing

(6) Food and Beverage Processing

(7) Forestry Operations: Logging

(8) Gas Terminal Systems

(9) Geothermal Projects

(10) Hazardous Materials Management

(11) Health Care

(12) Life & Fire Safety

(13) Occupational Health and Safety

(14) Office Buildings

(15) Offshore Oil & Gas

(16) Polychlorinated Biphenyls (PCBs)

(17) Pesticide Handling and Application

(18) Plantations

(19) Port and Harbor Facilities

(20) Rail Transit Systems

(21) Roads and Highways

(22) Telecommunications

(23) Tourism and Hospitality Development

(24) Waste Management Facilities
(25) Wastewater Reuse
(26) Wildland Management
(27) Wind Energy Conversion Systems
(28) Wood Products Industries

Bibliography

ABI, 2001, "Disclosure Guidelines for Socially Responsible Investment".

Accountability, 2003, AA 1000 Framework Series, URL: http://www.accountability.org (accessed 27 May).

Adetunji, L., 2005, "Animal Test Group Postpones US Listing", *Financial Times*, 8 September.

Alam, N., 2001, Head of Social Research, EIRIS, interview with author, April.

Alexander, M., 2001, Senior Campaigner, Ethics for USS, interview with author, November.

Alliance of Religions and Conservation, 2000a, "Ethical Investment of Faith Funds", for discussion on 16 November, ARC event, Kathmandu, 14 September.

Alliance of Religions and Conservation, 2002b, 3iG Meeting Summary, 18–20 June.

Amnesty International, 2000a, "Individual Action – Pensions: Protecting Your Future and Theirs", July.

Amnesty International, 2000b, "Human Rights Guidelines for Pension Fund Trustees", July.

Amnesty International, 2001, "Summary Evaluation Report on Amnesty Business Group's Pension Fund Campaign on Socially Responsible Investment", February.

Amnesty International and The International Business Leaders Forum, 2002, Business and Human Rights: A Geography of Corporate Risk.

Andriof, J., *et al* (eds), 2003, *Unfolding Stakeholder Thinking: Theory, Responsibility and Engagement* (London: Greenleaf Publishing).

ARC, 2002, 3iG Meeting Summary: 18–20 June 2002, Council on Foreign Relations, New York.

Arctic Power, 2003a, URL: http://www.anwr.org/gallery/pages/01-ANWR%20land% 20use%20map.htm (accessed 27 July).

Arctic Power, 2003b, URL: http://www.anwr.org/power.htm (accessed 27 July).

Aristotle, *c* 350 BCE, *The Politics*, Book II, Part III, URL: http://classics.mit.edu/Aristotle/politics.2.two.html (accessed August 2003).

Balfour, B., 2001, Company Press Release, 14 November.

Banerjee, N., 2002, "BP Pulls Out of Campaign to Open Up Alaskan Area", *New York Times*, 26 November.

BankTrack, 2003, "Summary, Collective NGO Analysis of EPs", URL: http://www.banktrack.org/fileadmin/user_upload/documents/J_Equator_Principles/Equator_principles/Summary_and_Full_NGO_Analysis.pdf, June (accessed 1 October 2005).

Barclays Global Investors, 2003a, "Corporate Governance Policy", March.

Barclays Global Investors, 2003b, "Profile 2003 – Barclays Global Investors", URL: www.barclaysglobal.com/repository/standard/europe/press/press_materials/bgi_profile.pdf (accessed 15 February).

Beattie, A., 2002, "Religions Pray at the Altar of Profit", *Financial Times*, 20 June.

Beattie, A. and V. Houlder, 2002, "Shades of Green", *Financial Times*, 19 August.

Bell, S., 2001, Research Director, PIRC, interview with author, October 2001.

Bendell, J. (ed), 2000, *Terms for Endearment: Business, NGOs and Sustainable Development* (London: Greenleaf).

Birch, S., 2003, "Dirty Money", *Guardian Society*, 14 May.

Blacconiere, W. and D. Patten, 1994, "Environmental Disclosures, Regulatory Costs and Changes in Firm Value", *Journal of Accounting & Economics* 18.

Borkey, P. and F. Leveque, 1998, "Voluntary Approaches for Environmental Protection in the European Union", Working Party on Economic and Environmental Policy Integration, OECD ENV/EPOC/GEEI (98) 29/Final.

BP, 2001, AGM Agenda and Shareholder Information.

BP, 2002, Shareholder Resolution 14: Requisition by shareholders under Section 376 of the Companies Act 1985 for giving notice of an intended Special Resolution for the circulation of a statement on the matter referred to in the proposed Special Resolution at the BP plc 2002 Annual General Meeting.

Brundtland, G., 1988, "Our Common Future", World Commission on Environment and Development.

Buckley, C., 2002, "Mapping Socially Responsible Investment Initiatives and Opportunities", Oxfam internal briefing, July.

Bulmer, M., (ed), 1984, *Sociological Research Methods: An Introduction*, 2nd edn (London: Macmillan).

Burns, J., 2000, "Pressure Groups 'have Influence on Investors' ", 22 May, p 2.

Business for Social Responsibility, 2003, URL: http://www.bsr.org (accessed 6 July).

Business in the Environment, 1994, "City Analysts and the Environment – A Survey of Environmental Attitudes in the City of London", Extel Financial.

Carbon Disclosure Project, 2001, "Confidential Executive Summary", December.

Carr, M., 2003, "Applying Socially Responsible Investment Criteria to Corporate Bonds", MSc dissertation, Cass Business School, London, September.

CBI, 2000, "Global Social Responsibility – Is the Business of Business Just Business?", International Competitiveness Brief, January.

Chan-Fishel, M., 1999, *Confronting Companies Using Shareholder Power: A Hand-book for Socially Orientated Shareholder Activism* (Washington, DC: Friends of the Earth).

Chatterjee, N., 2002, "Green Groups and Ethical Shareholders in BP Lose Vote", Reuters News Service, 19 April.

Christian Aid, 2001, "The Scorched Earth: Oil and War in Sudan".

Claros Consulting, 2002, "The Xstrata Listing: An Analysis of Climate Risks", for Friends of the Earth.

Commission of the European Communities, 2001, "Promoting a European Framework for Corporate Social Responsibility", Green Paper COM (2001) 366 final, Brussels 18 July.

Committee on Corporate Governance, 2003, "The Combined Code – Principles of Good Governance and Code of Best Practice", July.

Cowe, R., 2001, "Investing in Social Responsibility: Risks and Opportunities", Association of British Insurers' research report, September.

Davies, P (ed), 1997, *Gower's Principles of Modern Company Law*, 6th edn (London: Sweet & Maxwell).

Davis, S., J. Lukomnik, and D. Pitt-Watson, 2006, *The Civil Economy* (Cambridge, MA: Harvard Business School Press).

De George, R., 1990, *Business Ethics*, 3rd edn (New York: Macmillan).

De Grauwe, P. and F. Camerman, 2002, "How Big Are The Big Multinational Companies?", University of Leuven and Belgian Senate, URL: http://www.econ.kuleuven.ac.be/ew/academic/intecon/DeGrauwe/PDG-papers/(accessed 16 March 2003).

Dean, A. and J. Garin, 2005, "Socially Responsible Investment Market Commentary: Thoughts on SRI Research", Morgan Stanley Equity Research, July.

Delphi International, 1997, "The Role of Financial Institutions in Achieving Sustainable Development", report to the European Commission by Delphi International Ltd in association with Ecologic GMBH, November.

Dickson, M., 2001, "Behave Nicely Now – or We have Ways of Making You..." *Financial Times*, 19 October.

Dresner, S., 2001, "Engaging Companies – How Can Fund Managers Most Effectively Influence Corporate Environmental And Social Performance?", MSc dissertation, London School of Economics and Political Science, August.

Drucker, P., 1976, *The Unseen Revolution: How Pension Fund Socialism Came To America* (London: Heinemann).

Edwards, M., 1995, "Introduction", in Edwards, M. and D. Hulme (eds), 1995, *Non-Governmental Organisations – Performance and Accountability: beyond the magic bullet* (London: Earthscan).

Edwards, M., 2000, "NGO Rights and Responsibilities: A New Deal for Global Governance", UK Foreign Policy Centre, 29 September.

Edwards, M. and D. Hulme (eds), 1995, *Non-Governmental Organisations – Performance and Accountability: beyond the magic bullet* (London: Earthscan).

EIRIS, 1999, "Engaging with Companies", discussion paper, London.

EIRIS, 2002a, *Ethical Investor*, Spring.

EIRIS, 2002b, *Ethical Investor*, Summer.

EIRIS, 2002c. *Ethical Investor*, Winter.

Elkington, J., 2000, Chairman, Sustain Ability, interview with author, November.

Elkington, J. and S. Fennell, 1998, "Partners for Sustainability", *Greener Management International* (24), Winter, pp 47–56.

Ennis, E., 2002, "Politically correct!: a Review of BP's Exposure to Political Risk", SG Global Research, 19 July.

E-USS, 1999, "Meeting the Responsibilities of Ownership", URL: http://www.ethicsforuss.org.uk/report/report.asp. Accessed 19 July 2002.

E-USS, 2000, Summer Newsletter.

E-USS, 2003, URL: http://www.ethicsforuss.org.uk (accessed 12 July).

Financial Times, 2001a, "GSK to Review Drug Pricing Policy: Pharmaceuticals Giant Reacts to Criticism Over Costs to Poor Countries", 16 February, p 12.

Financial Times, 2001b, Editorial, 20 April.

Financial Times, 2002, "Human Rights and Accountability, Under the Skin", interview with Irene Khan, secretary-general of Amnesty International, 13 June, p 15.

Forum for the Future, 2001, "The Centre for Sustainable Investment – A Partner Invitation from Forum for the Future", Forum for the Future.

Forum for the Future, 2003, URL: http://www.forumforthefuture.org.uk/ (accessed 6 July).

Forum for the Future, PIRC, and the Co-operative Insurance Society, 2002, "Sustainability Pays", July.

Frankental, P., 2001, Director, Amnesty International Business Unit, interview with author, May.

Freeman, R. E., 1984, *Strategic Management: A Stakeholder Approach* (Boston, MA: Pitman).

Friends of the Earth, 2000a, "Capital Punishment: UK Insurance Companies and the Global Environment", prepared by FM Research for Friends of the Earth, January.

Friends of the Earth, 2000b, "Press for Change – Demanding Green Investment", Campaign Express pack, March.

Friends of the Earth, 2000c, "Campaign Express: Results of the Investor Pack", September.

Friends of the Earth, 2001a, "Balfour Beatty Counter Report – 2000: Balfour Beatty's *annus horribilis*", Ilisu Dam Campaign.

Friends of the Earth, 2001b, "Top 100 UK Pension Funds – How Ethical Are They?", briefing, July.

Friends of the Earth, 2002, "2001–2002 Annual Review", November.

Friends of the Earth, 2003a, "Investing in A Better Future. Ethical Pensions, Insurance and Investments", May.

Friends of the Earth, 2003b, URL: http://www.foe.co.uk/campaigns/corporates/issues/corporate_globalisation/index.html (accessed 9 July).

Gimbel, F., 2003, "Ethical Investors Unite to Strengthen Initiatives", 4 August, p 2.

Global Risk Management Services, 2001, "BP PLC Factsheet", 12 November.

Gower, L. C. B., 1969, *Modern Company Law*, 3rd edn (London: Stevens).

Goyder, M., 2003, "Twenty-first Century Investment: the Inquiry. Detailed outline of the programme", Tomorrow's Company, May.

Graham, B. and D. Dodd, 1940, *Security Analysis – Principles and Technique*, 2nd edn (London and New York: McGraw-Hill).

Green, D., 2001, Senior Policy Officer, CAFOD, and Project Manager, Just Pensions, interviewed by author, February.

Green, D., 2003, "Do UK Charities Invest Responsibly? A Survey of current practice", Just Pensions, 14 May.

GSK, 2001, "Facing the Challenge", June.

GSK, 2003, "The Impact of Medicines: Corporate and Social Responsibility Report 2002".

Guardian, 1999, 17 December.

Gummer, John, 2000, Secretary of State for the Environment 1993–7, interviewed by author, January.

Gunthorpe, D., 1997, "Business Ethics: A Quantitative Analysis of the Impact of Unethical Behavior by Publicly Traded Corporations". *Journal of Business Ethics* 16.

Hamilton, J., 1995, "Pollution as News: Media and Stock Market Reactions to the Toxics Release Inventory Data", *Journal of Economics and Environmental Management* 28, pp 98–113.

Hampel Report, 1998, *"Final report of the Committee on Corporate Governance"*, para 1 (London: GEE Publishing Ltd).

Harrison, H., 2003, UKSIF, Personal Communication. August.

Hawley, J. and A Williams, 2000, *The Rise of Fiduciary Capitalism – How Institutional Investors Can Make Corporate America More Democratic*, (Pennsylvania: University of Pennsylvania Press).

Henderson Global Investors, 2003, "Managing Pension Fund Assets as if the Long-Term Really Did Matter", 24 September.

Hewitt, P., 2003, *A Labour Economy: Are we nearly there yet?*, Pamphlet to Accompany Speech at IPPR Labour Party Conference fringe event, Bournemouth.

Hildyard, N. 2002, "Briefing 25: Financial Market Lobbying – A New Political Space for Activists," The Corner House, January.

Hildyard, N. and M. Mansley, 2001, "The Campaigners' Guide to the Financial Markets: effective lobbying of companies and financial institutions", The Corner House, May.

Hirschman, A., 1970, *Exit, Voice, and Loyalty: Responses to Decline in Firms, Organizations, and States* (Cambridge, MA: Harvard University Press).

HMSO, 1994, "UK Government's Report on Sustainable Development: The UK's Strategy".

HMSO, 1999, Statutory Instrument 1999 No 1849, "Pensions: The Occupational Pensions Schemes (Investment, and Assignment, Forfeiture, Bankruptcy etc.), Amendment Regulations".

HSBC, 2003, "All Share Constituents & Weightings, UK Monthly Quantitative Analysis", January.

ICGN, 2003, "Statement on Institutional Shareholder Responsibilities", 22 May.

IFSL, 2003, "Fund Management", City Business Series, 2003.

Innovest, 2002, "Brand Risk and Sustainability – is shareholder value at risk in the new BP? Environmental performance, brand equity and shareholder value", April.

Institutional Shareholders' Committee, 2005, "The Responsibilities of Institutional Shareholders and Agents – Statement of Principles".

IPPR, 2003, URL: http://www.ippr.org.uk/research/(accessed 6 July).

ISIS, 2003, URL: http://www.isisam.com/AboutUs.asp?pageID= 2.3.1.4.5. (accessed 6 July).

Johnston, J., 2001, SRI analyst, Morley Asset Management, interviewed by the author, May.

Jones, L., 2001, Deputy Chief Executive and Director of Finance, WWF-UK, interviewed by the author, 30 January.

Jones, M., 2002, "Alaska Drilling Cuts no Ice with BP Investors", *Financial Times*, 23 January.

Just Pensions, 2001a, "Socially Responsible Investment and International Development: A Guide for Trustees and Fund Managers", May.

Just Pensions, 2002, "Do UK Pension Funds Invest Responsibly? A Survey of Current Practice on Socially Responsible Investment", July.

Kahn, S., 2002, "The Right Way to Make the Green Case", *Daily Express*, 23 January.

Karpoff, J., "The Impact of Shareholder Activism on Target Companies: A Survey of Empirical Findings", 4th revision, University of Washington, School of Business, Fourth revision, 8 September.

Kernaghan, C., 1998, "Made in China: Behind the Label", National Labour Committee, March.

Kiernan, M., 2005, "Trustees of the World, Unite!", *Financial Times*, 8 August.

Kirk, D., 2002, BP, personal communication, May.

Knight, R. and D. Pretty, 2001, *Reputation and Value: the Case of Corporate Catastrophes* (Oxford: Oxford Metrica).

Koller, T., M. Goedhart and D. Wessels, 2005, *Valuation: Measuring and Managing the Value of Companies* (Hoboken, New Jersey: John Wiley & Sons).

Korten, D., 1995, *When Corporations Rule the World* (London: Earthscan).

Lake, R., 1999, "Governing Capitalism for International Development: Can NGOs and Financial Institutions Work Together for the Poor?", Traidcraft Exchange, paper presented at the NGOs in a Global Future conference, Birmingham – UK, 11–13 January.

Lam, J., 2003, *Enterprise Risk Management – From Incentives to Controls* (Hoboken, New Jersey: John Wiley & Sons).

Lascelles, D., 2005, "The Ethics of Influence: Political Donations and Lobbying", Institute of Business Ethics.

Litvin, D., 2003, *Empires of Profit: Commerce, Conquest and Corporate Responsibility* (London: Texere Publishing).

Loh, J., 2002, "Living Planet Report" WWF International.

MacGillivray, A. *et al*, 2005, *Towards Responsible Lobbying: Leadership and Public Policy*. AccountAbility.

Mackenzie, C., 1993, *The Shareholder Action Handbook. Using Shares to make Companies more Accountable. A New Consumer Guide* (Guildford, Biddles Ltd).

Mackenzie, C., 1997, "Ethical Investment and the Challenge of Corporate Reform". PhD thesis, University of Bath.

Mackenzie, C., 2001, Email to Howard Carter, Chief Executive of Friends Ivory & Sime (unpublished), 20 April.

Mackenzie, C., 2002, "Defining Global Business Principles – Towards a New Role for Investors in Promoting International Corporate Responsibility", Insight Investment.

Manifest, 2002, URL: http://www.manifest.co.uk (accessed September and December).

Mansley, M., 2000, *Socially Responsible Investment: A Guide for Pension Funds and Institutional Investors* (Sudbury: Monitor Press).

Mansley, M., 2001 Executive Director, Claros Consulting, interview with author, October.

Mansley, M. and A. Dlugolecki, 2001, "Climate Change – A Risk Management Framework for Institutional Investors", US$ 2001.

Matthew, E. and J. Willem van Gelder, 2001, "Paper Tiger, Hidden Dragons: The Responsibility of International Financial Institutions for Indonesian Forest Destruction, Social Conflict and the Financial Crisis of Asia Pulp & Paper", Friends of the Earth.

McIntosh, M., *et al*, 2003, *Living Corporate Citizenship – Strategic Routes to Socially Responsible Business* (London: FT Prentice Hall, 2003).

McLaren, D., 2001, Acting Director of Campaigns, Friends of the Earth, interview with author, April.

McLaren, D., 2002, "Corporate Engagement by 'Socially Responsible' Investors: A Practical Paradigm for Stakeholder Governance?", Judge Institute of Management, Cambridge.

McLaren, D., S. Bullock, and N. Yousuf, 1998, *Tomorrow's World: Britain's Share in a Sustainable Future* (London: Earthscan).

McRae, S., 2001, "Getting Engaged: The Evolution of the Environment NGO Sector and its Implications for Business", Friends of the Earth. Environment Council seminar, London, 27 June.

Miller, K. L., 2002, "Pin-Striped Protesters: Activists are Learning to Work the Capitalist System", *Newsweek International*, 25 February.

Mitchell, L. E., 2001, "Corporate Irresponsibility: America's Newest Export", New Haven: Yale University Press.

Monks, R., 1998, *The Emperor's Nightingale – Restoring the Integrity of the Corporation* (New York: Perseus Books Group).

Montagnon, P., 2002, "The ABI Guidelines – An Impact Assessment", Association of British Insurers, paper presented to IPPR seminar entitled "The Transparent Company", 20 March.

Moon, P., 2003, "Competition where Savers are the Winners". Financial Times Fund Management, 3 March, p 4.

Murphy, D. and J. Bendell, 1997, *In the Company of Partners* (Bristol: The Policy Press).

Myners, P., 2001, "The Myners Report of Institutional Investment in the UK: Final Report 2001", HM Treasury.

Napier, Robert, 2000, CEO, WWF-UK, Speech to the Local Authority Pension Fund Forum Annual Conference, 30 November.

Nesbitt, S. L., 1994, "Long-Term Rewards From Shareholder Activism: A Study of the 'CalPERS Effect' ", *Journal of Applied Corporate Finance*, Winter.

OECD, 1999, "Principles for Corporate Governance", Paris, 1999.

OECD, 2000, "Guidelines for Multinational Enterprises", Paris, 2000.

OECD, 2001, "Corporate Responsibility: Private Initiatives and Public Goals", Directorate for Financial, Fiscal and Enterprise Affairs, May.

Oxfam, 2001a, "Dare to Lead: Public Health and Company Wealth", briefing paper on GlaxoSmithKline, February.

Oxfam, 2001b, "Implausible Denial: Why the Drug Giants' Arguments on Patents Don't Stack Up", policy paper.

Oxfam, 2002a, "Mugged: Poverty in your coffee cup".

Oxfam, 2002b, "Annual Review, 2001–2002".

Oxfam, 2003a, "Oxfam's Strategic Plan for 2003/4–2005/6".

Oxfam, 2003b, "Statement of Legitimacy and Accountability", URL: http://www. oxfam.org.uk/atwork/legitimacy.html (accessed July).

Oxfam, 2003c, URL: http:// www.oxfam.org.uk/about.htm (accessed August).

Oxfam, Save the Children and Voluntary Service Overseas, 2002, "Beyond Philanthropy". July.

Pearce, B., 2000, "Capital Markets, the Financial Services Sector and Sustainability", background briefing, Forum for the Future.

Pearce, B., 2001, Director of the Centre for Sustainable Investment, part of Forum for the Future, interviewed by author, September.

Pearce, B. and J. Ganzi, 2002, "Engaging the Mainstream with Sustainability – A Survey of Investor Engagement on Corporate Social, Ethical and Environmental Performance", Forum for the Future, September.

Pearce, B. and S. Mills, 2002, "Financing the Future – The London Principles – The Role of UK Financial Services in Sustainable Development", Forum for the Future and Department of the Environment, Food and Rural Affairs.

Peck, J., 2002, "Post BP Response Headlines: Dissonance between Rhetoric and Reality?", WWF-UK, May.

Pener, A. M. and W. J. Casey, 2001, "Capital Markets Transparency and Security: The Nexus Between U.S.-China Security Relations and America's Capital Markets", Institute of the Center for Security Policy, 29 June.

People and Planet, 2002, "Annual Report 2001–2".

People and Planet, 2003, "About Us", URL: http://www.people-andplanet.org/aboutus/ (accessed 12 July).

PIRC, 1998, "Environmental and Corporate Responsibility at Shell – the shareholder role in promoting change", November.

PIRC, 2004, "Proxy Voting Annual Review 2004", November.

Rahman, S., 2000, "The Global Stakeholder's Message, the Firm's Response and an Interpretation of the Ensuing Internatio-nal Dilemma: Moving Children From Tin Sheds to Brick Houses", PhD dissertation, Nova South-eastern University, Fort Lauderdale, FL.

Reuters News Service, 2002, "Factbox – Wildlife, Jobs Part of Alaska Drilling Debate", 17 April.

Schroder Investment Management, 2003, "Dynamic Allocation for Pension Plans. Entry Form to: Managing Pension Fund Assets as if the Long-Term Really Did Matter". September.

SEC, 2003, "Final Rule: Selective Disclosure and Insider Trading", URL: http://www. sec.gov/rules/final/33-7881.htm (accessed 6 October).

Sevastopulo, D and V. Houlder, V., 2004, " 'Greening' of financial sector gathering speed", *Financial Times*, 4 June.

SHAC, 2005, URL: http://www.shac.net/FINANCIAL/said.html (accessed 1 October).

Short, C., 1998, Secretary of State for International Development. letter to Ethics for USS, 27 May.

Smith, A., 1776, *Enquiry into the Nature and Causes of the Wealth of Nations*, reprinted 1937 (New York: Modern Library).

Smith, M. P., 1996, "Shareholder Activism by Institutional Investors: Evidence from CalPERS", *Journal of Finance* 51, pp 227–52.

Spark, P., 2001, "BVCA Environmental Investment Survey Report", by Ecsponent for WWF-UK.

Sparkes, R., 2002, *Socially Responsible Investment: a global revolution* (Hoboken, New Jersey: John Wiley & Sons).

Stathers, R., 2003, SRI Analyst, Schroders, Personal Communication, July.

Sternberg, E., 1995, *Just Business: Business Ethics in Action* (London: Warner).

Stigson, B., 2003, "Future Trends in Global Sustainability", paper presented to the International Leadership Council meeting, Hot Springs, 31 March.

Suranyi, M., 1999, "Blind to Sustainability? Stock Markets and the Environment", Forum for the Future.

Svendsen, R. G., *et al*, 2001, "Measuring the Business Value of Stakeholder Relationships", Centre for Innovation in Management (CIM), Schulich School of Business, Canadian Institute of Chartered Accountants (CICA).

Tassell, T., 2003, "Guides on Social Risk Followed", *Financial Times*, 3 February.

Thamotheram, R., 2001, "Senior Adviser on SRI for the Universities Superannuation Scheme, Interview with Author", 25 April.

Times, 1997, "Business Ethics Don't Travel Well", 15 May.

Traidcraft plc, 2002, "Share Issue Prospectus", September.

Traidcraft, 2002, URL: http://www.traidcraft.co.uk (accessed 7 September).

Traidcraft Exchange, 1998, "Invitation to Ethical Investment Funds and International Development Seminar", September.

Traidcraft Exchange and War on Want, 2000, "Business Plan – Pension Funds and International Development: Enhancing Understanding of International Development in the Pensions Industry", February.

Traynor, J., *et al*, 2002, "ExxonMobil: Decision Time", Deutsche Bank, 17 September.

Triolo, P., M. Palmer, and S. Waygood, 2000, *A Capital Solution: Faith Finance and Concern for a Living Planet* (London: Pilkington Press).

TUC, 2003, "Working Capital: Institutional Investment Strategy", February.

Tunmore, S., 2001, "Senior Climate Campaigner, Greenpeace, Interview with Author", November.

Turner, A., 2001, *Just Capital* (London: Macmillan).

Tuxworth, B. and F. Sommer, 2003, "Fair Exchange? Measuring the Impact of Not-for-profit Partnerships", Forum for the Future, June.

Tyrrell, M., 2002a, "Socially Responsible Investment Research: Our Proposition", HSBC, 22 January.

Tyrrell, M., 2002b, "Socially Responsible Investment Research", Weekly Update 6, HSBC.

UKLA, 2002, *UKLA Sourcebook*, August.

UKSIF, 1998, "Saving the Earth by Responsible Investment", notes of presentation by Tony Juniper, 3 November.

UKSIF, 2000, "New Pressures for Corporate Disclosure", notes from a meeting of the All-Party Parliamentary Group on Socially Responsible Investment, 7 November.

UKSIF, 2001, "What's New in Social Investment", May.

UKSIF, 2002a, "What's New in Social Investment", May.

UKSIF, 2002b, "What's New in Social Investment", September.

UKSIF, 2002c, "What's New in Social Investment", November.

UNAIDS/WHO, 2002, "Global AIDS Epidemic Update", December.

Union of International Associations, 2005, *Yearbook of International Organizations 2005/2006* (Brussels: UIA).

United Nations, 1945, Charter of the United Nations, 26 June.

United Nations, 2003, http://www.un.org/MoreInfo/ngolink/ brochure.htm (accessed 5 May 2003).

USS, 1999, "New Stance on Socially Responsible Investment Announced by £20 Billion Pension Scheme", press release, 10 December.

USS, 2002, Voting Record for the Second Quarter of 2002, July.

USS, 2003a, Quarter 1 Report.

USS, 2003b, "Rules of Universities Superannuation Scheme", April.

USS, 2003c, URL: http://www.usshq.co.uk (accessed 12 July).

Vander Stichele, M., 2004, "Critical Issues in the Financial Sector", SOMO Financial Sector Report, Amsterdam, March.

Wade, M., 2000, Shell, Personal communication.

Walden Asset Management, 2001, Memorandum to selected socially concerned clients from Stephen Moody, Timothy Smith and Jane Chase. 12 January 2001.

War on Want, 1999, "Invest in Freedom – Charter for Fair Employment".

Waygood, S. and W. Wehrmeyer, 2003, "A Critical Assessment of How Non-Governmental Organisations Use the Capital Markets to Achieve Their Aims: A UK Study", *Business Strategy and the Environment* 12(6), November–December, pp 372–86.

Whittaker, M. and M. Brammer, 2001, "Climate Change and Shareholder Value: Case Study of BP", prepared by Innovest Strategic Value Advisors for Greenpeace, March.

Wicks, C., 2002, WWF-UK, Personal communication.

Willetts, P., 1997, "Political Globalisation and the Impact of NGOs Upon Transnational Companies", in J. Mitchell (ed), *Companies in a World of Conflict*, Royal Institute of International Affairs (London: Earthscan).

WWF International, 1998, "Investing in Tomorrow's Forests: Profitability and Sustainability in the Forest Products Industry".

WWF-UK, 1997, "Investment Policy", 17 July, p. 1.

WWF-UK, 1998a, investment questionnaire, pp 2–4.

WWF-UK, 1998b, "Response of WWF-UK to the Financial Services and Markets Bill Consultation Document", February.

WWF-UK, 1999a, "WWF-UK and NPI to Launch Socially Responsible Investment Partnership" press release, 26 January.

WWF-UK, 1999b, "Business and Industry Policy".

WWF-UK, 1999c, "Response of WWF-UK to the DSS Strengthening the Pensions Framework Consultation Document", February 1999.

WWF-UK, 2000a, "Environmental Report", p 5.

WWF-UK, 2000b, Investment Sub-Committee Minutes, 3 August.

WWF-UK, 2000c, "Mini-campaign Proposal for the Arctic National Wildlife Refuge", February.

WWF-UK, 2000d, "Challenging the Economic Myth: Oil & Gas in the Arctic Refuge, Alaska", June.

WWF-UK, 2000e, Autumn WWF News.

WWF-UK, 2000f, Business and Industry Core Group Briefing, WWF and ARC Meeting, September.

WWF-UK, 2000g, Presentation to European Network Meeting.

WWF-UK, 2000h, "2000–2005 Strategic Plan".

WWF-UK, 2003, Annual Review.

WWF-UK and Cable and Wireless, 2001, "To Whose Profit? Building a Business Case for Sustainability".

Zadek, S., 1998a, "Civil Partnerships for Social Cohesion", unpublished paper prepared for the WWF International conference "Partnerships for Social Cohesion", Copenhagen, 16–18 October.

Zadek, S., 1998b, *Strengthening Civil Regulation.* (London: Earthscan).

Zadek, S., 2000, Speech to the PIRC Environment and Investment Conference, London, 10 November.

Zadek, S., 2001, *The Civil Corporation – the new economy of corporate citizenship* (London: Earthscan).

Index

US Public Interest Research Group
(PIRG) 106
USS 44
(1999) 95–6, 101
(2003) 99
(2003a) 17, 143

V
Value driver
brand valuation 47
earnings 45
employee productivity 46–7
raw material 45–6
Vander Stichele (2004) 4
VSO 83

W
Walden Asset Management (2001)
114
Whittaker and Brammer (2001) 43
Wicks (2002) 111
Willetts (1997) 9
World Bank General
Environmental Guidelines
206–7

World Business Council for
Sustainable Development 17
World Commission on Dams
Guidelines 99, 198
World Conservation Union 115,
148
World Trade Organisation rules on
patents 144
World Wildlife Fund (WWF) 107,
137
(2003) 107
NPI Investment Fund 24
WWF-UK 3, 58, 77
(1999b) 107
(2000c) 108–9, 114
(2000d) 109
(2000e) 110
(2000g) 108
(2000h) 107
(2002c) 116
fund manager 55

Z
Zadek (1998b) 2, 12
Zeneca 126